'With remarkable candour, Petrea King reveals a life buffeted by emotional and physical trauma. That she survived, and thrived, and has helped thousands of others along the way, is testament to her conviction that it isn't our traumas and tragedies, but the view that we take of them, that determines the quality of our lives.'
Margaret Throsby

'So many hearts salved, so much joy, strength, consolation and wisdom given by this extraordinary woman. As another prominent Australian said to her not long after he was diagnosed with a life-threatening illness, "I have arranged to take my own life, but be damned if I will die before I've learnt to love."' David Leser, *The Australian Women's Weekly*

'Petrea King works and writes from a rare level of insight. She understands that true healing is more than a question of physical life or death.' Swami Kriyananda (Donald Walters), author

'I have personally observed Petrea King's work, and her work is both loving and beautiful.' Dr Jerry Jamposlky

'Petrea's support group is not about dying. It is about living. For these people every moment is precious, to be savoured and lived as vitally as possible. It is not the quantity of life that matters but the quality.'
Panorama Magazine, Melbourne

PETREA KING

Up Until Now

The inspiring story of the founder of
QUEST FOR LIFE

ALLEN&UNWIN
SYDNEY · MELBOURNE · AUCKLAND · LONDON

Certain names and details have been changed to protect the innocent and guilty alike.

First published in 2017

Allen & Unwin
83 Alexander Street
Crows Nest NSW 2065
Australia
Phone: (61 2) 8425 0100
Email: info@allenandunwin.com
Web: www.allenandunwin.com

Cataloguing-in-Publication details are available
from the National Library of Australia
www.trove.nla.gov.au

ISBN 978 1 76029 733 6

Internal design by Romina Panetta
Set in 12/17 pt Minion Pro by Midland Typesetters, Australia
Printed and bound in Australia by Griffin Press

10 9 8 7 6 5 4 3 2 1

Until you become a rebirth, you won't know what that is.

It's the same with anything.
You don't understand until you are what you're trying to
    understand.

Become reason, and you'll know it perfectly.
Become love and be a burning wick at the centre of yourself.

I would make this very plain, if someone were ready for
    what I have to tell.
Figs are cheap around here!
Mystical knowledge is easy to come by.
All you need is just to arrive, as a bird who loves figs lights
    in a fig tree.

Rumi, 1207–1273, excerpt from 'Dying'

Contents

CONTENTS

Part 3 In search of meaning

Part 4 A home for the bewildered

A note from the author

It's often not until we encounter a significant trauma that our desire for peace becomes paramount. This trauma might be the death of a loved one, the diagnosis of a serious illness, or a divorce.

When you're faced with the unfamiliar landscape of your own anguish, it can be hard to find good company, so it's a blessing to spend time with others who are familiar with the territory. They help normalise the powerful emotional roller-coaster that we find ourselves riding. We hurtle through space and time, unwilling passengers without a compass—but in their company, listening to their stories, we no longer feel isolated, that we're going mad, that God's out to get us, that life isn't worth living.

The stories we tell about our lives are comprised of bones and flesh. The bones are the historical facts: the dramas, traumas, disappointments, joys, tragedies and disasters that interrupt the unfolding of a life. The flesh holds our emotional reactions, often buried for years or even decades until the unconscious rattling of our bones demands acknowledgement, expression and healing. It's not enough just to hope that we'll survive our traumas. Hope has to have legs. Moving forward is always underpinned by effort.

I've sucked and chewed considerably upon the flesh of my story over the past thirty-plus years: in the therapist's chair, in lonely dark nights of the soul and in sharing details with hundreds of thousands of people. I've told parts of my story on television, on the radio, at workshops, in interviews with journalists, and through countless talks and speeches. Fragments of my story have also appeared in several of my other books, but many people asked for something more sequential and complete.

In writing this memoir, I found that it was still a challenge to explore so many deeply personal aspects of my life. I was confronted with raw emotions that I had assiduously avoided at the time, when tears were not an option. Ultimately, it has been healing to revisit past traumas now that I have more emotional awareness and understanding.

I am indebted to thousands of people who, over the decades, have helped me find words to describe the inner journey we are all embarked upon: the journey home to our essential self, a place where we stop needing life to behave in a particular way in order for us to be happy. The individuals and groups I've worked with have taught me that we can grow through adversity into more compassionate, wise and insightful people who choose courage in the presence of the unknown. We are designed to heal from trauma, though it certainly doesn't feel like that when we're in the midst of despair. Our bodies are designed to heal from injury and sickness and the brain can heal from trauma too.

If you're challenged by an unchangeable obstacle, the only option is to change yourself. The peace that passes all understanding is something we can all find. It's not easily won, but peace is possible—always.

PART 1

Growing up

CHAPTER 1

In the beginning, there was an end

1951

My first memory is of rainbows. I lay on the floor, staring at the bevelled edges of the small windows that enclosed the verandah of my family home in Brisbane. I was entranced by slivers of rainbow light.

My next memory is of being lifted onto a chair with my nose at the level of a table. In front of me lay a box encased in black leather. Someone opened it, and I was fascinated and captivated by an optometrist's prism sitting in purple plush satin, colours radiating from its facets. Rainbows have woven their magic throughout my life and, to this day, their sublime beauty fills me with joy and wonder.

***

According to my mother, Rae, I was very quiet and contented as a baby. She would often leave me under the trees in my bassinet, where I was mesmerised by the movement of the leaves in the breeze or the clouds drifting through the sky.

Rae already had two young children on her hands, my brothers Brenden and Ross. Brenden, twenty-one months older than me, was a handful and required a good deal of Rae's attention. He clung to her back like a frightened little koala as she attended to her household duties. She has often said there was no space for me because Brenden was always in her lap or being carried.

Ross, in contrast, was an easygoing child with a sunny disposition and a broad grin. He seemed to weather the emotional undercurrents in our home with ease, perhaps through oblivion. He was dark-haired, freckled and four years older than me. Brenden was fair haired and not so freckled as Ross, and his worldview was completely different from Ross's—and probably from that of every other family member. He once said, 'It's easy for Ross to be nice.' Yet Brenden dominated our household; everyone seemed to have a stronger relationship to him than to each other.

Brenden may well have had intense ADHD thirty years before anyone used that term. He was highly intelligent, funny, accident-prone and complex, and his moods could shift in a flash. As a small child, I found him quite unnerving—sometimes frightening— because I never knew what might happen next. My fight-flight-freeze button was perpetually switched on. Only one thing was predictable, a daily disruption that I awaited with a confusing mix of emotions. Each morning, the moment my mother's back was turned, Brenden emptied the porridge bowl over his head. I waited anxiously, watching him watching Rae. He would catch the one moment her attention was distracted from supervising him and, in a flash, the bowl was on top of his head. Porridge dripped down through his short hair, over his mischievous face, landing in splotches on his fresh, clean clothing. His enjoyment of this daily prank was tinged with my anxiety at the ensuing upset and Rae's frustration as she mopped up the mess and rushed to wash his hair and change his clothes.

Being the youngest, I tried to be as little bother to Rae as possible. Brenden filled the house with his chaos and was forever getting into more mischief than most: falling out of windows, cutting himself, breaking bones, setting fire to things, painting the walls with lipstick. I did my best to be invisible and not to take up any space or have any needs. This became second nature to me, along with a strong sense of responsibility for keeping Brenden safe. I loved him intensely and was always trailing along behind him, seeking his acknowledgement of my existence. He often roped me into an activity better left alone.

One sunny day in our backyard, Brenden discovered something strange in the fork of a tree: a nest of white fluff. When we scooped it up enthusiastically, we were stung all over our hands by baby hairy caterpillars. Brenden's screams were much louder than mine, and I was struck by an agony of fear at seeing him so upset. My tears were as much for him as for the stinging in my hands, which weren't as badly hurt as his.

***

My father, Geoff, had not long returned from World War II. He had lied about his age to enlist at seventeen, interrupting his education. He served in the Middle East and New Guinea. On his return five long years later, he and his fellow veterans were told to get on with their lives—and never to talk about the bones and certainly not the flesh of their experiences. Geoff married Rae shortly afterwards and was soon focused on building a career and providing for his young family. He did his best to put on a brave and confident face in the workplace, appearing happy and jolly in public, while at home he was often tense, irritable and guarded.

His father, Harold, was bound by suffocating social and religious strictures that had long ago quashed any sense of humour—if he'd ever had any. His presence alone instilled fear and hesitancy in me and my brothers. Not that he would ever raise his voice or hand.

He didn't need to: he could slice you in half with a look. I imagine he was no fun for Geoff to grow up with, and I've often wondered whether my father's harshness was born of his upbringing or the war or a combination of both.

He played some strange games with us when we were very young. He would often tickle me before I went to sleep at night, and while I couldn't stop laughing, I was also beside myself with near hysteria, because Geoff wouldn't stop. This agonising hilarity underlined the sense that things could look and sound okay but, in truth, they were the opposite. In an even stranger game, my brothers and I would lie in a line on the living-room floor, and Geoff would put matches between our toes. Amid the fear and nervous laughter, he would then light them and see who could bear the heat the longest.

These 'games' were more than confusing to me and, while I loved my father, I was also scared of him. I have no memory of sitting on his knee or receiving affection from him, though anyone hearing our nightly merriment would have been surprised by this. I found the combination of laughter and fear quite bewildering as a five-year-old girl finding her way into this strange world, dominated by the males within it.

Like me, Rae was dwarfed by the masculine energy in our home; and, like Geoff, she had her own complicated emotional history. Her father, Siegfried, married my grandmother, Phyllis, when he was forty-two and Granny was just eighteen. They had three children: two sons and Rae, the youngest. His Judaism didn't feature strongly in their early upbringing, but as he aged he wanted his sons to say the Kaddish prayers—the Jewish prayers for the dead—for him when the time came.

Judaism is passed down through the women, so to enable the boys to become Jewish, Granny and Rae, who was then just thirteen, converted at my grandfather's dogged insistence. This involved them learning Hebrew and being dunked by the rabbis in the Sandgate Baths, something that Granny and Rae resented and found excruciatingly embarrassing. My mother struggled as a newly converted Jew in a private Methodist and Presbyterian girls' school; she was forced to observe the Jewish holy days, which inevitably drew unwanted attention to her. She was fortunate to find a friend in one of her teachers, Jean, whose understanding was a balm to poor Rae.

The whole ordeal turned Granny vehemently against religion, and she lost all respect and love for her husband. She and Rae were very close, so when Rae became a talented contralto singer and was accepted into the Melbourne Conservatorium, Granny moved down with her as a chaperone. This allowed Granny to escape from the claustrophobia of her relationship with an increasingly demanding and difficult husband. In her sixties, long after my grandfather's death, she married a minister on the condition that he never mention religion in the house!

I adored my mother's voice, full of the warmth of autumnal colours. Her specialty was German lieder and, after her marriage to Geoff, as she became well known through her singing live on radio, her career began to overshadow his—a fact that he resented. Once he was mistakenly called by her maiden name, 'Mr Benjamin', he set about sabotaging her career, perhaps unconsciously. When my brothers and I were very young, Geoff would cancel his commitment to mind us just when Rae was due to leave for the radio station. She finally gave up her career in frustration, finding it a stress instead of a pleasure.

Granny's temperament was quite different to her daughter's. Like Ross, she was a delightful antidote to the shifting emotional undercurrents that pervaded our lives. She was a spectacular human being full of love, life and good humour. She had a keen wit, could play any tune on the piano after someone hummed a few bars, was heartily impressed with her own efforts at watercolour painting, and had generous arms that were always happy to hug me.

It was Granny who reassured me that farting wasn't a medical condition as she enthusiastically rattled the timber shutters of her Queenslander with her efforts. Her confidence in life was inspiring— she strode heartily into any situation with an unshakeable certainty about herself. I felt safe in her presence and relished her company.

At home, I was acutely aware of, and confused by, the emotional undercurrents within our family; they were never shared out loud except through unpredictable, angry outbursts. Geoff's frozen silences were hard to interpret and, at such times, I did my best to give him a wide berth. I grew into a quiet and anxious child, uncertain about the world or my purpose within it. I became preoccupied with existential questions while being too young to articulate them. Perhaps I had been born to the wrong family—or, more likely, on the wrong planet.

✳✳✳

When I was four, I had my first encounter with death.

Granny's companion, Peter, was a crusty old sea captain with a ready smile and a gentle disposition. The delicious smell of pipe tobacco hung about him and heralded his presence; nowadays, the very rare scent of it still melts my heart and brings tears of happiness. His hair was wispy white, his face crinkled with long exposure to sunshine and laughter, and I was fascinated with the white hairs that sprouted like grass tufts from his ears. While his features were chiselled and tanned, his eyes danced with a humorous twinkle and were full of softness, compassion and wisdom.

Peter and Granny were dear friends, and the warmth of their companionship was a safe and happy harbour in which I felt anchored and cherished. For one of his birthdays, Granny and I decorated a cake with liquorice straps for a roadway and a liquorice model of his car, including its running boards; in my mind's eye, it was an identical replica of the one he drove and loved. On very special occasions he'd let me stand on the running board of the car as he drove slowly to the bottom of our street. His warm delight when we presented him with our special birthday cake was memorable.

In Granny's backyard stood a mighty mango tree. Each year it bore a heavy crop of delicious, juicy fruit which Ross, Brenden and I gorged ourselves upon as we sat among its branches. In a hollow at the base of its gnarled trunk, Peter made a fairies' home complete with a little light that hung at its entrance above a white picket fence and gateway. Lying on my tummy, I could see deep into its magical interior: there were tiny chairs and a table with a red-checked gingham cloth, cups and saucers upon it. In my imagination, the fairies that he'd carefully carved and dressed came alive when I wasn't looking. He'd created an enchanted world for me to inhabit—no wonder I felt so loved by him.

One afternoon, Granny asked me to waken Peter from his nap. I tried to gently rouse him, but he had already left for other horizons. He seemed so peaceful; it felt so right. I can't recall the reactions of my mother and grandmother when I reported back— perhaps they protected me from their distress, which would have been a kindness.

His death remains in my memory as one of sweet calmness. I felt no fear, no distress. I had nothing but memories of loving him and being loved by him. After his death, I would bury my head in his clothes to catch a whiff of the remembering.

CHAPTER 2

Off to Sydney

In early 1957, I was uprooted from Brisbane as Geoff's employer, Exide Batteries, wanted him to start a branch in Sydney. He found a home for us in the leafy suburb of Artarmon, and we joined him some weeks later. This was an unwelcome adventure as it was hard to leave my beloved Granny, my refuge, behind.

I was also worried about 'Mum's bird'. On hearing the cooee-like call of a koel, Rae would always say, 'It's going to rain.' And, sure enough, it would. This fixed her in my mind as a magical person who conversed with wild birds.

But how would the koel find us in Sydney? My mother reassured me by standing on the back porch and telling the koel the timeframe of our move and our new address in Artarmon. I was mightily impressed, but not nearly as impressed as when, a month or two later, I heard the koel's call near our new home; my mother was clearly a woman of high powers.

I was in my teens before it occurred to me there was more than one koel and that rain often fell in Queensland!

***

Off to Sydney

Our relocation coincided with my first year of kindergarten at Artarmon Public School. Ross and Brenden were also enrolled there, and we used to walk together from home, though the boys would usually run ahead or hide from me. I remember those primary school years as being quite solitary, and I have no memory of spending time with my brothers in the playground. They were very active and close to each other, and I felt left out. They called me 'bus face' and 'tree face', which I tried to laugh about but found painful and isolating—no matter how I tried, I just couldn't take their teasing in my stride. Their playful arrows always found their mark in my tender heart.

Rae often asked Ross or Brenden to turn on my bedroom light at night as I was scared of the dark. Regardless of how often it happened or how I would prepare myself, I never got used to one or other of them leaping out from behind my bedroom door to scare me. Every time I was reduced to a shaking heap, which did nothing to build my resilience, let alone confidence. I was terrified of monsters under my bed and wouldn't let my feet protrude from the covers for fear of them being eaten.

While my brothers thought their teasing was fun, I became more anxious and worried about my sense of belonging. It was obvious to me from an early age that, in our household, men were more important than women and, as a little girl, I found it difficult to see any place for me in the family. Men's time, ideas, needs and desires were far more important than Rae's or mine, and getting things wrong or upsetting Geoff was to be avoided at all costs. Geoff had a short fuse, so we all tiptoed around him. Accidentally bumping his bed while he was reading the newspaper could unleash a torrent of terrifying rage.

One day, when Ross and Brenden were quarrelling, as brothers do, over some triviality, Geoff insisted on them having a fistfight in our lounge room to establish a winner. Neither of them were the least bit interested in fighting, but Geoff wouldn't take no for an answer, goading them relentlessly into violence. He insisted that my mother and I sit and watch them fight. I felt helpless and very small as my beloved brothers—their boyish chests exposed, their fists clenched—started dancing around the lounge room, jabbing at each other. Of course, Rae's and my distress went unnoticed in all the hubbub.

That time, my existence was inconsequential, but I didn't always escape Geoff's anger.

Early one Sunday morning, during a council clean-up, my brothers and I went around the neighbourhood to look for discarded treasures. We gathered enough bits and pieces to suffice as musical instruments and created a cacophony of sound that delighted only our ears. I had no idea that what we'd thought of as simple fun could provoke rage in Geoff until, on returning home, we were greeted with the strap.

I fronted up for the strap first, and then it was Brenden's turn. I sobbed and sobbed because I wanted my father to give me a double dose rather than hurt my beloved Brenden. While he was full of noise, energy and life, I sensed a fragility in him that needed protection, and it broke my heart to think of him being physically punished.

Only in his later years did Geoff share with us some of the appalling things he had seen and done during the war. He suffered from nightmares throughout his life, often waking in a lather of sweat and anxiety. I'd have loved to have known then what I know now about the awful impact trauma has on a person's life, but as a child, I was helpless in the face of his outbursts and bluster; his numb silences were somehow even more frightening.

***

A stark contrast to the ferment of our home life was our regular attendance at our local church. All five of us went to morning service each week, first at the Congregational Church in Chatswood and then, a couple of years later, at St Stephens Church of England in Willoughby, where my mother was baptised back into the Christian faith.

One Sunday when I was six years old, I plucked up the courage to ask the minister some questions. He towered above me in his long white robe as I said, 'What's behind the stars?' Without hesitation, he responded that God had placed all the stars in heaven inside a large egg.

Confused but undaunted, I continued, 'And how did Adam and Eve get here?' He looked down at me from his great height and answered, 'God put them in a big egg.'

I was incredulous. Was he lying to me? I asked, 'How did they get out of the egg?' From his lofty viewpoint, he replied, 'God gave them a hammer and a chisel.'

I was confused. I knew in my bones that what he said wasn't true, but perhaps I was somehow unworthy even to ask these questions. For the first time, I felt a sense of betrayal. A man of God was lying to me—and, clearly, he had an egg fetish. A conspiracy was going on here, and I was forbidden to know the facts. I was already feeling nervous about what life meant and what my purpose could possibly be, so this caused me to retreat further into my inner world, making me even more isolated than before.

This minister also taught me that if I didn't ask Jesus Christ into my heart, I would gnash my teeth for all eternity and burn forever in hell. I already ground my teeth at night—was this a sign that I was preparing for my fate?

I immediately welcomed Jesus in, so I had ticked that box, but then I was racked with worry because my beloved Granny, given her dunking to become Jewish, wasn't the least bit interested in religion. Scared of the monsters beneath my bed, I still spent hours on my knees at night, praying for the miracle of her conversion. When I would tell her, 'Granny, you only need to ask Jesus once into your heart,' she would laugh and say, 'Don't you worry, darling, I'll be with all my friends.' This gave me no comfort at all, and I fretted mightily at the idea of her experiencing eternal damnation and suffering. I fretted too over all the children in Africa who had never heard of Jesus and who were likewise condemned to hell. I couldn't understand the injustices in the world, the awful cruelty I saw against people, animals and the environment.

Brenden was also worried about damnation. He'd asked our minister if thoughts were as bad as actions, only to be told, 'Yes, they are one and the same.' He then had nightmares because he'd thought about taking money from Rae's purse or some other such crime that would condemn him to eternal burning and teeth-gnashing.

I have no idea why he and I took the world so literally when others seemed able to shake off what didn't suit them. But when I was seven, I had a strange but reassuring experience that enabled me to sack the God of the egg-fetish minister.

I was running around the side of our home in Artarmon with my pet dachshund, Brynner, when the entire physical world suddenly became completely insubstantial. I became rooted to the spot as I experienced everything within and around me as an interconnected, blissful energetic whole—there was no separation between me, Brynner, the earth, the sky and the trees. A blindingly beautiful light enlivened everything. The physical world was simply a dance of energy held within this blissfully beneficent light. I had witnessed the 'hand inside the glove': the 'glove' being the physical world, the 'hand' being that which gave life to everything. I had an unshakeable certainty born of the knowledge that the material world was transient while the invisible world was wondrous and eternal.

As a child, I didn't share this divine encounter with anyone because I had no words even to vaguely describe its intensity. While it was sublime, and I knew the truth of what I'd experienced, I didn't know how to reconcile this with the outer reality of my life. I tucked it away as a private but sustaining treasure for many years.

***

Animals and nature became my passions, and we were blessed as children to have an array of pets in our suburban garden that included kangaroos, a lamb, snakes, rabbits, hamsters, lizards, parrots, quail, bees, budgerigars and mice, along with the more traditional cats and dogs. I dreamed of becoming a game warden in Africa and spent hours studying animal behaviour in encyclopaedias.

In 1959, my father took up a management position at a transport company. On two occasions, when a truck driver killed a roo, Geoff brought home a joey that had survived in the pouch. We raised one, Josie, to adulthood while the other died from cold on a stormy night when the pilot light of the gas heater blew out; given her lack of fur, she was probably too young for anyone but her mother to raise.

Each morning, Josie would ascend our sixteen back steps, sideways and one at a time, to come into my bedroom and wake me up. She would climb onto my bed and settle herself comfortably while I read, went back to sleep or scratched her behind the ears. Josie and I became the best of friends. Animals seemed far more predictable and constant than humans in their affections.

In my six or seven years with Josie, we had many adventures together. She would regularly get out of our suburban garden and lead me on a merry chase through Artarmon, Chatswood and Willoughby. I would fret mightily until her return. We were all in awe of Josie's ability—despite traffic, dogs barking, people shouting and other disorienting factors—to find her way back to our garden.

One time, when I was beside myself with worry, my parents and I went out in the car looking for Josie. We stopped every now and then to ask pedestrians, 'Excuse me, have you seen our kangaroo?' only to be told, 'Yes, she went down that road,' or 'Around that corner.' But we couldn't catch up with her. Eventually, my parents decided we should go home for a cup of tea. I couldn't believe they would want tea in the middle of this all-consuming catastrophe! As we pulled up outside our house, there was Josie, sitting behind our low front gate as if to say, 'What's the fuss?'

Josie grew to adulthood and thrived but, as she matured, we realised she wasn't Josie but Joseph. And he took a keen interest in Rae when she was hanging out the washing at the Hills hoist. Sadly, his amorous intentions sealed his fate. After he knocked her flat behind a flapping bed sheet, Joseph was dispatched to a nearby nature park at Ku-ring-gai Chase. It was very funny to see people do double takes as we drove up the Pacific Highway with Joseph hanging his head out the window, enjoying the breeze.

My love for animals knew no bounds, so I was delighted when our local Sunday school decided to have its annual picnic at Taronga Zoo. After we'd eaten together, we kids were allowed to wander around and view the animals for hours with no adult supervision—things were certainly different in the 1950s! We just had to be back in time to leave on the bus. This freedom suited me and a small group of companions as we set off on our adventure. Before long, my friends kept racing ahead while I was quite happy to sit and study each animal.

By the time I'd found my way to the rhinoceros cage, I was alone. This enclosure was at the far end of an unattractive cement walkway that passed equally unattractive cement cages. As I drew closer, I could see that the two rhinos had been fighting. One was lying down with a trickle of blood running from the base of its horn to its lip. The other was on the far side of the enclosure, standing up but with its head lowered, snorting and occasionally pawing at the ground.

A small area of the enclosure's very strong crisscross wire had been cut away so that food could be put inside. Quick as a flash, I scrambled through this hole and, with hanky in hand, approached the rhino lying on its side. It didn't fret or even move as I dabbed at the blood on its face, or when I sat on its sizeable jaw to do a better job.

I was only there for a few minutes before someone raised the alarm. Shouting zookeepers descended from everywhere. I couldn't see what all the fuss was about, but they ordered me to climb back through the hole, then marched me up to the office where I was banned from ever coming to the zoo again without the supervision of my parents. I was mortified and confused—I had just been trying to help.

Another time, in teeming rain, I rescued a bedraggled galah swinging precariously from the overhead electrical wires. We'd arrived home in the car and my family had dashed inside out of the downpour, but I had stayed to call out, 'Scratch, cocky!' to this waterlogged creature, who flew clumsily onto my shoulder.

Fred was obviously somebody's pet, but no one claimed him, so he lived with us for several years. He sat on my shoulder and nibbled my ear while I was reading, and I could walk around the house with him quite content to join in whatever my activities might be. Then Fred laid an egg and so became Freda; I obviously had a lot to learn about picking the sex of an animal.

***

A life among animals appealed to me partly because I found human behaviour far too frightening and confusing. Animals seemed far more predictable and trustworthy. Deliberate cruelty was extremely hard for me to bear, and I sometimes felt others' pain as if it were happening inside my own body. This hypersensitivity drew me to the underdog, the mocked, the deformed, the disabled, the forgotten.

I still often questioned whether I had been born into the right family, and I began to wonder if my parents or brothers ever asked existential questions too. Soon, Brenden and I began having conversations about how weird we thought the world was—it turned out that he had also never felt as though a 'normal' life was his destiny. But I usually couldn't talk to him for too long because his moods fluctuated from morose to hyperactive.

I would often slip away to the nursing home at the top of our street. There I would tidy up the drawers in the old people's bedside cabinets and do other chores for them. They didn't talk much— sometimes not at all—but I found their company more tolerable than being at home where things were so emotionally volatile.

On one of our visits to family still living in Queensland, Geoff's sister, my Aunty Gwen, sat me down in what seemed like a cavernous armchair and taught me to relax. Aunty Gwen was a well-known theatre director and she told me that actors used these techniques to settle their nerves before venturing on stage. She asked me to close my eyes and focus my attention on my inward and outward breath. Aunty Gwen told me to breathe in while she counted to four, hold for two counts and then breathe out while she again counted to four. I don't know how long she did this for, but I entered a safe and calm space that felt wonderfully peaceful. This was my first experience of meditation, and I have always been grateful to her for giving me the gift of inner calm at a time when I sorely lacked it.

Another important person in my childhood was my godmother, Jean, the teacher who had befriended my mother. Only a few years lay between them, and they had formed a deep connection born of a shared understanding about feeling awkward: Rae because of her conversion to Judaism, and Jean because of her own difficult upbringing.

After Jean married and moved onto a farm at Cassilis, we frequently spent holidays there. These were very happy times that cemented my love of animals and living on the land; and, given that Geoff rarely accompanied us, there was a certain carefreeness and freedom that we three kids relished. Occasionally, I holidayed alone with Jean and her family, and I enjoyed horseriding, mustering, milking the goats and generally being involved in farm life, which was such a contrast to my home life. I sensed that Jean's family had some relationship tensions too, but I did my best to avoid these issues and only came to understand them better as I grew older.

No one except Brenden knew anything about my fiercely guarded private world, which was very much at odds with the image I tried so hard to present to others. Feeling awkward in social situations, I did my best to be invisible at home and at school.

And yet somehow I became a social activist.

When I was about nine years old, a serious car accident took place at the crossroads, a few doors down from our house. I was there in a flash, kneeling beside the injured man. He lay half in and half out of the car, unconscious and having a seizure. Adults stood around, seemingly content to watch this man's nightmare unfold; I couldn't understand why they weren't doing anything. I put a stick between the man's teeth to stop him from biting his tongue and kept his head safe until the ambulance arrived.

The next day, I wrote to the council about the need for a stop sign at the intersection of Tindale and Shepherd roads, where accidents frequently happened. Their reply shocked me: apparently there had been 'insufficient fatalities' to erect a sign at that corner. In frustration,

I retrieved a can of red paint and a brush from under our house and painted a line across the road and the stop sign myself.

Animal rights also concerned me, but while I read voraciously about game-hunting and poaching in Africa and India, I knew there was little I could do to help. Instead, I wrote a letter to the *Sydney Morning Herald* about finding a way to transport grass clippings from the city to drought-stricken areas where sheep were starving; I was pleased when my letter was published but frustrated by their reply about slow combustion dangers that prohibited the transport of grass.

I also wrote to Taronga Zoo about the way they confined sea snakes and other animals to pitifully small or inappropriate enclosures, but their response was only that they required more funds before animals could be housed more appropriately.

Later, when I was eleven or twelve, I established the first branch of the World Wildlife Fund in Australia and felt empowered to do something practical to help animals when the forms and badges arrived from England. I enrolled a couple of members, but then other events overtook me. I sadly returned what had been sent to me with a letter of apology for starting something I couldn't continue.

***

Brenden and I grew closer, and we had many conversations about the suffering we saw in the world. Our inner lives were in sharp contrast to the middle-class suburbia around us. We both felt the pain of others intensely, and we worried about how we could make a difference to issues like starvation and poverty when we were so helpless and small.

Meanwhile, our family continued to talk about what we thought or believed but never about how we felt—we had no collective vocabulary for feelings. Our Sunday lunches exemplified the subterranean nature of emotions in our household.

All five of us would attend church to sing in the choir while the lamb cooked by faith at home in the oven. On our return, I would scamper down to the backyard to pick the fresh mint growing under the regular drip of the tap; I would chop it up finely while its heavenly scent mixed with the aroma of the roasting lamb. The table would be set with a white damask cloth and matching napkins, and Spode china and silverware laid out neatly for five places. Geoff would ceremoniously carve the lamb at the table as we helped ourselves to veggies, gravy and mint sauce from the rose-patterned dishes.

And then we would wait for the bomb to explode.

Brenden would relentlessly tap his fingers on the table or rock in his chair, tipping it onto its back legs. Geoff would tell him to stop. That was a sure-fire way of getting attention, so Brenden kept aggravating Geoff until his patience was sapped. He would shout at Brenden and then, perhaps jumping to his feet, banish him from the table.

I would shrivel down into my chair, terrified by the violence of the outburst, the lamb a flavourless, dried-out ball of inedible fibre rolling around in my miserable mouth. Fortunately, our dog Brynner knew the deal and would wait patiently under the table for my spat-out offerings.

The meal would finish in deafening silence and, as soon as possible, we all escaped to our rooms or outside with the animals to recover.

***

I don't remember how I broke my arm, but I do remember my complete inability to speak up loudly enough for the pain of the greenstick fracture to be addressed. I told my mother that my arm was sore, then two weeks went by before I managed to make the true pain known and for the subsequent X-rays and sling to be administered. My lack of complaint was part of a deeply ingrained pattern that kept me trapped in a stifled silence. I felt that Brenden's needs always outweighed my own.

One grey and dismal afternoon Brenden and I were in our secret cubby under our house when my world irrevocably shifted on its axis. We were sitting on thick old phone books in our secret play area, which was inhabited only by a damp mustiness and the occasional funnel-web spider. Brenden was almost eleven and I was nine and a half when he told me that he knew he had to kill himself by the time he was thirty. The filtered light from the holes in the air vents did nothing to lighten the load I took on that day.

My purpose in life was now clear: I was born to keep Brenden safe, to ensure he would never fulfil this dreadful commitment. I remember thinking, *I have to grow up really quickly so I can look after Brenden.* It didn't occur to me to share his words with Rae, and certainly not Geoff or Ross, so their weight fell squarely on my shoulders.

At the time, Brenden and I were still at Artarmon Public School, while Ross had moved on to Chatswood High. Ross and Brenden maintained a close relationship, but Ross and I hardly ever interacted. My world revolved around Brenden with a strange mixture of fear, anxiety and love. I barely knew Ross as he was always so active, and he wasn't around when Brenden and I shared our confidences. We each had a powerful relationship with Brenden but a far more tenuous one with each other.

I didn't tell anyone about Brenden's declaration, an almighty burden for an anxious little girl to carry. His words about killing himself gave meaning and purpose to my existence and I didn't feel able to share the knowledge.

✳✳✳

In 1964, I entered Queenwood School for Girls in Mosman. Within weeks of starting, I fainted during morning assembly—my appendix was about to rupture, necessitating its urgent removal. Once I'd recovered, I tried hard to blend in with the other girls, but they all exuded a confidence that I completely lacked. Their cliques were already well-established, as many of them had been at Queenwood since kindergarten.

Though I was very small for my age, I was a nimble runner, and winning at school sports carnivals was my forte.

But I also remember overhearing two teachers talking about me in the playground, one trying to describe me to the other by saying, 'You know the one, that mousy-haired, sickly-looking child.' These words left me feeling even more flawed and deficient. The teacher named out loud how I saw myself: pale, sickly, ugly and the runt of the litter.

I was a keen student and full of questions, but not helped by my small Austrian science teacher who told me I would go mad if I continued to ask so many of them. My English teacher, Mrs Rose, was my favourite—she saw something in me worth cultivating and was very kind to me. She encouraged my love of writing and literature, and my escape into the world of books afforded me considerable comfort.

I also became tremendously fond of classical music. I could sit for hours on the lounge-room floor in front of the radiogram speakers, listening to Rachmaninov's Piano Concerto No. 2 or Grieg's Piano Concerto in A minor over and over again. The strong romanticism of such works felt like a balm to me; with the volume turned up as high as I was allowed, they drowned out every thought. Such music conveyed a powerful emotional expression that delighted and comforted me.

Occasionally, my mother would sing a solo piece with the church choir's backing or she would sing in some other setting. I adored the warmth and depth of her voice and its resonance nourished my inner being in mysterious and unspeakable ways.

But it was often easier to access books than music. Geoff had changed jobs again, this time moving into managing the retail division of Angus & Robertson on Castlereagh Street. It was in this shop that my great love of books was nurtured through the advice of Mrs Rose and my own adventures.

Shops traditionally closed at midday on Saturdays, which meant my family could have the whole place to ourselves on rainy Saturday afternoons. Geoff would pull back the mighty timber and glass sliding door to reveal the dark interior full of mysteries to be discovered. The lights would flicker on, revealing the vastness of the shop's interior and, slipping inside, we would fan out to wherever our interests lay, while my father worked upstairs in his office. We'd meet there at 3.30 pm for cheese and Jatz biscuits.

It was both eerie and wonderful to have this cavernous space full of the undiscovered written word at our disposal. Tall timber ladders led to the higher shelves, and I'd perch on a rung, pulling out whichever books captured my interest. I was enthralled by the whiff of new books and the information they contained. The solitude and echoing silence intensified the wonder of my explorations about animals, medicine, nature, science, astronomy and birds.

In my father's office, a secret door led to a small turret that housed nothing but a desk and a chair. In times long gone, Geoff told us, the inebriated Henry Lawson would arrive at the front sales desk with a new manuscript tucked under his arm, demanding to see the publisher. Henry was never satisfied with the sales clerk's claim that the publisher wasn't in, and he would insist upon lurching unsteadily up the stairs to see for himself. The clerk pressed a bell under the front counter that rang in the publisher's office, providing sufficient time for him to slip through the secret door to the turret where he could continue working. Henry would burst into the office only to find it frustratingly empty.

This lovely titbit of history was demolished with that beautiful building in Castlereagh Street many decades ago. But my love of books remains.

***

I was never sure why, but on the completion of my first year at Queenwood, the principal suggested I find a school closer to home in Artarmon. This deepened my sense of not belonging anywhere—I believed that she saw how inept I was as a human being, lacking in any potential. My parents decided that I should attend Chatswood High School, where Ross and Brenden were already enrolled.

In early 1964, Geoff and Rae established their own book-publishing business, the Australian and New Zealand Book Company Pty Ltd. As it was based in Chatswood, my brothers and I would often go there after school to pick out orders, pack books, collate catalogues or help my parents however we could.

Around this time I had a growth spurt which led to sore feet and legs. The one activity I was good at—running races—became impossible. Since Brenden had told me about his suicide plan and I'd urged myself to 'grow up quickly', I'd gone from being small for my age to shooting up by 23 centimetres. Considering I'm just 156 centimetres tall now, it was a substantial amount! Painful calluses developed on the balls of my feet; then, a few months later, my knees swivelled inwards and began dislocating.

I was only a couple of months into the rough and tumble of Year 8 at a large public school, where I found the sheer number of students overwhelming. While I did my best to fit in, my sense of being different was all pervading. Given that my running prowess was gone, I didn't feel I had much to contribute to school life, and being on crutches occasionally made me the subject of ridicule.

My inner world was completely at odds with the outer appearance I tried hard to promote. I felt painfully shy and inadequate and ached for an escape to another way of being, so I was relieved when I couldn't continue my schooling due to my inability to walk. The pain and swelling from the dislocations seemed a tiny price to pay for my freedom.

CHAPTER 3

The bones
of my story

1964

Months of physio and daily swimming in the Balmoral Baths did nothing to fix my legs. Clearly, something was amiss with my hormones and ligaments. My joints were unstable and unusually flexible—so flexible that they couldn't stabilise my knees.

Finally my orthopaedic doctor, John McGlynn, decided that surgery was the only option. So began three years of surgeries in which my femurs were cut and my lower legs rotated outwards by eleven degrees and then plated into place; three months later my tibias were cut and my lower legs were rotated inwards by nine degrees until my legs were more or less straight. John transplanted tendons below my knees to account for the changes in bone alignment, and several of the leg muscles were shortened or lengthened.

Dalcross Hospital in Killara became my home away from home for months at a time. It wasn't a children's hospital, and so from the age of thirteen I was plunged into the world of adults. This was a huge relief to me, as I didn't feel emotionally equipped to grow through my teen years and was far more comfortable in adult company. I hadn't the stamina to match my peers and wasn't interested in the things that preoccupied them—I had no breasts nor

27

any sign they might materialise, no periods, no boyfriend—and not much interest in having one, due to my extreme shyness.

I attempted correspondence lessons to continue my schooling, but the trauma of the multiple surgeries, the ensuing painful cramps and the endless physio made it impossible to keep going. My formal schooling effectively finished when I was thirteen.

This didn't bother me. I'd been bored by school lessons; my existence and purpose were far more tantalising subjects, along with nature, animals, spirituality and science. I have always been blessed with an insatiable curiosity and wonder about life, and being in hospital allowed me to pursue my learning as I had on those rainy Saturday afternoons in the Angus & Robertson bookshop. I consumed encyclopaedias and other volumes about many subjects and gave little time to novels: life in its myriad forms was so rich and extraordinary, and exploring its reality as a full-time occupation suited me better than attending school.

A library of sorts was wheeled around by volunteers on a twice-weekly route: a trolley that bore a wondrous load of unexplored tomes. I listened keenly for its squeaking wheels, impatient to devour the subjects that really interested me. Among the books were some with brightly coloured covers from the Hare Krishnas. I'd already read the Bible from cover to cover a couple of times, and now I moved on to the Bhagavad Gita, the Upanishads, the *Autobiography of a Yogi*, as well as the writings of Alan Watts, Jiddu Krishnamurti, Aldous Huxley and Thomas Merton.

***

My mother's daily visits were among the highlights of my time in Dalcross. She would bring messages about the family, our animals and their doings. I recognised her footsteps long before I sighted her. I also knew the footsteps of most of the staff and regular visitors, and my heart would shrink or enliven with the recognition of who was approaching.

Being in hospital also meant I got to see a little more of Granny, who came from Brisbane whenever she could. She and I played Scrabble for hours and, in between her visits, I studied the dictionary diligently so I could catch her out on new or unusual words. Indeed, I can thank Scrabble for most of my vocabulary and a good deal of my education, though I'd always had a passion for words and as a child had collected them in little notebooks.

Because my family were so busy with the publishing business, I only occasionally saw Geoff or Ross and Brenden on weekends. My brothers were preoccupied with their schooling, though Brenden's anxiety was now leading him into more serious depression. Between setting up a business, getting help for Brenden and their worries about me in hospital, it was a wonder that my parents, particularly my mother, managed at all.

While Ross was studying to enter university, Brenden couldn't always face going to school. My heart ached for him and his words about ending his life haunted me. I was enduring my own emotional turmoil, but I covered it up because Brenden seemed to have 'baggsed' depression—I saw no point in trying to compete with him. I simply couldn't plummet in the way he had as I didn't feel entitled to be as 'down' as he was. I felt the agony of his despair but assiduously maintained a facade of happiness so that my parents' worries would be minimised.

Being confined to hospital relieved me of the pressure of living with Brenden. I still loved him intensely but found it increasingly difficult to watch him descend into his inner hell. Physical pain was something I could manage and live with; the emotional pain I saw in Brenden was harder for me to witness. But I could—and would—cope with anything, so I worked hard at maintaining my highly polished facade, behind which lay a somewhat bewildered, overwhelmed and frightened little girl.

My parents tried everything under the sun to help Brenden. Psychiatrists were ineffective, as were newer and more alternative therapies such as orthomolecular nutrition. When Brenden was hospitalised, other patients often unburdened themselves to him rather than to the staff; he could often help them to see past their depression but was unable to fathom his own torment. His compassion, humour and insight were legendary. When he was well, his wit and wisdom were a joy to everyone who knew him. Any happiness we felt was largely dictated by the fluctuations in his mental health.

When I was in my mid-teens, my mother and I visited his psychiatrist to hear about Brenden's diagnosis and prognosis. From across the doctor's large timber desk, he pronounced, 'Brenden suffers from a Messianic Complex—he believes he is in the world to do good, to make a difference, to help people.' I felt a sense of dread because I too had such a disease, though just like Brenden, I didn't have a clue how I might make a positive contribution to the world.

***

Each surgery resulted in three months in hospital and a month on morphine, and then I had to learn to walk again on a leg that was fundamentally changed in its alignment. Pain, discomfort and loneliness were tiny concessions to make and were preferable to living with Brenden and dealing with growing through my teenage years. I felt alien and different to other young people who weren't preoccupied with questions about their own existence. I thought I was fundamentally flawed in some essential way that made me different from everyone else—except Brenden—who understood my inner world better than anyone, though he was always more preoccupied with his own troubles than with me and mine, which didn't rate by comparison.

I also felt terribly guilty because, at some deep level I believed I'd created the abnormal growth spurt and the subsequent problems with my legs. I knew I was causing my parents and Granny added worry and stress but the alternative of growing up with Brenden at home seemed insurmountable by comparison. This only added to my desire to be the perfect patient who could cope with any amount of pain, distress and discomfort and never let it show.

After one surgery, my femur wouldn't unite and I was in traction for nine months. In this operation they had cut through my right femur about 5 centimetres above the kneecap and rotated my lower leg outwards by eleven degrees. They had plated the fracture in place with four screws. There was a very good reason why the femur wouldn't heal, something I dared not tell anyone: I was dispatching most of my food through the large sliding window beside my bed.

At the awkward ages of thirteen, fourteen and fifteen, I found the lack of privacy around daily ablutions excruciatingly embarrassing. Although nurses swished the curtains almost shut around my bed, 'almost' was unbearable. Being in traction meant being bed-bound twenty-four hours a day, seven days a week. The bedpan was no friend of mine, so I figured that if as little as possible went in, the need for our encounters would be minimised. Flocks of birds arrived throughout the day to take care of my regular offerings.

I became thinner and thinner, and my poor bones were starved of the nourishment they needed to heal.

Outside my window, a driveway led to the doctor's carpark. The game was up the day a sausage bounced off my surgeon's wind-screen as he arrived for his morning rounds; he came to my bedside with a scowl on his brow and sausage in hand. From then on, the window was securely closed during mealtimes, so I found another

31

way to dispose of food. Patients' rubbish was placed in little paper bags sticky-taped to the tray table, and the cleaners and nurses never asked why I needed so many.

No one ever asked me what was going on in my mind. Perhaps it was because I was in an adult hospital that didn't cater for the psychological needs of young teenagers—or perhaps it was because I had long ago perfected not being a bother. It was second nature for me to wear a brave and cheerful front, to cope, to never complain, no matter what. My mother was an exemplar of that way of being, and I had fully absorbed her lessons in the concealment of all emotions. I was so adept at having as few needs as possible that everyone assumed I was okay.

While writing this memoir, I visited Dalcross and asked the staff if I might see the room in which I'd spent so much of my teenage years. They welcomed me kindly, though they warned me that the old part of the hospital had been completely gutted and modernised; where my bed once stood is now a waiting room, freshly painted and furnished. Even so, I easily conjured up the feelings of that little girl as I stared at the trees on the far side of the driveway—the windows had been replaced, but the view was the same. My eyes grew moist remembering the lonesomeness of that little girl, the pain and fear beneath her bright pretense. The body holds the traumas of the past; the feelings are enmeshed in the flesh. As I brought those long-submerged emotions to consciousness, allowing them space to breathe, I acknowledged and released them.

It wasn't all awful at Dalcross, though. There were many light moments during those long, tedious hospitalisations.

One weekend, my parents were visiting when I became aware that 'someone' was watching me. After a few minutes, I looked inside the basket my mother had placed on my bed, and looking back at me was the dearest little puppy I had ever seen.

Mandy was a miniature dachshund, and I fell immediately and irrevocably in love. I beseeched the hospital staff to let her stay with me. Given my long incarcerations, they allowed me some concessions, so Mandy stayed overnight; they made a snug little nest for her between the traction on my right leg and the plaster on the other.

My surgeon occasionally checked on me on his way home, late at night. On this particular evening when he visited, I was sound asleep. As he quietly slid his hands under the covers to check the traction unit was in order, he was greeted by the yelping bark of little Mandy disturbed from her sleep.

Later we laughed, but at the time he swore it took ten years off his life! Mandy was promptly sent home, where I joined her a few weeks later. Once home, whenever I sat on the floor and dragged myself around with my arms, Mandy was happy. She spent her days nestled between my legs as I pulled myself around the house; we were inseparable. The moment I started to use crutches and became vertical again, she became completely neurotic and took to eating the furniture. Finally, after destroying the legs of several expensive items of furniture, and with my next hospitalisation on the horizon, we had to find a new home for her.

***

Probably due to my lack of nutrition, I experienced excruciating cramps every day while my leg was imprisoned in traction. The cramps started in my toes, then extended into the arch of my foot, my calf and finally my thigh and hip. There was no escape, and I occasionally passed out from the pain as the cramps continued relentlessly for weeks.

After nine months, my legs were two white, lifeless, hairy sticks attached to my body. Even with every ounce of my willpower, I couldn't move either of them. It was creepy having these monstrosities extending from my body like strangers with no relationship to me. The muscle wastage was so complete that I lifted them with my hands when nurses changed the sheets. Once my left leg was released from plaster, I could circle my calves with my thumb and third finger. How there was enough muscle left to cramp, I do not know, but the pain was searing, brutal and exhausting. My face bore wrinkles from its intensity.

Around this time, I had an uninvited visitor.

I actually had many uninvited visitors, as I was a sitting duck, bound to my bed, and it was really during these nine months that my counselling career began. Adults would pull up a chair and tell me their problems. Sometimes it was a staff member from my parents' publishing business, one of whom confided that he was gay (I had no idea what that might mean, but it seemed deeply troubling to him and caused him to weep). The cleaners stopped by to tell me about their son, daughter, parent or partner who was depressed, sick, unemployed or the source of some other worry. Other patients' visitors stopped by to tell me of difficulties in their lives.

People treated me as their confessor, so I gave them a listening ear—though I didn't really have a choice—and sometimes they cried. At most, I made sympathetic noises. Once they'd talked themselves into silence, they would generally pat or squeeze some bit of me, a hand or an arm, or give me a hug and then leave, their step a little lighter.

But this visitor was different. She wanted nothing from me and brought me a gift. I never knew her name, but she seemed to know everything about me. She wore a hat and gloves complete with handbag over her arm and, next to Granny's, she had the kindliest face I had ever seen.

Somehow, she knew about my daily cramps and suggested that the next time one came, 'Take a deep breath and go to a quiet place inside yourself where you can just watch.' After telling me that, she turned to leave, hesitated and then came back and took my hand in hers while she added, 'And never let a man touch your panties.'

The second part of her advice I forgot, but the next time I had a cramp, I did as she'd instructed.

Much to my surprise and delight, I found myself above my body, looking down on it from the ceiling. My body went through the motions of the cramp but there was no pain, just an 'intensity', a bit like the sensation of having my leg tightly squeezed.

It was such a relief to be free of my wretched body. Soon, with practice, I could get out and about quite easily. The freedom was wonderful, but I also felt guilty for using the technique for my pleasure rather than as an escape from the relentless pain of the cramps.

My deep sense of shame and embarrassment about my body—and even my presence on the planet—was a result of my strong desire to be invisible. In our household, men were in all ways considered more important than women. Brenden, in my world, was king. But I couldn't fix him, and my prolonged hospitalisation was worrying my parents and Granny. I felt stuck between a rock and a hard place. If my legs mended I would need to return home and probably to school, and this was simply beyond my ability to cope. No matter what I did, I felt guilt and a deep sense of shame about my existence.

One day, after escaping from my body, 'I' was hiding in the cupboard because I wanted to surprise Granny when she visited. My body was clearly on the bed and, as she walked towards it, I realised she wouldn't be able to see 'me'. I had the strangest 'shlooping' sensation of re-entering my body in an unpleasant rush.

I never saw my visitor again. Was she a figment of my imagination? An angel? Whoever she was, I remain deeply grateful for her presence and instruction. It was a rarity to find anyone familiar with the world of the invisible. Other than my reading around spirituality, she was the first person who seemed aware of its existence and felt comfortable talking about it. Not that she said more, but her instruction landed me in a reality I found wonderful—a reality full of wonder, freedom and possibility.

***

During those months, I had X-rays two or three times a week. The technician trundled in a newly purchased portable X-ray machine to measure the progress—or non-progress—of the uniting of my right femur. Most of the time, he covered me with a heavy blanketing shield to protect my body from the radiation, but not always. I had dozens of X-rays during those years and since.

After nine months, the surgeon said my femur was unlikely to unite and I was either destined for a wheelchair—or, at best, a permanent calliper to support the useless leg. On hearing this, I thought, *No way! I'll make myself walk*, and I established a new routine which added to my sense of guilt because I knew I wasn't allowed out of bed.

At night, between nurses' rounds, I would unbandage my tethered leg and lower the heavy traction weights to the floor. The pulley would *squeak, squeak, squeak* as the metal weights were released and lowered. This was totally nerve-racking—I was so afraid I would be discovered and get into trouble for interfering with the traction unit, let alone being out of bed. I carefully arranged the bandages to reattach the equipment as quickly as possible after my escapade. I lifted my useless legs over the edge of the bed and rested. Even slightly bending them caused intense pain, as the ligaments and tendons had adapted to being straight while my legs had lain inert for so long.

I would wait while I caught my breath, the sweating stopped and my pulse rate subsided. When I was ready, I would carefully slide out of bed with my legs dangling precariously until they reached the floor. It is hard to convey how weird it was to have these two lifeless sticks attached to my body. They felt alien and unrelated to me. Twisting around, I took the weight of my body on my arms and gently exerted pressure onto my feet. This too was painful, as my ankles were unused to supporting my weight and the arches of my feet had dropped. The stretched muscles in my arches ached while I shuffled around the bed, keeping the majority of my body's weight on my arms. I felt the grating sensations of my unhealed femur— but I was determined to walk.

Finally, I collapsed exhausted and sweating back onto the bed, hauling first myself up and then the weights so I could reattach them to my leg with the bandages before the night sister made her next round.

After three weeks of this nightly ritual, the X-rays showed two things. One, the femur had healed, the bones had united; two, the screws holding the plate securing the join in my femur were dislodged. Two of the four screws were stuck in the wasted muscle at angles that necessitated a return to theatre, where they finally removed both the plate and screws.

I never let on to my doctor or family about my nightly adventures, but I imagine they must have wondered what had happened.

The day finally arrived when I was officially allowed out of bed. My crutches were retrieved from the cupboard in my room and were close enough for me to reach. But instead of waiting for the nurse or physio to assist me, I waited until the nurses were doing their early morning handover. Weak as a kitten but full of gritty determination, I made my slow and shaky way past the closed door of the nurses' office to the sanctuary of the bathroom beyond.

Once inside, I placed a chair under the door handle to ensure my privacy and poured myself the finest bath I've ever had. I flopped unceremoniously into its divine warmth, soaking in the glorious balminess of the water and my first bit of guaranteed solitude in nine months. Before long I heard an anxious pounding on the door—the nurses had realised where I was and what I had done. I took my time revelling in the sheer deliciousness of undisturbed isolation, while contemplating how I could possibly get myself out of the bath.

CHAPTER 4

The love of country

In the months between hospitalisations, I often stayed with my godmother, Jean, and her family. They had moved from Cassilis to the Hunter Valley, and were living on a sheep and cattle property a few kilometres from Merriwa. Country air, fresh food and outdoor activities (within my abilities) were considered good therapy for strengthening my muscles. My visits also allowed my parents to focus on their budding business and Brenden's mental health, rather than having my mother at home to care for me as well.

Jean had been shy and introverted when she'd married a handsome and charismatic man, Peter Evans. He dominated a strange household of women who adored him: his mother, Florence, his sister, Sarah, and their housekeeper, Maggie, all competed for his affections. This put a great strain on his early marriage with Jean, who tried desperately to establish her place in this busy household of strong women.

Although Jean was highly educated and refined, she was also shy and apologetic, so finding her niche was no easy task. It didn't help that the other women had clearly designated roles: Maggie and Florence took care of the inside chores and cooking, while Sarah worked with Peter outside, caring for the livestock and her herd of beloved Saanen goats. Jean wasn't a country girl and found it difficult to acclimatise to the lifestyle, especially without an obvious purpose. If she baked an apple pie, Sarah would bake a better one the following day. If Jean made scones, next day Florence would outdo her efforts. Whatever Jean attempted, one of the other women would do it better, bigger or more bountifully, causing Jean's confidence to plummet further.

They were all ardent Christians, which added a disturbing veneer of niceness—but anyone with a shred of intelligence could sense Jean's subterranean struggles for a sense of place in Peter's affections. He did little to help her with this, as I imagine it worked quite well for him to be surrounded by several doting women.

Maggie would say, 'God led me to this special family,' and I heard Jean mutter, on more than one occasion, 'It's a pity He never led her away again.'

She gradually found some sense of purpose, though hers was not a happy life. Many years later and in her final months, the veneer of apologetic propriety dissolved to reveal in Jean a more authentic representation of her personality, long subjugated.

The Evanses descended from British colonists in India. Their house was full of magnificently carved timber furniture, its walls adorned with carpets featuring Bengal tigers and other exotica. Beautiful blue willow-patterned china plates featured at the enormous table, around which we gathered daily for meals. After Florence's death, Peter would grace one end of the table with Sarah at the opposite end, while Jean was relegated to a lesser place on one side. At the age of six, Ross was clearly unsure about how she fitted in, and he once asked her, 'Aunty Jean, are you boss of the cats?'

My perspective on these mealtimes was undoubtedly very different from Jean's. To me, they were formal affairs full of stimulating conversation and education, with a different kind of tension under the surface from the one at home. The subject of the prickly pear plague and its effect on farming might come up—and, before I knew it, dictionaries and encyclopaedias were on the table as the subject was deeply explored. I found such conversations fascinating as they taught me more about the natural world.

***

I flourished during my stays with the Evanses. They treated me as though I was completely able to participate in all the farm's activities, regardless of callipers, plasters or crutches. I milked the goats, fed the dogs, helped butcher a male kid goat for roasting, and moved irrigation pipes in the middle of the night during the 1965 drought—no easy task, as my crutches sank deep into the sticky, black mud. I learned how to mend fences, collected 'dead' wool from sheep that had succumbed to the drought, assisted malnourished cows to give birth to deformed calves, worked in the shearing shed, and put the chooks away at night and collected their eggs. As my strength and flexibility improved, mustering also became a favourite pastime.

I came to love these people of the land who knew their country and felt a part of its fabric. Sarah, in particular, fascinated me: she was a magical woman who knew the ways of the land and its natural inhabitants. She could pick up a clod of dirt and, by smelling it or even tasting it, tell me what minerals it lacked or when rain had last fallen upon it. As we rode through the paddocks, she would spot a bird long before I did and call out to it in its native tongue, only to have it reply. She imparted her knowledge generously, interwoven with our companionable silences. I was an eager sponge, soaking up every titbit while relishing the sounds, smells and sights of the ever-changing landscape.

No matter what the activity of the day, everything stopped for lunch and the latest episode of *Blue Hills* on ABC Radio. If we were to be out mustering on hot and dusty days, we wrapped grapefruit, cold from the fridge, in wet tea towels, then packed them into our saddlebags along with the radio. Come one o'clock, we'd be under a tree eating the refreshingly tart fleshy fruit while listening to the saga of the Tanimbla townsfolk.

But my favourite part of the day was towards its end.

My last responsibility was to milk the goats with Sarah, my legs splayed among theirs. Then, as the omnipotent sun succumbed to the magnetism of the western hills, I would begin my journey up the slope behind the homestead to a water trough overlooking the expansive length of the valley. This was no easy trip for an awkward teenage girl on crutches, brandishing a calliper or plaster on one leg or both, but for me it was the most magical time of the day—my time. The smell of dry earth hung deliciously in the air, and the last rays of the sun illuminated eddies of dust that swirled around my feet and found their way into my nostrils.

No one would notice me slipping away, as everyone was pre-occupied with the final chores of their day. Jean would be inside the house stoking the Aga and preparing the beginnings of the evening meal—if Maggie allowed her. Sarah would be settling the goats and their kids in their pens with fresh hay; they would acknowledge her ministrations with nudges and high throaty murmurings. Peter would likely be in the shed wiping his creased, oil-drenched hands on a rag that could barely absorb another drop, after tinkering with some machinery. The final tasks of another day on the land.

I would haul myself up to sit on the thin but sturdy support beam across the top of the water trough.

The jangling of the sheep dogs' chains, their occasional barks and the cracking of a bone as they ate drifted to my ears, along with the familiar and comforting sound of the squeaky spring on the verandah's gauze door when it swung closed after Maggie's chores were done. Galahs, cockatoos, currawongs and magpies shrieked, whistled, sang or chortled in the dying rays of the sun as they sought a final morsel or jostled for roosting spots in the mighty she-oaks down by the creek. Piping plovers jealously guarded their nesting spots, their haunting call piercing the dusk. The gaggling of the geese would settle as they nested in their usual spot on its grassy banks. The galahs, my favourites, swooped and screeched like crazed delinquents, while in the distance the melancholy caw of a crow sounded, so evocative of the Australian bush.

In between the birds' ruckus, the shroud of evening silence soaked into the deepening folds of the darkening landscape.

Though it hadn't been at full torrent for many months due to the drought, the pristine creek that ran between the homestead and the front gate could turn from a joyous babble to a raging torrent in the space of a few hours, cutting us off from town. Sometimes this would happen when rain had fallen high in the ranges towards Willow Tree while not a drop would have fallen at Kilmarnock.

Up behind the water trough stood the grapefruit tree. Even in the drought, this generous tree's branches required support so as not to break beneath the weight of its golden, thirst-quenching orbs. The slow leak in the tank behind the trough no doubt helped the tree produce such abundance. These were the grapefruits we took with us when mustering. Nothing was more refreshing than to peel away the skin to reveal the cool, juicy tartness within. My mouth still waters at the thought.

From where I perched, my gaze was always drawn to the soft, rounded hills on the far side of the valley, first turning pink and then a deep plum as the shadows lengthened and the air cooled. That pinkish plum is such a singularly Australian colour born of the fading sunlight, the dust, the vegetation, the marvellous lazy landscape.

While sitting above the water trough, I'd ponder questions about life and existence. 'Does Merriwa exist if I can't see it?' 'Does anything exist if I am not there to witness it?' 'What purpose is there to our endeavours?' 'What makes for a meaningful life?' Given my experience of seeing everything as energy held by some awesome beneficent power, along with my out-of-body experiences in hospital, these questions came naturally to me, though I felt no pressure to find immediate answers. It was enough to contemplate the deeper mystery of my own and others' existence, the motivations behind our words and actions, the beliefs we collect, the meaning we ascribe to our daily trivialities as well as the larger, looming, more consequential matters of our existence.

There are so many ways to live a life. I wondered if life fundamentally involved a simple choice to align ourselves either with fear of the other or with love and compassion for the other. Which would I choose? And if I was to choose love, why was I so fearful of 'the other'?

I'd wait for the evening star and, even then, find it hard to pull myself away from my immersion in the peace, solitude and my reverie. When I contemplated the night sky, I felt incredibly insignificant in the grand scheme of things, but also profoundly significant in my life and grateful to even ponder the questions of my existence. I was acutely aware of my surroundings both immediate and more cosmic. I relished the mystery of my existence; my body, a collection of stardust infused with awareness. Here I sat upon a water trough at Kilmarnock, in New South Wales, in a country we called Australia, surrounded by oceans, which encircled all continents on this beautiful blue-green jewel of a planet as it floated through space in a prescribed pathway within the larger cosmos of the Milky Way and its planets, suns and stars. How extraordinary it is to have a human life. Is it only human beings who contemplate the source of their own existence? Mine felt like both nothing and everything.

Far in the distance, maybe 2 or more kilometres away as the crow flies, the first wisp of smoke curled out of the neighbours' chimney while a light flickered on. They too were completing their day and retreating to the warmth of house and hearth. Did they ponder such questions? Was I alone in my wonderings? The books I devoured addressed many of my concerns and—because of the great blessing they were to me in my lonesome ponderings—I knew these to be age-old questions that many before me had also considered. Reading other people's answers was important and instructive, but I yearned to experience the truth of their answers; to know the truth in my bones. I knew peace would remain elusive while I only added more knowledge to my beliefs. I yearned for the experience of oneness, the interconnectedness of all life, which I had been blessed to know in my childhood. Before, and since then, I had collected a host of beliefs that left me feeling inadequate, flawed, ashamed and unacceptable. The knowledge of the interconnectedness of life and the experience of feeling separate and imperfect were diametrically opposed, but that was my daily reality.

In the gathering dusk, I listened and watched, a voyeur of life unfolding in the twilight, the space between the busyness of the day and the deep rest of the night. Jean would have collected vegetables ripe for picking for our evening meal. A bucket or two of still-warm goat's milk, duly delivered by Sarah, would now stand in the cool room in the scullery. The distant horizon faded into darkness and the quality of the air noticeably changed. The cacophony of birdsong subsided with only the occasional squawk or shriek piercing the quiet, and I would pick my way carefully down the hill to join life once more in the homestead.

***

These periods in the country not only strengthened and healed my body, but they also nourished my soul in special ways. I treasured my independence, which the Evanses fostered and encouraged. And I was away from Brenden, whose depression was overtaking him. While much in my life didn't make sense, nature did. Living in its presence and working alongside people who saw me as just a kid was profoundly healing. Nature was more predictable than people—it moved in rhythms and cycles I could trust, even though the drought brought harsh lessons in loss.

I had plenty of amusing experiences at Kilmarnock too. My surgeon probably wouldn't have encouraged many of the activities I engaged in, but I knew when I had really stretched the boundaries of what was sensible—not always by intent!

Late one day, when the goats were eager to get to their stalls where fresh hay awaited them, I was opening the race—a swinging gate—for them to pass through. Being on crutches made me a little slow and clumsy, so the first goat ducked her head and pushed between my legs before I could get out of her way. Once her head was through, she decided it was safe to stand up and lifted me straight off the ground.

I was facing towards her tail, so I grabbed it as she took off in surprise with the unexpected weight upon her back. My crutches went flying, which only startled her more, and we were a jumble of legs, plasters and callipers as she bucked around the sheep yard, finally dumping me in a pile of poo. I laughed myself silly and was both sorry and relieved that no one had witnessed the spectacle.

Incidents like this didn't put me off developing more independence. Sometimes I travelled out to Merriwa on the rail motor from

Muswellbrook, having arrived by the New England train. Merriwa was the last stop, and the rail motor delivered not only passengers but also the mail, packages, mechanical spare parts and supplies. People were kind and helpful to me, as managing a suitcase along with crutches wasn't possible. But for the most part, these journeys increased my autonomy, and I was grateful that my parents allowed me such freedom.

On my return home, I sometimes wrote heart-breaking letters to Jean, beseeching her to let me live in the country because city life didn't make sense to me.

I didn't want to put up with the craziness of people piled on top of each other in tiny cubicles for homes while they didn't even know their neighbours' names. I didn't understand how people could spend a lifetime shuffling bits of paper from one side of the desk to the other. People seemed so willing to settle for such a mediocre life—a huge judgement on my part, but indicative of how strongly I felt that what the world seemed to value was pointless.

It was a heartache for Jean to receive these tear-stained letters, as she understood my unhappiness but wasn't able to offer what I yearned for: a life away from most people, living on the land, surrounded by animals.

***

I didn't always stay with Jean between surgeries. One time I was with my beloved Granny, staying in a holiday shack on the tranquil shores of Currimundi Lake in Queensland. The shack—called Kembalak, an Indonesian word meaning 'return'—was a simple structure with everything you could possibly need for a gentle life. We spent our days reading, fishing and cooking mud crabs or fish over the fire outside, transfixed by the dance and hiss of the flames and relishing each other's company. There's simply nothing on earth quite like staring into the mysteries of an open fire and giving it the odd poke with a stick.

Granny and I loved the companionable silence of fishing. Our vessel was an old but sturdy timber rowboat with faded and peeling blue paint on its sides. We happily spent hours together on the lake, listening to the gentle slap of the waves against the boat, feeling the heat of the sun on our skin. I loathed wearing hats, but without one I'd have been burned to a crisp, and Granny insisted on my wearing it anyway.

Out in the boat, I felt a persistent tug on my fishing line. This wasn't the spasmodic darting of an alarmed fish. I carefully pulled on the line as my heavy catch surfaced inch by inch. Finally, over the side came the biggest mud crab we had ever seen, angrily snapping its formidable claws at us as it ran up and down, imprisoned in the bottom of the boat.

With a burst of adrenaline, Granny and I scrambled unceremoniously out of our vessel. Clinging to opposite edges, we laughed helplessly until the crab found its way out and returned to the quiet of the deep to recover from the indignity of capture.

Granny was frantic because I had one leg in plaster and the other in a calliper—should I let go, she knew, I would surely sink to the bottom of the lake. But neither of us could stop laughing. We wet ourselves with the hilarity, which didn't matter given we were up to our necks in water.

It took some time, but once our laughter subsided, and after several failed attempts that propelled me into the air as her weight tipped the boat's balance, reducing us to even more hilarity, Granny finally hauled herself in and set about dragging me up and over the edge. She held me close as we lay in the rowboat with the hot sun drying us, feeling such happiness and relief to be safe in each other's arms.

CHAPTER 5

Putting one foot in front of the other

At the end of the surgeries, and when I'd mastered walking without crutches, Geoff thought it sensible for me to train as a secretary. I still walked with a peculiar gait, not only because of all the surgeries but also due to early osteoarthritis in my knees. But I finally felt I could begin some sort of adult life, and learning secretarial skills seemed as good a place to start as any. I completed the course at Gore Hill Technical College and then worked in my parents' publishing business.

During this time, Brenden was in and out of treatments and hospitals, while Ross was finishing his university education. I'd grown distant from my brothers during my long hospitalisations and my stays at Kilmarnock or with Granny. Ross was preoccupied with his studies, and Brenden was dealing with his own challenges. He endured electroconvulsive therapy, and it broke my heart to know what was being done to him. I was failing miserably in helping him. When he entered St John of God Hospital at Richmond, he became a zombie, overweight and absent because of the heavy medication. I shared with him some of the books that had given me strength, and while he sometimes read them, he always seemed relentlessly determined to follow his own path.

Rae and I talked about the unfolding nightmare with Brenden, including his treatment plans. We also wondered about the spiritual significance of what was happening to him and whether his psychological issues were biochemical or spiritual. Was he living out some karmic consequence that we could only guess at? Brenden had oceans of compassion for people and animals but not a great deal for himself. Like me, Rae loved him deeply and was willing to do anything to help him. She stoically put one foot in front of the other, and I knew all about doing that too, quite literally. Without a doubt, having two children with health issues was heartbreaking for Rae, but most of us don't discover how resilient we are until we encounter a major challenge or tragedy in our lives. My mother has an indomitable spirit, although—or because—it was sorely tested by Geoff, Brenden and me.

***

I've always been grateful that I learned to type, as it has stood me in great stead over the years, but I knew my life wouldn't be fulfilled through secretarial duties. I felt alien among the other girls in the class: they seemed to walk and talk with all the confidence in the world, which I still so sorely lacked in social situations.

We had to take a deportment and make-up class, and as I limped around the room I felt awkward and different. Some of the girls tittered, thinking it funny that I should even try. When the deportment teacher asked the girls what you had to do first when applying eye make-up, they chorused, 'Open your mouth.' Again, I felt alien—this was obviously common knowledge to everyone but me, because I lacked worldly experience. I was pitifully self-conscious about this and a thousand other trivialities.

After such a long confinement in hospital, I felt that nursing would suit my disposition more than being a secretary. It might not have been the wisest choice, given the amount of walking it required, but I was very familiar with hospital culture and well understood the needs of patients. I returned to Gore Hill Tech to complete the Nurses Entrance Exam and started my training at a nearby hospital.

I treasured this opportunity to give loving care to people who were sick or in pain. I understood their need for dignity and privacy, and I did my best to serve them well. When I drew the curtain around a patient, they were sealed within its confines, and I'd always have a pocket full of safety pins to ensure their privacy.

I took very much to heart what we were taught and lapped up the facts about anatomy and physiology. I studied far more than was necessary, for the sheer enjoyment of learning about the miraculous and intricate ways in which our bodies functioned.

I became increasingly interested in the body's innate healing power, fascinated by what might hinder or speed a person's recovery. If my femur had healed in a more timely manner, I would have had to return to school—and yet, the idea had seemed emotionally and psychologically impossible to me. I knew I'd probably slowed the healing of my femur through dispensing with much of my food, but I also wondered whether I had engineered my body not to heal during those long months in traction.

I found myself intrigued by the slower and more gentle approach of herbal medicine. I was a frequent visitor to Rosemary Hemphill's herb garden just outside Sydney, near Dural; this amazing garden was marked by little signs indicating each herb's medicinal uses. I read everything I could find on herbal remedies, along with hydrotherapy, homeopathy, massage, fasting and what comprised a healthy diet.

The more I read of the old philosophers and European naturopaths, the more I became interested in harnessing lifestyle choices as part of managing the osteoarthritis that still brought me pain and, along with the changes in alignment, caused me to limp.

At seventeen, I became a vegetarian and began a regular twice-daily practice of meditation. I knew from my reading that the mind is a powerful ally if harnessed, and I knew equally that the stories we tell ourselves have an impact on our bodies. The word 'psycho-neuroimmunology' hadn't yet been invented, but I was certain that my mind had influenced both the non-healing and then the rapid healing of my femur after that particularly long hospitalisation. Beliefs are powerful, as they motivate our behaviours—if I'd believed what my doctor had said about my femur never healing, I may not have tried to get out of bed and walk.

***

We were taught in nursing school that the last faculty of an unconscious person is their hearing, and I was particularly mindful of a patient who'd been unconscious for several months. Mrs Granville had been in a car crash, and while her body appeared to have healed, she hadn't regained consciousness. She was often my patient for my scheduled shift, and I chattered away to her while I washed her face or body, or generally cared for her. I would tell her about what I loved, my favourite music, what the weather was like, and any other titbit that would pass our time together pleasantly.

I'd also tell her about what I got up to on my days off. I would frequently visit Kilmarnock and, if I had a longer period off duty, I would head to Nyngan or Bourke. I loved the spaciousness, the lack of people, and the vast and magical landscape. The people I did meet were characters who didn't indulge in pretences.

One day, on a drive out towards Louth, I picked up an older man pushing his motorbike. It had run out of petrol, so I drove him to his home some distance away, where we sat on kerosene tins while he insisted on making me billy tea on the open fire outside his primitive hut. We chatted about our love of the bush as we poked at the smouldering fire. When the time came to take him and his full petrol tin back to his bike, he insisted I take the carcass of half a hogget back with me to the Nyngan caravan park where I had pitched my tiny tent. Vegetarianism was beyond his comprehension and he wouldn't take no for an answer to his generous gift. He had killed the hogget the day before, and it was hanging in the meat room, a simple gauze-covered cubicle outside his tin and wattle-daubed hut.

When I brought back my booty, the other campers were delighted and enjoyed a mighty barbecue. They too couldn't understand why I didn't indulge.

The atmosphere in these campgrounds was full of camaraderie and good cheer; people shared whatever they had as well as tales of their travels. My simple little tent was a nonsense in comparison to some of the converted buses, trucks hauling caravans and campervans. Many of the campers lived on the road: they were contractors who travelled the stock routes looking after the windmills that pumped water from artesian bores, or they ensured that the fencing was sound and in good order. I met some tough characters, both men and women, who mostly seemed good-natured and willing to share conversation, experiences or food with me. I would often watch the way a man treated his dog as an indicator of whether I would engage in conversation or give him a wide berth.

After the barbecue, I returned from four days off to find that Mrs Granville had woken. As I greeted her, her eyes lit up and she said, 'You're the one! You talked to me.' She grabbed my hand and didn't want to let go.

Mrs Granville went on to describe how the doctors often stood around her bed and talked negatively about the likelihood of her recovery. She'd felt trapped inside her body and wanted to scream at them. She also said she'd been roughly treated by many nurses who left her exposed and vulnerable, or spoke about her in uncaring ways as if she was already 'gone'. She had so appreciated someone who'd treated her respectfully as a human being, and she described my words as her 'lifeline'.

I realised that I'd played this role years before, without meaning to. When I was about fifteen, a good friend of mine and my brothers had a serious bike accident. Robbie lay unconscious and unresponsive at a hospital near where we lived and little hope was held for his recovery. Instinctively, when I visited him I held his hand and talked about how we all loved him and were wishing him a full and speedy recovery. I asked him to squeeze my hand if he could hear me—and, ever so slightly, he did.

But when I told the nurses about this, they weren't interested and dismissed my comments as wishful thinking. They scoffed and said that because he was unconscious, he couldn't have responded. Their certainty didn't convince me and, as it unfolded, Robbie went on to make a full recovery.

These experiences and many more instilled in me the certainty that we are more than our bodies, and they allowed me to cultivate comfort around the presence of mystery and the world of the invisible.

✶✶✶

I was naturally drawn to patients who were nearing death or were unconscious. My own experiences gave me a keen sense of what they needed in this difficult time when they couldn't speak for themselves. I've always had an aversion to whispering, as it takes me right back to the murmured conversations of loved ones as I struggled through the haze of anaesthesia, so I neither whispered nor raised my voice as if a patient were deaf.

Often the curtains would be drawn around a patient nearing their death; occasionally a nurse would part them just enough to see if the person was still breathing, and then move on. As often as possible, I'd slip into their cubicle and read or talk to them quietly, or massage their neck, hands or shoulders, hoping I wouldn't be discovered and subsequently criticised or mocked by the other nurses. They would look askance at me as if it were a waste of time or some silliness.

The first patient whom I had the privilege to be with when he died was Mr Bradley. He had the bluest eyes, and a face crinkled by a lifetime of love and laughter. He had no family or visitors whom I ever saw; perhaps one of the greatest of agonies is to outlive everyone you have ever loved? But I felt guilty when I spent time with him, nervous that I might be found by other nurses.

I knew that Mr Bradley was a Christian because his much-loved and well-thumbed Bible lay on his bedside cabinet. Not long before he died, I quietly read him Psalm 23. A tear of recognition slipped from the corner of his eye. I experienced a deep sense of fulfilment in the simple act of accompanying another human being to the edge of their life. Since then, I've been privileged to accompany many people on this precious last journey. The great mystery of death has never perturbed me, and the way that people approach their own—with openness and peace or with trepidation and fear— has always fascinated me. Is a willingness to gently embrace death a sign of having embraced life as well?

An acute care hospital is often not the best place to die, given the busyness of the nurses and the daily rounds of treatments. Often-times I would encourage a visitor to massage the hands or feet of a loved one nearing death or suggest that they say whatever lay in their hearts. Although it's never too late to speak to the dead— sometimes we need to say the words, whether the person needs to hear them uttered or not. It is in the speaking that we find healing.

My being at ease with the sights, sounds and smells that are present at such moments has often helped loved ones to feel comfortable or confident to touch, laugh, speak and weep while not being distressed by the physical process. This enables them to connect with the love that has woven them and the dying person together into one sacred fabric of treasured memories.

I was often distressed by the suffering I witnessed, particularly when so much of it could have been avoided by healthier lifestyle choices. We were so often treating people for diseases that, had they made healthier choices, would have been avoided. I became increasingly interested in what could be done to prevent the disaster and suffering of illness before drastic measures were necessary.

During my training, we were studying the life cycle of bacteria when an epiphany struck me like a lightning bolt: there's a critical point where natural healing methods and modern medicine diverge in philosophy. In the life cycle of a bacterium, it needs a suitable host to continue its replication. At this point, modern medicine looks for a drug to kill the bacteria without killing the host, while natural medicine looks at strengthening the individual so they are an unsuitable host.

Prevention of illness saves an enormous amount of unnecessary suffering, along with a great deal of taxpayers' money. So little education was provided to help patients make healthier choices, or to inform doctors and nurses about the principles of creating vibrant health—rather, the focus remained firmly on treating disease.

***

I was still a very naive young woman and not educated about many things that other girls seemed to have acquired quite naturally. An embarrassing example of this was my encounter with Mr Conroy, who'd had an unfortunate accident with a blowtorch—it had viciously attacked his penis and accompanying treasures when it blew up. Mr Conroy required daily dressings to his poor scorched bits, but fortunately I wasn't up to doing dressings so was saved from this dubious pleasure.

During my morning shift, an insistent ringing of his buzzer brought me flying to his side. He grabbed my arm, his eyes watering. 'Nurse, nurse, I'm having an erection!'

My God, I thought, that sounds serious, having not yet studied this medical catastrophe.

I ran the length of the ward to the senior nurse, who was talking to the sister and on-duty doctor. Junior nurses never addressed the sister directly, let alone the doctor, so I interrupted their conversation and breathlessly said to the senior nurse, 'Nurse, Mr Conroy is having an erection,' fully expecting all three of them to rush to his bedside with the necessary equipment.

She turned to the sister and said, with a slight sneer, 'Oh, Sister, Mr Conroy's having an erection.'

The sister, smirking all the more, said to the doctor, 'Oh, Doctor, Mr Conroy's having an erection.'

I stood there bewildered by what was unfolding.

The doctor turned to the sister and said, 'Cold spoon, Sister.'

The sister, still sneering, said to the senior nurse, 'Cold spoon, Nurse,' and then she told me to take him a cold spoon.

How they laughed as I dutifully went into the kitchen to deliver one cold spoon to poor Mr Conroy. Never was there a longer journey down that miserable corridor to his bedside.

∗∗∗

While I loved working with patients, nursing wasn't a sensible career choice after all my surgeries. Just over a year later, I damaged my back when lifting a patient; I couldn't take the weight in my knees. This landed me in a back brace for some months, so my career came to a halt. I moved from the nurses' quarters back to my parents' home in Artarmon while I undertook physiotherapy to regain my flexibility and strength.

I was happy to see that Brenden was in relatively good spirits while he worked at George Patterson's advertising agency in the city. He was wonderfully creative, clever and artistic, and they were kind and supportive even though he needed time off every now and again when his depression or anxiety flared. They were terrific people who kept the door open to him when many would have lost patience.

I too had a support network outside our family. Some of my most regular visitors when I was in Dalcross had been from our local church, St Stephens in Willoughby. The curate was particularly kind and visited me most weeks during those long years. We would discuss religious principles, both of us baffled by the mysteries of life and death. I found this refreshing after my encounter with the egg-fetish minister.

Not long after he was assigned to St Stephens, the curate had visited us at home. That day we happened to have a very sick rabbit in the lounge room, tucked up in a towel in front of the heater. Rae's remedy for most animal ills was a generous swig of brandy—and, just when the curate asked us to bow our heads in prayer, the rabbit crawled out of the towel to flip-flop around the room in a haze of brandy fumes, finally collapsing dead at our feet. To his credit, the unfazed curate included the rabbit in his prayers, but then hurriedly left so we could deal with the deceased.

Now that I was living at home again, I regularly attended our church fellowship meetings, which were rotated through parishioners' homes. It was at one of these meetings that my relationship with the church and the curate came to an abrupt, irrevocable end.

During the meeting, my back was so painful that I had to excuse myself to lie down. I was resting in a bedroom when a man I barely knew walked in and quietly shut the door.

While this man had no gun or knife, he approached me with confidence. After running his hands over the scars on my legs, he moved them up my body and roughly removed enough of my clothing to allow him to penetrate me, even though I was in pain and a body brace enclosed my trunk.

At first I didn't understand what was happening, as my naivety about human sexual relations was truly profound—but it didn't take long for the searing pain of rough and unprepared intercourse to reduce me to a traumatised heap.

Afterwards, I blamed myself and felt guilty and ashamed. If I had called out, someone would have come to my rescue, but I had no voice—I was so familiar with splitting off and going 'elsewhere' in my mind while people did painful things to my body. I believed it was my fault, not his, that this had happened; my fault that this was my first sexual experience. I gathered myself together and quietly left the house, never telling anyone about this abuse. I berated myself harshly for letting it happen.

This experience deepened my confusion about the motives and actions of other human beings. How could this happen at a church fellowship meeting where people ostensibly met to understand the mysteries of faith? Was there no refuge from pain, from abuse, from fear, from cruelty?

After the sexual attack and once my back recovered, I decided to look for work as far from cities as possible. I'd given up on people—they were much too complex for me to understand—and my long stays with Jean and her family, along with my escapades out to Nyngan, Louth and Bourke, had given me a deep love of the land. The sanity-saving respite of Kilmarnock and my visits with Granny had provided connection with nature and animals. My breaks with them also provided time for reflection and solitude, which was always a wonderful relief from the fears I harboured about Brenden and his—and my—future.

I took a job 90 kilometres north-east of Cunnamulla in western Queensland as a companion/helper to the women of the house, a mother and her two adult daughters.

CHAPTER 6

The great outdoors

When the plane banked and came in for landing, I looked out the window and wondered how on earth I'd survive in this barren wasteland. It looked dead, flat and empty—but, of course, I was completely wrong. The land teemed with life, and I grew to love the lazy rivers, the waterholes, the bore drains, the gorgeous river gums, the goannas, lizards and birds, the astonishing night skies and the laid-back people. Although my employers weren't quite so laid-back.

Indeed, the women of the house were anything but. They didn't step their high-heeled feet outside the sprawling house unless it was to board the light plane to fly to town, a dinner or a party, often two or three hundred kilometres away. And they always wore stockings, high heels and very formal dress in the house. I never understood the need for such attire—it wasn't as if people dropped in for social visits. I still limped and preferred riding boots and jeans that covered the long scars travelling from mid-thigh to well below my knees.

The homestead was a strange and lush oasis in the middle of a dusty desert. Maintained by plentiful bore water, the garden sported a bright green lawn and hundreds of roses and other luscious plants, while beyond its perimeter the land was red, parched and unyielding.

The house had been built during the wool boom, when the sheep's back brought great wealth. Eight bedrooms with ensuites were housed in one wing, and the living and formal dining rooms, kitchen, family room, laundry and cold room were housed in the other wing, connected by a breezeway, though a breeze was a rarity. Windstorms, however, were not so uncommon. Fine red dust from the surrounding landscape, with the consistency of talcum powder, found its way into every crevice and fold—and even inside sealed bottles and jars that were stored in the sealed pantry, within the closed kitchen. I quickly got used to an ever-so-slightly gritty texture to many staples.

Formal 'drinks' in the breezeway were a daily ritual, while my preference was to watch the sunset and listen to the earth settling into the stillness of eventide. But given my role was to be a companion and a help to the women of the house, the preparation of snacks to accompany the drinks usually fell to me, so I often missed the setting sun.

My sleeping hut was situated just outside the main house, which allowed me the privacy and solitude I craved. On mild nights, I occasionally slept out in my swag, which my employers found particularly odd, but I never tired of the shifting heavens full of sparkling stars. The skies in these far western areas, so distant from city lights and pollution, are always spectacular. There's something incredibly special about sleeping on the earth and witnessing the slow rotation of our planet as the heavens discernibly shift. When the generator was shut down around 10 pm each night, the deafening silence of the heavens was all pervading.

I enjoyed being outdoors and would sometimes work alongside the Aboriginal stockmen who were forever laughing at private jokes. They seemed to take to this lily-white girl from the city who walked in a slightly ungainly way and who preferred their company to the confines of the house. They liked that I was always eager for useful physical work, and they readily taught me skills and shared their knowledge.

But while being outside suited me and nourished my spirit, it wasn't the advertised job, and I could see that my time there would be limited. I wondered whether I would ever find a sense of belonging given that I felt more at home with the Aboriginal stockmen than with the women of the house.

✳✳✳

I came to love the slow rhythms of this land. And, not long after my arrival, I met a gorgeous man whom I almost married.

John was my first love. He lived 150 kilometres away, on the other side of Cunnamulla near the banks of the Warrego River, and we met at a Bachelor and Spinster Ball. He and I were wonderfully compatible—we had both escaped the hubbub of the ball and were staring at the stars that seemed so close you could reach out and touch them. We struck up a conversation about our love of the bush, and I found that he too was from the city and had a deep love of the land—and, like me, he felt his destiny lay in its embrace.

Every weekend he travelled to see me, and under the mighty river gums we shared stories and laughter while friendship grew into love. He was gentle and kind, with a quirky and endearing sense of humour. He loved working the land and dreamed of owning his own cattle and sheep station; he was managing one for a distant and disinterested owner.

Keeping secrets in the bush was impossible given the telephone line was a 'party line', and other people frequently listened in to conversations with the sole intention of increasing their armament of gossip. A private chat was out of the question unless John and I were together, and our every move was broadcast throughout the district. Word of our romance spread like wildfire.

We spent every spare moment together on weekends, and we did our best to avoid social situations, preferring each other's company. We often drove to distant towns like Eulo where we met wonderful bush characters like Isabelle, the Eulo Queen. Followed by several scrawny dogs wherever she went and with a shotgun always close at hand, she ruled the roost in Eulo. Many men and quite a few women eked out a living from the elusive opals that flashed rainbow colours in deep caverns, laboriously dug by hand. Simple tin and wattle-daub shacks were scattered around Eulo, each inhabited by a crusty character who fiercely guarded his or her patch of dirt. The surface temperature often reached into the fierce forties, while underground it remained a comfortable twenty or so degrees.

An air of secrecy surrounded any conversation about the miners' search for the elusive 'big one' that would ensure their financial future. But some of them showed us into their caverns, which were accessed vertically down carved-out holes with small hollows for hands and feet. At the bottom, perhaps 6 or more metres down, tunnels big enough to stand up in spread to our left, right and straight ahead. The glint of brilliant and fiery colours flashed magically from the dark red earth as our torchlight fingered its way into the tunnels. It was easy to understand the allure of—if not addiction to—the search.

Sometimes John and I drove even further out, all the way to Thargomindah, just to have some private time away. I loved that he understood and shared my desire for solitude and reveries in nature. Our privacy was an illusion, however, because even though we might drive 200 or more kilometres from town, John's vehicle was bound to be recognised. The bush telegraph crackled alive with the news and, after one such weekend, I returned to the homestead only to be greeted with a question about the state of the road out to Thargomindah.

When you're with someone you love, it's like being with the best parts of yourself, and so it was with us. We often camped out in swags on these journeys and shared the joys of cooking simple meals on an open fire, then staring into the depths of the heavens as the stars put on their nightly show.

John was a gentle and undemanding man who preferred our love to grow from friendship. This suited me well, as I was reluctant to have any man come near me after my first disastrous sexual experience. I couldn't bring myself to share my shame about the attack, so John believed my shyness was due to my scars—he was deeply respectful of the trauma I'd endured in hospital. It was easier for me to let him believe this than to tell him that my hesitancy around physical intimacy was a result of feeling sexually violated. In time, his gentleness, respect and love provided the safe harbour I needed to heal and grow past this trauma, though I never told him about it.

By the time the question of our marriage loomed on a nearer horizon, we both reluctantly realised that the life of a country woman isolated in the bush wouldn't work for me in the long term, and we sadly and gently took our leave of one another. We both recognised the inner restlessness that kept me searching for fulfilment.

When I did marry some years later, John visited me to ensure that I was happy and as he said, 'With a man worthy of loving you.' I was very touched by his kindness and concern for me, and I've often wondered what became of him. I never saw him again, though I did hear that he left Australia to volunteer his agricultural skills in a developing country.

CHAPTER 7

The land of the long white cloud

By 1969, after a year out west, I was limping less and decided to apply for work as a roustabout in the shearing sheds of New Zealand. A tiny ad in *The Land* newspaper leapt off the page at me: I was ready for another adventure, and I wanted to remain in the countryside because I still found the intensity of cities beyond my endurance. I also thought that I could continue improving the strength in my legs by engaging in hard physical work, but I had no idea what lay ahead!

The shearing ganger, Hector, was based in Palmerston North. My parents had friends there, the Cartwrights, so I set off on this wonderful year of freedom with a base among friends. The Cartwrights were very welcoming and gave me my own bedroom along with a key, encouraging me to come and go as I pleased. I got along well with them, though I was still a very private person. While I was adept at putting others at ease by getting them to talk about themselves, I largely kept my own self quite private— maintaining a facade was a well-practised art.

The day after I arrived, a motley crew of Australian girls met in Palmerston North to get to know one another and hear a little of how the shearing gangs worked. This included understanding the rhythm of the days, our duties and what would be expected of us. We eagerly piled into dilapidated vehicles and followed Hector's equally decrepit truck as we left the city's confines behind and entered the luscious green New Zealand landscape. The contrast with where I had come from was profound.

***

New Zealand sheep are very different from the merinos I was familiar with. These were smooth-skinned British breeds without the many skin folds under the neck that slow down any shearer's progress towards relieving the sheep of its fleece. A 'gun' shearer could shear about one sheep per minute from 5 am to 5 pm with an hour each for breakfast and lunch, and half-hour breaks for morning and afternoon smoko.

For a gun shearer, divesting four hundred sheep per day of their wool was standard. And, after nine months, I was working in a gang of twenty gun shearers, which translated to eight thousand fleeces processed each day. But initially I worked with a team of four or five shearers and the same number of roustabouts, as we moved from farm to farm to shear each flock.

We worked every day that the sheep were dry—which meant, at one time, forty-two days straight. When it rained, we downed tools and took a rest while we waited for fleeces to dry. On these days, I limped through mile upon mile of the lush and beautiful countryside, loving the sound of water that trickled, bubbled, splashed, cascaded, dripped, babbled and flowed so abundantly everywhere. After my time in western Queensland, the amount of free-flowing water seemed extraordinary.

The shearers and roustabouts called me 'the Abo' because of the frequency of my wanderings. Some days I joined them at the pub after our work was done, then had to drive them back given they could barely find their keys, let alone their car. But mostly I preferred my own company and would drag my leg up hill and down dale, determined to see what I could of this bounteous and luscious land. The brilliance of green grass dotted with white sheep was such a novelty.

I was determined that my legs wouldn't stop me from living my life. Motivated by a sense of frustration, I forced myself to do things best done more judiciously or perhaps not at all. I would, for instance, if no one was watching, make myself ascend stairs two at a time, even though holding the handrail while walking more slowly and consciously would have been kinder.

The shearing sheds provided plenty of opportunities to strengthen my muscles, as did my wanderings. I loved being out in the elements, and rainy days never stopped me.

✱✱✱

I buddied up with a great girl from northern New South Wales who was likewise looking for adventure as a roustabout. Barbara had left school at fourteen to work on her family's dairy farm, and I liked her straightforward manner and innate good humour and confidence. She was a rough diamond and had a heart of gold.

Barb was of nuggety build and could give the shearers as good as she got. There was a lot of chiacking and sending one another up, and the shearers were forever playing tricks on us.

We were quickly initiated into many of the delicacies that the Maori shearers ate, some of which were delicious while others required a stronger stomach. They used coat hangers to hook eels in nearby rivulets, then they hung them on the clothesline until they stopped writhing. The taste of their flesh was strong and oily, and the Maori shearers loved eating them, while I found this to be quite character-building.

We occasionally went to the seashore to gather shellfish or paua, and they made fritters from them. Paua is a kind of sea snail, called 'abalone' in other parts of the world, but the flesh of the paua we gathered was a rather unappetising, inky bluish-grey colour.

Hector, the ganger or 'boss of the gang', was a big Maori man whom you wouldn't choose to mess with or question. One frosty morning, Hector told Barb and me that he'd prepared a special dish to warm us up before work, as the mornings were crisp and our starts were early. He removed the lid of the simmering pot on the stove, breathed in deeply and, with a satisfied look, ladled the contents into our bowls.

Greeted with grass, leaves, snails and other bugs steaming in our bowls, Barb and I didn't want to offend Hector by refusing or throwing up! We gingerly dipped our spoons into this awful concoction while the shearers watched. It wasn't until the spoons were at our lips that they fell about laughing.

***

The bigger shearing gangs mostly worked in the South Island, where vast stretches of land hold many more sheep than the smaller properties of the North Island. It was good that we started in Hawke's Bay with a few shearers and the opportunity to familiarise ourselves with the rhythm and demands of roustabout duties.

Our gang would arrive at a shearing shed in a variety of clapped-out cars and Hector's battered truck piled high with our food. The shed and sleeping quarters always felt empty and deserted; they hadn't been used since the last season. The night before our work began, the shearers prepared their combs and equipment. After the first day, when I walked into the shed in the evening, I would feel the buzz of humanity's presence—the walls still hummed with the intensity of our activity. Only the day before, there had been nothing in the shed but cobwebs and an air of abandonment.

If anyone got in the way of a shearer busy about his work, they could be knocked off their feet or laid flat out across a pen full of sheep—without apology. This generally only happened to someone once, or twice if they were very slow. The simple rule was to never get in the way of a shearer: he was paid by the number of sheep, and anything that slowed him down wasn't appreciated, to put it mildly.

Each roustabout had one of three jobs, and we rotated through them during the day. One job was to work with three shearers, broom in hand, keeping the area meticulously clean and carefully separating the top-knot wool, the belly wool and the crutch wool; each of these was swept in a different direction, and the roustabout needed to quickly synchronise their efforts with the shearers, who might all be at different stages of releasing the wool from the sheep. Then, as the fleece gradually fell away in soft folds from the sheep's body, the roustabout arranged the wool so it would be easy for the pick-up roustabout to whisk away before the shearer brought out the next sheep—and so the cycle would start again.

The second role was picking up fleeces and throwing them onto the wool table for cleaning and classing. A capable roustabout could pick up three fleeces, drop two and throw one on the table. It was imperative that fleeces were picked up the moment the shearer finished, or he would walk right through the soft folds of wool on his way to choosing his next sheep. For the roustabout, being mindful of where each shearer was up to was vital if you wanted to work as a skilful member of the gang. Three or more fleeces on the floor created havoc but were also hard to avoid at times. Given that the shearers took no heed of anyone or anything other than shearing as many sheep as possible, it was the roustabouts' responsibility to deal with the resulting chaos.

The third role was on the table, where any contaminated wool around the leg, crutch or neck was removed so that the fleece was clean and consistent in quality. Nimble fingers were necessary, and no matter how fast I became, the Maori roustabouts were always faster. It was mesmerising to watch their dexterous fingers flying through the wool, removing grass seeds, thistles or dirt and ensuring a uniformity of the fleece.

I loved the speed and precision of all three roles, but my favourite was working with the broom and closely monitoring each shearer's movements while reading his next intention. This was like mindfulness meditation, as we needed to remain present to what was happening moment by moment—the consequences of not being present were brutal. When our gang synched with one another, we were in 'the zone', though that term hadn't yet been invented. It was just a joy to work together silently and so intimately, with no time to think or to feel inadequate. I found a deep satisfaction and sense of fulfilment in the quietness it brought to my mind.

I was already familiar with practising a sense of presence due to the instability of my legs. It is easy for me to rip ligaments, tendons or muscles if I move carelessly, so the increased imperative of coordinating my efforts with the shearer's added another layer to the intensity of concentration, which I loved. A quiet mind is a delight, especially when it provides respite from self-criticism or self-consciousness.

Because of my experience as a nurse, I was also given the job of sewing up the sheep that were accidentally gouged by the shears. I found it hard to witness these wounds, which were inflicted upon the poor creatures when they struggled and caught the shearer unawares. It didn't happen often, as the shearers were highly skilled; I probably stitched thirty gaping wounds during the year I was there.

Not only did I have to accept the suffering of these sheep as part of the job, but there was also no point in maintaining a vegetarian diet. The amount of food we consumed was staggering, and special diets certainly weren't catered for. Occasionally I would score the job of cooking for the gang, a mammoth task given the considerable appetites of up to fifty people. The kitchens were often basic or worse, and occasionally we needed to remove livestock from our quarters or the kitchen before we could settle in and unpack.

We woke at 4 am, showered, dressed and ate a couple of rounds of hot toast and tea before starting work when the bell sounded at 5 am. For breakfast we ate a large bowl of steaming porridge followed by two lamb chops or sausages, two eggs, mashed potato, steamed cabbage, toast and tea. Morning and afternoon smoko were the same: cheese on toast or scones, butter and jam, and mugs of hot tea. Lunch was roast lamb or lamb curry plus rice, veggies, toast, pudding and tea. Dinner was soup, a casserole with lots of vegetables, plus pudding. And we would always have toast and tea before bed.

I weighed fifty-five kilos when I arrived and fifty-two when my year was up. I had never eaten more in my life, but I'd never done such hard physical labour either!

***

The rhythm of our days was interrupted when a member of our gang, Brad, had a terrible car accident. I was particularly fond of him. On learning that he lay unconscious and badly injured in Palmerston North Hospital, I immediately hitchhiked down from Hawke's Bay to take part in his bedside vigil with his distraught parents and siblings. I didn't feel very well myself, but I was so preoccupied with Brad's precarious situation that I put my own needs aside.

At the end of the first night, I was about to go to the Cartwrights when I collapsed in a chair near the hospital entrance. A kindly doctor was passing by, and on inspecting me found that I had the beginnings of what became a 10-centimetre band of shingles extending from my bellybutton around to my spine. I was admitted into the hospital.

I'd succumbed to pneumonia every winter for years after my hospitalisations, and now shingles had laid me low. I'll never forget the searing, stabbing pain: each jab was like a burning knitting needle being thrust through my body.

It took some weeks until I was ready to return to the Cartwrights and ultimately back to the gang. I resumed the daily routine of a roustabout but stayed on the sorting table for a while, which was less physically demanding than the other two roles.

Sadly, Brad never rejoined us. His brain damage was severe, and I left him to the care of his loving family.

***

After nine months, I was considered a 'gun' roustabout by Hector and the shearers. This meant that I was put into the fastest team of twenty shearers and twenty roustabouts, all Maori except me. They were a wild and wonderful group who told amazing stories, and it was a great privilege to work with them. If they didn't go to the pub, they would build a fire outside for after-dinner gatherings and sit around telling stories.

I never quite felt I belonged among them, even though they did their best to make me welcome. We worked as a skilled and cohesive team, but when knock-off time came I was mostly left to my own devices: long walks, writing letters home to family, meditation or reading.

It was difficult to find books that I wanted to read, given we were usually miles from the nearest town—and, when the opportunity arose, I often chose not to go in. The shops were generally closed by the time the shearing gang descended upon the nearest pub.

Occasionally I'd join them, and we'd down jug after jug of beer before weaving our way up winding and sometimes precipitous roads to our quarters. I often wondered how the men functioned after the previous night's drinking; I suspect they sweated out the residue by lunchtime. Shearers weren't known to live long lives, and often their later years were painful, with damaged backs and arthritic knees and hips. Drinking helped them cope with the demands of the job.

I enjoyed a beer or two, but my main distraction came from the natural world. I've always found nature to be a wonderful teacher, so I spent many hours savouring the abundant wonders of the rugged south of the South Island. I would sit on a rock and gaze at the sublime view, smell the rich fecundity of the earth, listen to the drip of water or watch the industry of insects.

Meditation and contemplation were my closest companions, and mostly I was content to keep that part of my world private and separate from my outer life and relationships. My inner world flourished while I still struggled in social situations. I was painfully preoccupied with my own shortcomings and failures, and guilt and shame continued to infiltrate my sense of self. I became more adept at deflecting interest in me by asking questions of others, and they were happy enough to talk about their own lives without seeming to notice my tactic.

✳✳✳

I found it hard to warm to the presser in our gang. His job was to pack wool into boxes, then ratchet the pair of boxes together to create bales. These bales were sewn closed with a large needle and string, stamped with the name of the farm and set aside for collection.

To pack the boxes, the presser would jump up and down on the fleeces to compress them as much as possible. It often took the strength of two men to accomplish this feat, but our presser was quite singular in his abilities. He was a giant man who had lost one tattooed arm above the elbow. He also had tattoos on his face, chest and back—and I imagined elsewhere, but certainly didn't ask if I could inspect them.

I was totally insignificant in his world, a fact for which I was most grateful. I never saw him smile or talk to anyone, or heard him articulate more than a grunt, which he could do with emphasis or inflection so his meaning was obvious. When I was game enough, I'd watch him at work because it was a wonder to see his sheer strength and agility. With his good arm, he hauled on the rope that lifted the weighty box, tucking it under the stump of his right arm with each pull.

One night, I woke in terror when something furry and warm dropped onto my face. A tiny kitten! The presser was standing beside my bed, and I thought my heart would leap out of my chest. He just grunted and ambled off to some other drunken mischief.

My time in the land of the long white cloud had created a lasting love of New Zealand and its people, and I returned to Australia with a wad of money to contemplate what I might do next.

CHAPTER 8

Travel broadens the mind

1969

Granny, my mother and I had maintained regular contact by post. While our letters were always loving, they focused on the doings of our lives rather than our inner journeys. News of the family and their various activities was always welcome, and I learned to read between the lines of Rae's letters to decipher Brenden's emotional state.

By the time I returned home, Ross had flown to Europe to do what many young Australians did: work and travel for a period before settling into a career. He'd graduated from university with an honours degree in commerce, but he wasn't yet ready to enter the Australian workforce. Brenden, meanwhile, was creating a life for himself; though he still had ups and downs with his mental health, he'd managed to travel through Asia and India before flying on to Switzerland. Now my brothers were working together in a restaurant at the ski fields.

My parents' book company was flourishing, and my father generously suggested that my parents, Granny and I travel through the United States, Ireland, the United Kingdom and the Netherlands while he did some business and we enjoyed ourselves. We'd all meet up with Ross and Brenden in Basel, Switzerland, and then return home via Greece, Hong Kong and Singapore.

I was still overwhelmed by cities, so my parents thoughtfully planned the itinerary to avoid them. We worked our way through the spectacular national parks of the United States and on to the beautiful Emerald Isle. My father went ahead to work on the continent and stay with my brothers, while Granny, Rae and I enjoyed exploring the countryside and villages, staying in bed and breakfasts and small hotels. The generosity of the Irish was wonderfully welcoming.

This was a wonderful adventure to share with Granny in particular, as she had never been overseas and was tremendously excited. Her zest for life was legendary, and she was a great travelling companion because she found everything fascinating—she would let no experience pass us by without giving it her best shot. Her seventy-two years didn't slow her down one bit, and it was all Rae and I could do to keep up with her enthusiasm and interest in everything. She readily struck up conversations with complete strangers who warmed to her immediately.

Granny had the greenest thumb of any person I knew, and she collected seeds of exotic plants wherever we travelled. She seemingly knew the name of every plant, and I would gape at her and wonder if she was having me on when she unhesitatingly declared that we were witnessing the blossom of a 'greater thumbergia' or some such. I now see exactly the same look on my granddaughter's face when I name plants just like Granny did all those years ago!

During our journey, Granny and I shared a room each night. I fervently chastised her about her seed collections, reminding her there was no way she could carry them into Australia. But she was never one to abide by the dictates of authority, a trait that I admired tremendously given I was so often crippled by shame, guilt or embarrassment. Not Granny. When she and I had gone for walks in my childhood, she would always bring secateurs and a basket.

She'd take cuttings from the edges of people's gardens—and, if she was convinced no one was home, she wasn't above going into their yards. I would cringe, terrified that the police would descend upon us, but she was gaily oblivious to my turmoil. She could take on the world and have it love her right back!

In Singapore, on the last leg of our journey, I again reminded her that she must leave behind whatever seeds she had collected. 'Yes, dear,' she assured me. She was ample-bosomed and flirtatious, and she looked like butter wouldn't melt in her mouth as she assured the customs officer that she had nothing to declare but her fondness for men! If you were to visit her garden in Brisbane today, you'd see a tangled jungle of plants from around the globe—the seeds of which she'd secreted in her bra. I found her audacity inspiring, and as a young person I ached for her confidence and the sheer joy she felt in every day she lived.

On my travels with Granny and Rae, I learned that when my mother was away from Geoff and Brenden, she was a chip off the old block. Together she and Granny were a heady mix. Men gravitated to them because they were such good fun, and I became their chaperone instead of needing much supervision myself. Not knowing the local language posed no problem for them, as the language of laughter and flirtatiousness is universal. I loved seeing them together—particularly Rae, who was rarely so carefree in her manner.

***

Eventually the three of us embarked upon a luxury cruise up the Rhine from Rotterdam to Basel, on our way to meet up with Geoff, Ross and Brenden. I hadn't seen my brothers for well over a year and was hungry to spend time with them. Our reunion was sweetened by Brenden's apparent happiness and good cheer.

We set off together for several weeks, driving around Switzerland in a van that comfortably carried us all. We wound our way through tiny quaint villages, stopping off for fresh bread, cheese, sausage, *vino* and fruit, and we had many a cheerful picnic on the carpet of flowers that graced the lush hillsides. Brenden seemed genuinely happy that we were all together without stress or strain; and although Switzerland is a spectacular country, for me the highlight was being with a contented Brenden. He appeared mentally well, and his heavy, dark inertia seemed to have lifted.

During his most desolate days at home in Australia, I'd open his bedroom door and be assailed by the smell of fear. It was rank and cloying and stuck in my nostrils. But that smell was a distant memory now in the glorious sunshine of the Swiss Alps. Our hearts were light and our laughter was frequent.

Ross told us that Brenden had none of his natural caution on the ski slopes and skied without fear—which translated to 'he took almighty risks'. So long as he was alive and happy, though, I was content. I enjoyed the odd risk myself, so this behaviour didn't concern me at all.

Those precious few weeks are etched in my memory as the happiest time our family ever enjoyed together. And Granny was the happiest of us all. We could barely keep up with her—she was usually ten paces ahead.

***

We finally returned to Basel, where we reluctantly took our leave from my brothers. Then we turned our noses towards home, travelling through Greece, Hong Kong and Singapore. After smuggling her exotic seeds with us into Australia, Granny headed off to plant them in her Brisbane garden, and Rae and Geoff reconnected with their staff.

But I didn't know what to do with myself. I was nineteen and still living with my parents, who had moved from Artarmon to a spectacular penthouse overlooking Chinamans Beach. It was a beautiful and spacious home, and Rae and Geoff were happy to share it with me, but I needed to keep moving forward. I worked for a time at Royal North Shore Hospital as a ward clerk in the outpatients' clinic while I contemplated what to do next.

John McGlynn, my orthopaedic surgeon, also operated at that hospital. One day, while walking behind me, he noticed my gait and suggested I make an appointment to see him. The limp wasn't new and the pain had been increasing, but I hadn't noticed that my knee had swivelled in again, putting strain on the arthritic joint. I had two more surgeries to realign my leg, and afterwards I embarked on physio to strengthen and stabilise the knee.

The surgeries went relatively smoothly, but I was in a cast for several weeks after each one, so I was back to being cared for by my mother. She was always so good-natured about driving me around and generally looking after me, but I wondered whether I'd ever be able to start an independent life.

***

A few months later, when I'd recovered from the surgeries, I decided to join Ross and Brenden, who were now living on a boat in Amsterdam. We had navigated our teen years quite separately, and I wanted to re-establish our connection. My parents felt content knowing we would be together, and Amsterdam in 1971 was a very happy place—something they were probably less aware about. I bought an open return ticket to London with a stopover in the capital of hippiedom.

Brenden and I still had a lot in common. We philosophised about existential questions, and we discussed the state of the world:

the lack of compassion and care for the underdog, the inequality and poverty, the abuse and deterioration of the environment, the cruelty towards animals—and what, if anything, we could do to make a meaningful contribution. He and I also discussed our anxieties, though his always seemed deeper and more relentless than my own. I still didn't feel entitled to his depth of despair—surely one in a family was enough.

Ross appeared to skate skilfully across the surface of these conversations and was satisfied to make a contribution in his own particular way, whereas Brenden and I were disturbed by the world. We both lived with a sense of impending doom.

While we lingered in the doldrums, a political freshness was in the air. Many institutions and social norms were being questioned or dismantled. Feminism, anti-war protests and civil rights were on the rise, and the sexual revolution was in full swing. 'Make love, not war' was a common slogan that heralded the hope of a better tomorrow.

Brenden was working at a youth hostel, and I happily joined him. Every day brought people from all over the world to our doorstep, and once our chores were done we were free to talk to the guests or explore the city. I loved meeting people from so many cultures, and listening to and sometimes participating in their conversations.

While Brenden and I were friendly with many guests, most only stayed a few nights. But one young woman, Hagit, lingered for a couple of weeks and became a good friend. She was a dark-haired Israeli beauty with soft and gentle eyes. And, like me, she had a passion for animals and the environment. We spent days exploring Amsterdam on our bikes, and I was fascinated by her stories of living in a kibbutz. I soon gained some understanding of how Judaism permeated her life.

The pursuit of understanding spirituality through religious pathways continued to interest me. However, religious dogma seemed an obstruction to the direct experience of the divine that I'd encountered as a child and for which I yearned. I found it fascinating that religious people seemed so consumed by rites and rituals, without expressing a deeper wish to unite with the divine.

Like the eccentric opal miners of Eulo, forever in search of the flash of light and colour in the dark, I was driven by the desire to experience divine luminosity in every waking moment.

***

The boat that my brothers and I lived on was a deserted barge in a canal. While the amenities were basic—indeed, very basic—living there was free and at the heart of the action. We cooked on a precarious and potentially lethal portable gas stove and relied on bicycles for transportation. The barge was virtually empty, so we salvaged some discarded furniture to make it 'home'. Our sleeping bags kept us warm, and the subtle rocking of the barge was a comfort. There's a delightful simplicity about living with the bare essentials and bringing home only what can be carried by hand or bike.

We didn't spend a lot of time on the barge, given our responsibilities at the hostel, and our desire to explore and share easy times with friends, who mostly hung out in the Vondelpark. Amsterdam was a leafy, sprawling maze of low-rise buildings and streets with a friendly and welcoming atmosphere. Hundreds of people were sleeping in the Vondelpark, wearing flowers in their hair, and the smell of marijuana wafted around their gatherings. They played guitars and discussed building a better world based on personal liberty, compassion, justice, freedom and equality. I wasn't overly fond of smoking but I gave everything my best shot, never wanting to be left out and always keen to explore altered states of consciousness.

When I tried LSD, I thought, *That's better!* For the first time in a long time, I felt and saw the world of energy that I'd encountered at the age of seven. Being both a risk-taker and familiar with drug use—given how often I was kept on morphine throughout my teen years—I took to LSD with gusto. In fact, I took it every eight hours for the first three weeks, barely sleeping during that time. Living in a slightly altered reality suited me, as I was often at a loss about how to effectively deal with my day-to-day existence. But gradually my enthusiasm waned, and I functioned more normally while still sometimes exploring my inner landscape via the psychedelic.

One night, I felt a sudden urgency to share with someone what had happened to me at the church fellowship meeting four years previously. I still felt too ashamed to confide in my brothers, but the desperation to tell someone was all consuming. I decided that I could tell my friend Raymond, so I set off to find him and spent hours wandering streets where all the houses seemed identical.

Raymond was a Belgian with a mop of curly dark hair and a gentle manner. He usually wore braces to hold up his jeans. While he had a ready laugh, he also carried a deep sense of calm and appeared content within himself—silence was his friend. This had drawn me to him while we worked together at the hostel.

That night, I finally found him by lighting matches under the nameplates on every door in his district. It was two in the morning when, with a thumping heart, I tentatively rang the bell. A sleepy Raymond finally appeared and led me up the steep, winding steps to his bedsit. I could barely talk. He sat opposite me, gently holding my hands, and waited as I tried to get the bones of the story out. His kindness and patience enabled my long held-back distress to find expression.

It was Raymond who said, 'You were raped.'

I was so shocked, I could only say, 'Was that rape?'

Raymond made tea and held me close while I shivered and shook with the memory of the sexual violation. He murmured soft and soothing sounds as I gradually slid into sleep, relieved to have shared the story with someone at last.

***

After a couple of months, Ross continued his journey through Europe, while Brenden, Raymond and I moved to a tiny coastal village in Zeeland, Oostkapelle, where we rented an old stone farmhouse and continued to live a simple life. We were within easy walking distance of the traditional Dutch village where staples could be purchased and mail collected or dispatched.

Our farmhouse was clean, rustic and comfortable, and it had plenty of space for the three of us plus visitors from Amsterdam, Israel, Belgium, France, Italy and elsewhere—sometimes half a dozen people at once. Downstairs we had a kitchen, a bathroom, and living and dining rooms heated by an effective wood-burning stove; and upstairs were several bedrooms along with another bathroom. Attached to the house was a huge stone and timber barn that could be accessed through the kitchen. It was mostly used for food storage or the drying of vegetables, and it housed a tractor that looked like it belonged in a museum.

Behind our farm, fields of beetroot spread to a horizon dotted with similar-looking farmhouses that stared back at us. We had a productive vegetable garden where we mostly grew brussels sprouts, silverbeet and other leafy greens, as the growing season was relatively short and only the brassicas really thrived.

Our days took on an easy routine. We attended to the necessities: preparing and eating meals, tending the garden, and exploring the countryside and coastline. Each day I baked bread and traded it for goods from local farmers.

Within a short walk of our house was a dairy of magnificent Friesian cows. Every couple of days I left a clean billy there alongside my loaf of bread, returning an hour or so later to retrieve the billy full of fresh, frothing milk still warm from the cows.

Another farmer supplied us with eggs. His house was an enormous, thatch-roofed white building with old stone steps and tiny windows. Its kitchen housed an ancient fireplace big enough to stand in, as well as a wood-fired oven; a hundred or more years of smoke had stained the walls and beams that supported the low roof.

The farmer was short and stocky, and he looked as worn down but not nearly as handsome as the square black and white tiles on his kitchen floor. When I told him, in my hesitant Dutch, that he had the most beautiful farmhouse in the area, he gave me a hearty, toothless grin and embraced me enthusiastically—a hug that went on far too long. I escaped and pedalled home as fast as my legs would allow. When I told Raymond what had happened, he laughed: I'd said that the man was the most beautiful farmer in the area!

At another nearby farm, I traded my bread for the right to pick through their fields after the potatoes and onions had been harvested. There were always many that had either been missed by the pickers or were considered too imperfect to be sold.

All in all, Brenden, Raymond and I subsisted on what grew around us or what could be traded, with the addition of flour and rice that we purchased by the sack from the nearby Demeter organic farm.

I'm sure that the locals—fitted out, as they had been for centuries, in clogs and wide flannel trousers or traditional dresses with aprons and headwear—were bemused by the small influx of hippies into their village. We were certainly a novelty, but we were also industrious when not otherwise occupied with hobbies or books, and they admired our flourishing veggie garden when curiosity drove them to our door.

The seashore was a short ride away, and the three of us would often go down at low tide to retrieve mussels from the timber piers that stepped their way out into the water. Sometimes we made a fire on the beach, cooking up the mussels for a simple feast while we watched the sun sinking into the sea.

We were having fun together, but it couldn't last.

✳✳✳

The darkness was seeping into our days, not much helped by Brenden's alcohol and my drug consumption. He never used drugs, but he had hallucinations without them. He and I were often unreachable, and we weren't always a healthy combination.

Raymond would sometimes get angry with me for taking LSD, which was readily available in a nearby town. Most people I knew used LSD as a recreational drug, but I used it to disappear from reality. I was tired of physical pain and my sense of responsibility for Brenden, along with my worries for the world at large, and LSD provided an escape into another dimension. Although not all my LSD trips were happy ones—I had some terrifying experiences from which there was little relief—this didn't stop me. I was unsure which was the scarier reality: the one induced by drugs or the despair I often felt.

After some months, I only had to be in the company of people affected by LSD for me to feel that I'd consumed the drug myself. These were often very unpleasant experiences, because while other people would return to their usual selves when the drug wore off, I could be stuck in an altered state for days.

Brenden was always absorbed with his inner turmoil, and the nature of our relationship was always weighted towards me looking after him rather than the other way around. I'd been preoccupied with him since I was a little girl, but most of the time he couldn't see beyond his own suffering. Of course, while I craved his acceptance and acknowledgement, I also did my best to be invisible and without needs, which helped him remain oblivious to my suffering.

I craved being with him so that I could watch over him—and, at the same time, I lived with my constant concern about the commitment he'd made to me when we were children.

Brenden was getting restless and toying with the idea of returning to Australia—which he finally did. I felt relieved because I was frightened for him and thought our parents might be able to get him the support and assistance he needed.

Without Brenden at the farm, I spiralled into a precarious mental state where panic assailed me each day, often keeping me housebound. The LSD didn't help, of course, but I found that my reality became distorted even without the drug. During that year I took LSD more than a hundred and fifty times, so I'm fortunate to have survived.

My world shrank into pain and anxiety. Music, meditation and nature were my only comforts, and I confined myself to the farmhouse. I stopped talking to people, as conversation about trivialities seemed pointless. Raymond watched over me but knew there was little he could do to alleviate my turmoil and despair.

At times I felt myself disappearing into an abyss of anxiety. I would walk in circles, my bare feet on cold stone being my only connection to reality. The aching chill kept me in the present moment, and I used it as a way of avoiding the panic that assailed me. The practice of 'coming to my senses' began then and has been a blessing many times since. When focusing on my senses, I was distracted from the chaos of my mind; I guess that's why we say to people, 'Come to your senses!' when they're having a panic attack. While I concentrated on my cold feet, I could also feel the touch of my clothing against my skin, any taste in my mouth, any aroma in the air, any sight behind my closed eyes, and all the sounds within and outside of the space I inhabited. I also developed an awareness of my inward and outward breaths.

As weeks passed, I only managed the simplest of chores. Each morning I got up early to sweep out the lounge area, remove the incense and ashtrays, put fresh water in the flowers and plump up the cushions. It was a bit like the film *Groundhog Day*—I went through the same motions and waited for something to change.

On one bleak and heavy grey morning, so typical of Dutch weather, having completed my routine, I sat listening to Vivaldi's Four Seasons in the lounge. A ray of sunshine broke through the clouds, illuminating the yellow chrysanthemums in a vase. I heard, as clearly as if a voice were in the room, 'If you don't leave the farm within the hour and Holland today, you'll lose all power of discrimination.'

CHAPTER 9

Escaping madness

Without hesitation, I went upstairs, left Raymond a note, put my few belongings into my rucksack and a plastic bag, and left the farm. I hitchhiked to Schiphol Airport. I had my ticket to London and $10 in my pocket, and I felt that I'd just escaped the clutches of impending madness.

This was early in 1972 and, as there had been a bombing in London's Post Office Tower a few months before, security was high.

Passengers were shoulder to shoulder as we boarded the aircraft through the concertina corridors. After months in the spacious countryside, I found the close proximity of people quite daunting, especially after my precipitous departure from the farm. Then we were informed that we would be searched before boarding the plane. *No problem*, I thought, as they were obviously looking for weapons—then I remembered the two-ounce block of hashish in my coat pocket, along with some marijuana seeds.

I dropped the seeds down a tear in my coat lining and, under the pretence of coughing, I popped the chunk of hashish into my mouth, chewed it thoroughly and swallowed.

Clearly I looked like a hippie, given my long plaits and clothing, and the leering American passenger in the seat beside me kept questioning me about life in a commune. As the effects of the hashish spread through my bloodstream and tickled my cannabinoid receptors, I'm sure he doubted me when I assured him that it was anything but a continuous sexual orgy.

By the time we arrived, I was off with the pixies. While my parents knew many people in London, I was in no fit state to contact them. I remembered that Piccadilly Circus was in the middle of everything, so I took the train into the hubbub of the city.

There was only one person in all of London whom I felt I could contact—my Israeli friend, Hagit, who was living and working in the city. Neither of us had expected our paths to cross again, though we'd exchanged contact details in the hope she might one day visit Australia or I, Israel. I only had her American Express Mail Service address.

With my last bit of money, I ordered a cup of tea in a tiny cafe off Piccadilly Circus. I was contemplating my next step when who should walk past but the beautiful, dark-eyed Hagit. I almost knocked people off their chairs as I rushed to the door, where we fell into each other's arms.

Chattering like monkeys, we returned to her home where she put me to bed on her couch. She was returning to Israel in two days' time, so I needed to act quickly.

***

The next day, having recovered from my drug-induced haze, I went to Australia House, which contained a large book of employment opportunities for Australians. I thought that being a nanny would be a quiet and gentle opportunity to live in the country, recover from my overindulgence in drugs and generally mend myself.

One ad stood out, so I jotted down the number, made the call and went for the interview. And I got the job. Given the state I'd been in just a couple of days before, it all seemed like a miracle.

At the time of the interview I had no idea that my employer, Minnie Churchill, was none other than Winston Churchill's wife— this Winston being the grandson of Sir Winston Churchill. She provided me with my train fare to Sheffield Park Station, along with the assurance that I would be greeted and transported to their home near Chailey. So began a restorative year with their three delightful children: seven-year-old Randolph, six-year-old Jennie and five-year-old Marina.

The company of young children was perfect and my duties were simple. There were already two Japanese au pairs who lived in the house and attended to cooking and cleaning. Winston's elderly nanny also lived in her own wing of their home and, being an 'old school' nanny, she guided my efforts when they occasionally fell short.

My duty was to care for the children. Each morning I supervised their dressing for school and oversaw their breakfast in the nursery. After breakfast, they brushed their teeth and went up into the main house to greet their parents. Once inspections and cuddles were complete, I drove them to school about half an hour away. During the day I ensured their beds were made by the au pairs, and their rooms and clothes were clean and respectable, none of which was onerous as I didn't need to attend to these chores myself.

I blended into the home life of the Churchills, having been brought up with appropriate manners instilled by my parents. And as the daily schedule became a familiar routine, I managed quite well on automatic pilot.

Only once or twice did I step out of line—for instance, when I thought it might be good for the children to learn how to make their own beds. I turned it into a game where we sang as we accomplished the task: 'This is the way we make our beds, make our beds, make our beds, this is the way we make our beds, all on a sunny morning.' This caused a bit of a stir, and I was reminded that these were 'Churchill' children and we were there to 'do' for them.

When I'd first arrived, the children had been restless and jumped around like fleas in a bottle. They had very short attention spans, their incomplete puzzles and projects were strewn all over the nursery. I thought that being outside would be a great blessing for all of us, so every afternoon, weather permitting, we walked the moors and relished the joys of nature. Perhaps a caterpillar would catch our attention, and we'd get on the ground to watch it navigate its way through the long grass. The children would be off in a flash while I was still mesmerised by the caterpillar—my year on drugs had no doubt deepened my wonder at the intricacies of nature. The children would circle back, asking what on earth I was doing, before they too settled into the moment of intently watching the caterpillar. In time, they slowed right down so each of them could read quietly or complete a project without becoming distracted. Together, we grew and healed.

During breakfast one morning, I was surprised to discover that Jennie thought milk just came in bottles from the supermarket. She had no idea about its relationship to an animal, so I arranged to take the children to a local dairy farmer where they could learn the story behind what they put on their cereal. Their eyes were like saucers as they watched the farmer at work, and they even had a go at milking themselves. Of course, the children weren't destined to do farm work—or any physical work—on a regular basis. I was often reminded to ensure they were familiar with their heritage and lineage. Behind the nursery door was a family tree mapping out their ancestry, all the way back to the First Duke of Marlborough.

On one particularly hot day, when driving the children home after school, I saw an elderly woman waiting for a bus and stopped to give her a lift to her home. She gratefully sank into the front seat and started talking to the children. On finding out their names were Randolph, Jennie and Marina, the penny dropped and she said with emphasis, 'What special children you are because you're Churchills.'

I felt this was an unnecessary burden to place upon young children, and I frequently told them they were special because all children are special and no child is more special than another. I also spoke about the importance of making a life guided by kindness and a personal sense of meaning. I hoped my words would be remembered when unexpected traumas presented themselves—a proud family history doesn't necessarily equip a person to stand on their own two feet; happiness can only be found living in an authentic way congruent with a person's values. Perhaps, I thought, I could teach the children what I was desperate to experience myself.

I was still learning and reading everything I could. One of the great joys of working with the family was that Sir Winston's library and letters were housed in the Churchills' home and in the lodge that stood in its grounds. I offered to catalogue these documents, as a display of them was planned for the ten-year commemoration of Sir Winston's death. It was quite something to handle the correspondence between, for example, Lawrence of Arabia and Sir Winston. I also came across a small book that had hurtled across the House of Commons and clipped Sir Winston on the ear, along with many author-signed first editions. My experience in my parents' publishing business had given me a knowledge of cataloguing, so while the children were at school I immersed myself in this pleasurable task.

I was also learning a new skill: Minnie Churchill was a keen equestrian-trained horsewoman, and sometimes I accompanied her to her class. This was most definitely *not* the kind of riding I was used to, but it was good training and I enjoyed learning the finer points of professional riding. Heels down, toes in, back straight . . .

quite different from the skills I'd picked up at Kilmarnock when droving and mustering.

***

My parents visited twice during the year, and the Churchills generously made the lodge available to them. Geoff was captivated as he immersed himself in the extraordinary library. He held Sir Winston in the highest regard, so he spent his days happily going through the books shelf by shelf, and we loved his frequent cries of delight as he discovered some treasure that sparked his interest.

Rae and Geoff also brought news of Brenden's mental health. Since returning from Europe he'd been hospitalised from time to time, and this made working difficult for him. Given his immense creativity, it was hard for him to have no formalised channel in which to express himself. He taught himself the guitar and drew intricate designs, but he was often like a caged animal who lacked the keys to release himself.

Ross, meanwhile, was working in the family business and gradually taking the reins from Geoff—although that was a rather bumpy transition, given that Geoff found it difficult to relinquish control. The business had recently built a warehouse and offices in Frenchs Forest, a short drive from Geoff and Rae's home, while Ross had purchased a beautiful unit on the harbour's edge in nearby Cremorne.

While my mother and I were close, our love for each other was demonstrated more through actions than words. We didn't discuss our feelings of insecurity, but I knew they existed for her. She lacked the confidence to confront Geoff about his behaviours and lived by the saying, 'You've made your bed, now lie in it,' followed closely by, 'Peace at any price.' My struggles for identity and self-confidence were beyond my articulation and therefore her knowledge, though perhaps not her suspicion.

While I happily told Rae about my psychedelic explorations into both light and dark experiences, I withheld such information from Granny; I knew she would find it beyond her comprehension. Our regular correspondence was still focused on the doings of life. Granny was an uncomplicated woman who lived a simple spirituality based on a firm foundation of kindness. She often wrote to me about her visits to Currimundi Lake and the happy times she shared with her friends there—fishing, reading and relaxing—along with news of her latest exploits in her beloved garden. Granny simply wouldn't have seen any need to distort her reality; she was completely content in the moment.

But she eventually learned of my drug use from Rae, and she was mightily relieved that I'd found greater stability and a better lifestyle with the Churchills.

✳✳✳

The Churchills had friends with two unruly children who could easily have been described as rude, disobedient brats. They would, for example, deliberately drop an item on the floor and then, with an air of disdain, tell the 'help' to pick it up without a 'please' or a 'thank you'. Given they weren't yet ten years of age, I thought they were an unfolding disaster both for their own happiness and for anyone unfortunate enough to know them. It was hard to see children who seemed so indulged, snooty and superior.

Their parents were impressed with the impact I had on Randolph, Jennie and Marina. They beseeched me, did I know anyone in Australia like me who could come and sort out their children?

Yes, indeed, I knew the perfect person for the job! My friend Barbara from the shearing sheds would whip these two children into shape.

We still wrote to each other irregularly, though Barb's letters were a jumble of phonetically spelled words and sometimes didn't make sense. You might remember that she'd left school at fourteen to work on the family farm—she certainly didn't have the vocabulary, spelling and grammar I was fortunate to have acquired. Barb's manner was kindly but uncompromising, and in person you always knew exactly what she thought even though she had a colourful way of expressing things.

I tracked her down to a South Australian cannery and offered her the nannying job. Despite my warnings about the children's behaviour, she was undaunted. She seemed eager to leave the cannery and travel to a distant land, and the family were happy to pay her fare. Within two weeks, she had arrived.

As I'd predicted, Barbara was perfect for the job. The family loved her; they found her use of the English language and her broad accent endearing. She treated the children fairly but gave no ground and had them using their 'pleases' and 'thank yous' in no time. They had clearly met their match and were much happier too—they now had clear boundaries, and knew what was on and what was most definitely not.

After Barb had settled in and worked for a couple of months, the two of us took a holiday in Wales. We were standing on a bridge above a swiftly flowing river when her attention was caught by something in the water. She said, 'That really raises my curiosis!' This wonderful word has remained in my family's vocabulary ever since.

On this same holiday, Barb and I got hopelessly and delightfully lost in the lovely hills and dales of Wales. We had stopped at an intersection far from civilisation to consult a map when a farmer pulled up beside us on his tractor. He found it strange that two young women were quite content not knowing exactly where they were, and he invited us for a cup of tea with his wife at his nearby farm. As we entered his handsome old stone cottage, with its low ceilings and rooms filled with the scent of homely cooking, I spotted a harp in the corner. We were then treated to a beautiful concert by the woman of the house; she had played for the Queen and been the harpist on the maiden voyage of the *QE2*, the magnificent ocean liner built by Cunard for their transatlantic service.

The memory of this enchanting, spontaneous moment always brings a smile to my face. Travelling with Barb was such a joy.

Much to my amusement and delight, she went on to become nanny to the Shah of Iran. She lived with his family for several years, travelling to their various homes around the world—and teaching the younger children English! I lost track of where she ended up and have often thought of her fondly.

***

When I worked for the Churchills, my heart particularly went out to young Randolph, who was a delightful dreamer and loved his Snoopy toy. At eight years of age, he was dispatched to a Swiss boarding school where he knew no one. I was told that he would only be allowed to speak English at prescribed times so that he would become fluent in French. He looked very small and bewildered as he waved goodbye.

Shortly after, my year with the family ended. Nannies were generally employed only for one year, as children developed strong bonds with their custodians. It was difficult for parents to watch their children run to the nanny for comfort or celebration.

I left the Churchills feeling fully restored and embarked upon travelling around the United Kingdom. I returned to beautiful Wales, where I visited Arabella Churchill, Winston's half-sister. She was a couple of years older than me, and I'd first met her on one of her visits to the Churchills' home. She was the black sheep of the family—they obviously disapproved of her lifestyle choices—but

I immediately warmed to her and we shared many ideals. As I got to know her better, I came to love her creative eccentricity and commitment to following her dreams. Like me, she was passionate about the peace movement, but she was in it up to her ears whereas I hadn't yet found my place—a fact that still disheartened and disturbed me at twenty-two.

It wasn't until I visited her in the remote hills where she lived with her partner, Jim, and ten-month-old son, Jake, that I realised just how different she was from the rest of her clan. Arabella had unhesitatingly and cleanly turned her back on the social norms that held the Churchills in high esteem, preferring to eke out a simpler existence and only use her position if it furthered a political or cultural cause of her own choosing.

Her small stone house sat squat at the end of a long and lovely green valley. The furnishings were rudimentary, and the only cooking facility was a wood-burning stove upon which a pot of stew or soup would simmer, its steam creating a delicious and welcoming aroma. There was also an open fire around which we huddled when the temperature dropped, hot drinks cradled in our hands.

Our discussions about the state of the world heightened my sense of displacement—I still hadn't found any clear direction in life, aside from wanting to protect Brenden however I could. I admired Arabella's belief in herself and her ideals, her confidence and *joie de vivre*, and her willingness to forgo the trappings of a comfortable life to do what she felt was right.

Every evening around dusk, Arabella would leave Jake in my care and climb to the top of the range far above the house. A distant scream would eerily descend through the valley and, a little while later, she'd return rosy cheeked and content, having discharged the day's frustrations. I admired how content she seemed within herself and wished I could feel confident enough to do the same.

It was from the upstairs window of Arabella's cottage that I witnessed one of nature's greatest spectacles: a murmuration of starlings. I sat in the deep window cavity, gazing out over the peaceful valley, as the last rays of sunlight illuminated the bright green hilltops. A dark smudge formed in the sky at the far end of the valley, then became a mesmerising liquid cloud that soared, swirled and swooped up the basin towards me. I felt a glorious thrill of awe as I watched this eddying mass of birdlife, millions of starlings perfectly synchronised to move as one.

I often felt that Brenden and I were the odd ones out; Arabella, the starlings and everything and everyone seemed to have a direction while he and I hesitated on the fringe of life. I would have to find my own route, as would he, but the how remained beyond my knowing. Soon after my visit to Arabella, I decided to return to Australia.

PART 2

A quest for love

CHAPTER 10

Naturopathy, Leo and love

1973

Back in Sydney, I gravitated back to training as a nurse. Then, given I was immersed in a medical environment, I decided to have some tests to explore why I was still growing taller. My pants and skirts were getting shorter—at first I'd assumed they were shrinking in the wash, but finally I measured myself and discovered the truth.

To ascertain what was going on with my hormones, I had daily blood tests for a month. The doctor was surprised by his findings. He told me, among other things, that I had never ovulated and that getting pregnant was out of the question. He suggested that the anaesthetics and drugs I'd been given in my early teens had stopped my reproductive capacities from maturing. I wasn't deeply distressed because I hadn't considered having children, though to have no choice in the matter came as a surprise.

My interest in natural healing methods still greatly fascinated me. I experimented with a range of diets, supplements, fasting and medicaments to try and help my legs, which continued to be problematic and painful. I was limping noticeably and at times used crutches, particularly if the terrain was uneven or if the walk was long. I could just manage nursing and did my best not to draw attention to the fact that pain occasionally slowed me down. Mostly I simply wouldn't let it, but by the end of every shift my knees would be swollen and sore.

My training ended abruptly a year later when something dreadful happened to a patient. Evie was eighty-two years old and close to dying from leukaemia. She had no family or loved ones who visited, and looking after her was one of my responsibilities during my shifts in the several days leading to her death.

On that afternoon, I tenderly sponged her and made her as comfortable as I could. She was breathing peacefully and seemed in no distress. While it was sad that no loved ones were there to hold her hand or sit by her side, I did my best to be with her as much as possible given my other responsibilities. I was present when she died.

Afterwards, I stayed for a few minutes to allow us both space and time, then I gently closed her eyes, combed back her hair, arranged her bedding appropriately and told the sister on duty that Evie had died.

To my complete astonishment, the sister called in a 'code blue', which meant the crash trolley was raced into the room while nurses and doctors came running. They swung into action as if to resuscitate Evie.

I stood rooted to the spot in shock. This couldn't be happening. Surely there was a mistake. I stumbled out of the way, traumatised by what was unfolding. Paddles were attached to Evie's chest, and she heaved off the bed as the shock passed through her inert and unresponsive body. Heart-stimulating drugs were injected into her poor dead chest. Had I said something wrong? Had the nursing sister not understood that Evie had been dead for at least five minutes before I told her?

Finally they stopped and, without a word, perfunctorily left Evie's cubicle. I returned to her bedside to find her tousled and in awful disarray, her body skewed and dishevelled. I gently straightened and re-covered her body, placing her hands on her chest. I was still shaking with dismay and distress at what had been done to her. I again combed her hair and arranged her as gently as possible, but I didn't think she looked nearly as peaceful as before. Her body seemed racked with abuse.

The sister dismissed my concerns and gave no explanation for what had transpired. At the end of my shift, I walked off the ward and down to the matron's office, knocked and went in. I could barely contain myself. I reported what had just happened and my belief that it wasn't right. After a few minutes, the matron lost patience with me and said, 'Nurse, they have to practise on someone!'

Incredulous, I resigned on the spot. Just because a person didn't have someone to advocate for them was no reason to treat them so disrespectfully. In my view, it was an appalling assault, and I couldn't be part of a system that condoned or encouraged it.

***

I decided that day to start my formal studies in naturopathy and was soon enrolled at what was then called the NSW School of Naturopathic Sciences. I was given recognition of prior learning, which shortened the course by a year. I never looked back—although my great love was always that first year of nursing, where our principle responsibility had been to ensure the care, comfort and dignity of our patients.

Naturopathy was fascinating, and I became a dedicated student. Again, I studied far more than necessary, and I found that my nursing experience and my understanding of the medical system added a valuable and enriching perspective to my studies.

Early on in my training, I met a tall, blond and good-looking man at the annual dinner of the college I was attending. He asked me to dance, and I hesitated because of my uncoordinated legs and arthritis; I have never felt very stable on my feet. However, Leo wasn't one to take no for an answer. He was perhaps the most enthusiastic man I'd ever met. He was also very tall, and he swept me off my feet, quite literally. I had the strangest experience in his arms, as if we were dancing our way through the stars. I had never experienced anything like it—even with all my psychedelic trips!

In the noise and activity of the dinner there wasn't much time or space for conversation, but we spoke to each other as Leo escorted me home by cab. The next day, a mighty sheaf of roses was delivered along with a basket of fruit.

I soon learned more about Leo. Born in the Netherlands in 1938, he had lost his father when he was a toddler and experienced starvation as a young child during the Occupation—his family lived in a farming community, and all their food was handed over to the German army. Leo had strong memories of his mother concealing potatoes under her traditional Dutch skirts to bring home from the fields to feed her children, and of others who would happily trade diamonds for potatoes.

After school, Leo rose to the top of his profession as a chef, working in prestigious restaurants in France and Holland, and sometimes lending a hand to his friend Pierre, who was chef to Queen Beatrix for decades. In 1967, Leo orchestrated the food for the coronation of King Taufa'ahau Tupou IV of Tonga. Leo's enormous ice sculptures and other decorations were legendary at such events; silver foil animals and intricately carved fruits and vegetables turned dishes into extraordinary works of art.

Like many others, Leo came to Australia in search of adventure and to create a better life for himself. He was accepted into the country as part of the influx of immigrants to help build the Snowy Mountain Scheme. He worked there as a cook and relished the multicultural community that had instantly developed. Fluent in six languages, Leo had an easy way with people and a gift for making them laugh. He treated everyone the same and was happiest in company where genuine conversation took place. He was full of fun with a twinkle in his eye and often used humour to soften or avoid difficult circumstances.

When I met him in late 1974, Leo was still working as a chef. But, like me, he'd developed a strong interest in natural medicine and the powers of the body to heal itself. He felt that many of the extraordinary dishes he created were nutritionally deficient, and he wanted to eat and prepare healthier meals. He had studied many of the philosophers who intrigued me, including Vincent Priessnitz, Paracelsus, Sebastian Kneipp, Louis Kuhne, the great faster Arnold Ehret and, of course, Hippocrates.

While my interest was driven by my physical suffering, Leo's was born out of a natural curiosity about health, healing and wellbeing. We had much to talk about and quickly became inseparable as love wove its magic around us. I was enjoying my studies in naturo-pathy, hydrotherapy, botanic medicine, massage and homeopathy, and Leo was always interested in whatever I was learning.

He was interested in fasting too, and we both undertook quite a few fasts. I found a spiritual clarity during the two twenty-one day fasts we undertook together. My spine seemed to come alive and become an extra sense organ, and I noticed a heightened intuitive ability. I went on to do much longer fasts and, each time, I noticed the pain and swelling of my arthritis diminished and my flexibility improved.

Leo also shared my love of nature, and we spent as much time as we could enjoying the beauty of both beach and bush. Every weekend was an opportunity to explore the natural world through camping or bushwalking.

Leo's other passion, however, was for something I knew nothing about: he followed the stock market, understood its patterns and was very skilled at interpreting his meticulous charts. Frequently he could predict when a penny dreadful was about to take off. In the middle of the night he could often be found perched on a stool, elbow on knee and hand on chin, studying the patterns of charts that stretched down the hallway into the lounge. He said they 'spoke' to him.

But Leo wasn't interested in accruing wealth. I once found a briefcase under his bed stuffed with letters and certificates of appreciation from more than a dozen charities to whom he regularly donated sizeable amounts—some in the tens of thousands. He was content to live in a rented apartment overlooking Bondi Beach and happy to disperse his successes to worthy causes.

***

Leo belonged to a School of Philosophy that, as the name implies, exposed students to all the great philosophical teachers and teachings. It also provided a structured pathway to ignite spiritual awakening. I was keen to join Leo in this exploration, as it aligned with many of my interests; meditation and the practice of being present were fundamental to the School's teachings, and this resonated strongly for both of us. I was already a keen practitioner of meditation, and because of my legs I had to move with heightened awareness, otherwise I could easily tear ligaments, muscles and tendons.

The word 'mindfulness' hadn't yet been invented, but at the School we participated in activities designed to keep us firmly focused in the present moment—which is, of course, the meaning of the term. These included calligraphy, the sounding of Sanskrit, gardening, cleaning, woodwork, dressmaking, lace-making and crocheting. One of the School's mottos was 'wake up, get up', and we arose every morning at four to undertake a series of disciplines made up of these activities, beginning with three hours of spiritual discipline.

Though I had no desire to crochet, I found that focusing on the space between the hook and the thread was a fabulous mindful activity. Our hooks could barely be seen by the naked eye, and our threads were of the finest cotton available. In groups of about ten, we would sit with our spines comfortably erect while focusing on our work, which was held at eye height without any support for the arms or back. The finished products were crocheted spider webs no more than a fifty-cent coin in diameter and edged in gold thread. Our group produced two thousand of these to be sewn into a magnificent bedspread, although any attachment to the outcome wasn't encouraged.

The purpose of this activity was simply to keep the attention focused and the mind under observation. It went for three hours every Saturday afternoon, and silence was maintained throughout. As you might imagine, this was a perfect opportunity for the mind to go wild: 'What the heck am I doing this for?' 'I could be at the beach or bushwalking.' 'Whose bright idea was this anyway?' 'Surely there are more preferable pathways to enlightenment?' and so on. It was a great discipline in observing the ego's resistance, and this rigour and focus was applied equally to all our disciplines.

Another of the School's valued activities was cleaning, and I soon came to understand the expression 'cleanliness is next to godliness'. Bringing one's whole attention to the act of cleaning turns a mundane activity into a more sacred one. When a surface is pristine, there's a simple purity to it—everything that doesn't belong has been removed. This reminds me of sculptors who say their task is to remove everything extraneous to their artwork, which already exists within the stone or wood. It also echoes the age-old spiritual philosophy of removing the falsehood of separation so the unifying principle that enlivens everything is recognised and experienced.

In the School, I learned to observe my mind by simply watching the thoughts and feelings without acting on them. This mental training, along with meditation, has been an invaluable asset throughout my life, giving me great focus and concentration.

After I joined Leo at the School, I moved into his Bondi flat—a big step for us, and one that brought us happiness. Until then, when not travelling or staying in the nurses' quarters, I had always lived with my parents. I was finally making my own way in life, though I was also happy to be swept along by Leo's enthusiasm and certainty about our combined future. Our marriage in 1975 sealed our commitment to each other. A simple, civil ceremony suited us both and we celebrated the occasion with my family and a few friends at a restaurant at The Spit.

CHAPTER 11

Life's surprises

Only a few months passed before a great sense of tiredness overcame me. Whenever I had a spare half-hour, I just wanted to lie down and sleep. This went on for several weeks—I slept soundly at night and grabbed a nap during the day if possible. Between my work in a health-food store, my studies, my School commitments and my weekend activities with Leo, life was full, but that didn't account for my profound exhaustion.

At first, pregnancy as the cause of my tiredness didn't occur to me. I had resigned myself to the fact that I couldn't bear children. But when my exhaustion didn't abate, I decided to eliminate the possibility before seeking medical tests. I picked up a kit at the local pharmacy, went home, used it and sat there waiting for the negative result.

You can imagine my amazement and delight when the test confirmed that, indeed, I was pregnant!

It was also a considerable shock. Restless and excited by this unexpected news, I went down to the rocks at Bondi to take in the enormity of this revelation before Leo arrived home. I had no idea how he might react—I'd only ever broached the subject to tell him that I couldn't fall pregnant, and he hadn't seemed perturbed.

As I sat on the rocks above the pounding surf, I silently repeated to myself 'I'm pregnant' several times with the emphasis shifting from the first word to the second, back and forth: '*I'm* pregnant' to 'I'm *pregnant!*'

Bizarrely, a naked man with a healthy expression of his manhood stood up from behind some nearby rocks, no doubt to shock me. I stared at him blankly and blurted, 'I'm pregnant.' It was amusing to see his subsequent deflation!

Back at the flat, when I told Leo the news, he was instantly thrilled. He danced around like a large praying mantis—he was 195 centimetres tall—and then picked me up and held me close.

It turned out I was already well past the first trimester. I was lucky to have had no morning sickness, only the overwhelming tiredness.

***

Pregnancy, while welcome, changed our relationship as it does with all couples. We had been living very simply and concocting schemes that didn't involve children.

Recently we'd been learning about wild edible plants, and we'd made plans to walk to Queensland via the stock routes with a donkey to carry our meagre belongings. We'd already purchased the travel permits along with the donkey, Jenny, who was living with friends at Mulgoa.

Leo drove to Paddy's Markets twice a week to pick up and then deliver fresh produce for Jenny, which she devoured enthusiastically. On weekends, Leo and I brought her a bonanza of cabbage, lettuce, other leafy greens, fruit and whatever vegetables we could pick up freely from the city markets. Leo had a great relationship with the Chinese market gardeners, and they kept leaves especially for Jenny. On days when we couldn't get out to feed her, our friends gave her hay.

A note for anyone contemplating such an adventure: donkeys eat voraciously. By the time we unloaded the many boxes of produce from the car, dumped their contents into Jenny's enclosure, and attended to the cleaning of her water trough and stable, she had eaten every last morsel of this mountain of vegetation.

Now that I was pregnant, we realised our carefree dream of travelling with Jenny would have us resembling Mary and Joseph by Christmas. And so, Jenny had to go.

***

As soon as Leo needed to earn a better income with a family on the near horizon, he found that his knack for picking penny dreadfuls wasn't so good. It had been easier when he hadn't wanted or needed the money; he didn't respond well to pressure. His heart was also no longer in being a chef—he didn't want to return to the stressful kitchen environment. I understood and supported his decision.

Like everyone who has experienced childhood trauma, Leo had been affected by the suffering he'd endured as a young boy. The behavioural patterns we develop to cope with childhood trauma become habitual ways of dealing with stressful situations as we grow into adulthood. Leo and I had both developed coping strategies to compensate for the individual stresses we had experienced in our younger years but these weren't always useful or compatible with each other.

Whenever there was upset or the potential for conflict, my tendency was to disappear—if not physically, then emotionally. My pattern as a child had been to freeze, mainly because I never knew how to respond to the unpredictable behaviours of Geoff and Brenden. Fighting or fleeing obviously weren't options for me, so I vanished as if into a submarine, battening down the hatches, waiting for the storm to pass.

Leo's reaction to conflict was the opposite. When he felt under pressure or threatened, he would use his size, volume and bluster to intimidate, dominate or bully his way through. But this only made me want to disappear further into the recesses of my being. Clearly, our strategies were a lethal combination.

At the time, neither of us had enough awareness of ourselves to skilfully deal with the stress that's inevitable in every relationship when the first glow of love loses its brilliance. Being in love only takes you so far—when pressures come on the scene, our maladaptive patterns surface and are played out. Trying to resolve the challenges of adulthood, let alone parenthood, with the reactive physiology and thinking of young children is unlikely to lead to a mature collaboration and a respectful outcome.

If I'd understood then what I came to understand much later, perhaps things would have played out differently. But, as they say, it takes two to tango, and neither of us had a clue how to deal with stress in more mature or creative ways. While I was keen to ensure that the little one growing within me would only be bathed in an atmosphere of love, on several occasions Leo's temper flared to the point of violence.

The first time I felt the back of his hand against my cheek, it propelled me across the room to where I landed in a heap. I was shattered, of course, but my focus had to remain on bringing this precious being into the world as safely and lovingly as I could.

When Leo's storm passed, he was apologetic and assured me it would never happen again. But it happened again. And again.

It's a strange thing when a woman keeps quiet about violence occurring behind closed doors. I didn't want my parents to know, so I played out their expected scenario of 'everything's fine'. That might have been as much to reassure myself as it was to protect Leo from their disapproval. Making excuses to explain my injuries compounded my sense of shame, guilt and embarrassment. This was meant to be a happy time, and everyone's focus was on the imminent arrival of new life into our midst.

I didn't mention to anyone what was happening at home—upholding the facade of the happy family was easier than dealing with the consequences of disclosure. Perhaps the lessons learned in watching Rae tolerate a different kind of abuse from Geoff had laid the foundation for my own inability to address the situation. Our family had always maintained appearances regardless of how things felt and I had perfected the art of not complaining about anything.

***

My parents had given Leo work in their publishing business, although it wasn't a natural fit for him. We rented a two-bedroom duplex in Fairlight to be closer to my parents' business in Frenchs Forest.

Leo had strong and definite ideas about my preparation for the birth. He insisted on daily exercise and a rigid diet. As he became increasingly controlling of my behaviour, I still had no voice to object. The old patterns of not speaking up, of not being a bother, of believing that others knew best continued to undermine my ability to have an opinion, let alone express one.

I'm embarrassed to admit that Leo's regimen included my running the entire length of Manly Beach each day. The stupidity of this activity after all the difficulties with my legs was tantamount to sabotage. While my legs were functioning quite well in my mid-twenties, anyone should have known that with my history such an activity was unwise. But Leo would encourage me to keep going, and I didn't want to let him down, so I kept doing it literally until the day of the birth.

Along with Leo, I had developed a scepticism about doctors and their advice, and I'd avoided consulting them given I was keen to have as natural a birth as possible. Leo didn't want me to see a doctor at all, but I saw our family physician in Mosman from time to time without Leo's knowledge. We intended to have a home birth with an experienced midwife, and my physician was supportive if not enthusiastic.

Leo and I studied and diligently practised the Lamaze techniques for natural birth, and I practised yoga for a minimum of two hours a day along with my regular practices of meditation, calligraphy and the sounding of Sanskrit.

Leo had me on a strict eating regimen that I followed obediently. Some years later, my parents and Ross told me that they were singularly unimpressed when they saw him gorging himself on chips and burgers at a cafe near their office. The fact that he couldn't control his urges probably made him more determined to control mine.

Despite Leo's severity, I gained much pleasure from preparing for our first child. I sewed and stitched, painted and decorated, and generally feathered our nest. We had no accurate due date, as we had no idea when conception had occurred. My physician's best guess was February, though I couldn't share that with Leo.

∗∗∗

On a balmy Saturday evening, we went into the city and ate at our favourite vegetarian restaurant. Then, leaving our car parked, we walked up through Kings Cross. We were about to walk down William Street to collect the car when I went into a hotel for the inevitable pee. Someone had just smoked a joint in one of the cubicles; moments after I smelled it, my waters broke. By the time I joined Leo outside on the pavement, my contractions had begun in earnest and I couldn't make it back to our car. We hailed a cab and returned home to continue our well-rehearsed routine of breathing through the contractions.

Leo called the midwife, who arrived from the other side of Sydney four hours after my waters had broken. By then I was desperate to push this baby out! She gave me the go-ahead, and for the next five and a half hours I pushed with every ounce of my strength.

I'm forever grateful that Leo finally said 'enough'. He telephoned and then took me to the nearest hospital, whose staff were exceedingly unhappy to meet me. The midwife didn't want us to go and certainly wasn't going to accompany us, which is just as well as they may have eaten her alive. Arriving relatively unannounced at six on a Sunday morning via Emergency to give birth is not recommended, especially when the hospital has no record of your pregnancy. The staff clearly thought—quite rightly, from their perspective—that I was a stupid young woman for trying to give birth at home.

The doctor could barely control his disgust with me and only said, 'Hold her down and keep the mask on her face until the baby's out.'

Though they confirmed that my baby wasn't showing any signs of foetal distress, they didn't wait for a contraction before dragging her unceremoniously out of my exhausted body with forceps, into the light of day.

The dearest little baby girl was finally reunited with me as they placed her in my waiting arms. I was still shaking inside from the trauma and brutality of the birth, but she was here. My dream of a natural birth in a quiet and loving environment was shattered by the nightmare of her arrival, but she was perfect.

Leo and I hadn't discussed names because we thought the baby might bring a name with him or her on arrival. Names were now the last thing on my mind—as I was terribly shaken and tried to stay focused on learning how to feed this beautiful infant.

On the third day, Leo stood in the doorway to my hospital room and announced with indisputable confidence and enthusiasm, 'Her name is Ada!'

My shaking stomach lurched and turned, and my heart shrank to meet it, but I was in no state to argue with Leo, so Ada became her name.

Soon afterwards, I was grateful to go home where we could rest, recover from the trauma and get to know our gorgeous baby. Leo adored her as much as I did, and we felt so blessed to have her with us. She was generally happy, though she suffered badly with colic, so the usual exhaustion of parenthood in that first year was compounded by the endless walking of her up and down for hours at a time, day and night. Leo was a wonderful support and did more than his share of the walking, rocking and cradling.

But although little Ada was alive and kicking, I had dreadful nightmares about her birth for more than three years.

***

When Ada was just five months old, my beloved Granny became very unwell and uncharacteristically tired. When Granny didn't sound well on the phone, my mother flew to Brisbane and brought her—and Jacqui, her precious cat—back to Mosman, where our family physician conducted some tests. They confirmed the diagnosis of advanced breast cancer, so Granny underwent surgery.

When we visited her in hospital, the sound of raucous laughter usually greeted us long before we entered her room. The nurses, other patients and doctors loved her humour and waggish ways. Rae feared that her mother hadn't fully absorbed the impact of her prognosis, though the doctor assured her that he'd given Granny all the facts. She began but immediately stopped chemotherapy, as she didn't like the side effects and was quite a pragmatist, preferring to let nature take its course.

One day, while still in hospital, Granny said to Rae, 'It's a bugger, isn't it?' That was the first and last time she mentioned her impending fate. When Rae asked Granny if she wanted anything, her response was, of course, 'A party.'

Granny's sister Edna arrived from Brisbane to spend time with her, and Jacqui would only leave her for the bare necessities, immediately returning to her side or lap.

I visited as often as I could, and Granny looked the picture of contentment when she nursed young Ada. It was lovely to see them cuddling quietly together and I know it brought her great joy to cradle new life as her own seeped away.

Leo, of course, had some strange ideas about babies and their environment. When he visited Granny with us, he wouldn't let her hold Ada, and I saw the look of hurt and sadness in her eyes. I was helpless against his determination—and, the truth was, I feared his anger and had taken to avoiding anything that might provoke it. The way that I was repeating the pattern developed with my father wasn't lost on me, but recognising these deeply entrenched patterns doesn't necessarily equip us to change them.

Although her home was in Queensland, Granny was much loved by many, many people in Sydney, and her party was a very happy occasion. It was meant to just be drinks in the early evening so as not to exhaust her, but people were still there at 10 pm, while Granny made all the jokes and entertained everyone with her wit and charm. The photo we have of her on that joyous but poignant night shows a beautiful woman with no evidence of illness, dressed in her favourite lilac frock, radiating life and happiness.

The following week Geoff left for business in the United States, having been assured by Granny's doctors that she probably had about six months to live. Early the next morning, Granny started struggling for breath. Edna sat with her while Rae called the doctor, who didn't come soon enough. Everything unravelled so quickly, and unfortunately Rae sat with her beloved mother all alone as she died.

I weep more now in the writing of this than I did at the time, as tears seemed taboo in our family. After Granny's death, Rae continued to maintain her veneer of normalcy. Through traumas and tragedies, she protected her children from her own deep grief, and I have never seen her break under pressure. I had certainly learned well from her.

Geoff returned immediately, composing the eulogy on his miserable flight home. At Granny's funeral we were all in shock, unable to take in how swiftly events had unfolded. We still frequently recount stories of her life and use her favourite expressions, and it's a rare day that some memory of her doesn't cheer my heart.

***

The next couple of years passed happily enough as Ada brought me and Leo great joy.

But something was bothering her. The first sentence I remember her stringing together is, 'I hate the name Ada.' While I completely sympathised with her and would have happily let her change it, Leo wouldn't hear of it and that was that.

When Ada was about three, we were sitting at the kitchen table eating breakfast when she gave me a fixed stare and her face clouded.

She said, 'I get up, I have breakfast. I go outside and play. I eat lunch and have a nap. I get up and play. I have dinner. I have a bath and I go to bed and sleep. I get up, I have breakfast. I go outside and play. I eat lunch and have a nap. I get up and play. I have dinner. I have a bath and I go to bed and sleep.' She repeated it for a third time and then looked plaintively at me as she concluded, 'On and on until I die?'

In less than two minutes, she had postulated a somewhat defeatist view of existence.

***

We saved diligently for a home, and soon we moved to a tiny house in nearby Manly Vale. It was a small fibro and stone cottage with two bedrooms and a large garden, and it had plenty of room for play. As a newly graduated naturopath I sometimes saw clients in the sunroom, but my main focus was on caring for Ada and Leo.

Enough time had passed since the traumatic birth that I felt able to face the idea of having another child. After a disappointing miscarriage, I fell pregnant with Simon. I vacillated between having a home or hospital birth, until Leo and I finally decided upon another attempt at a home birth given my reluctance to be in hospital.

But this time I was under the care of an obstetrician, as I'd been damaged by those long hours of pushing and by Ada's rough arrival. Fortunately the obstetrician was a kind and gentle man who supported either a home or hospital birth, and he took on the role of guiding me through my pregnancy. He respected my choices, telling me he would only interfere if he felt any concern for my safety or the baby's.

Because I'd fallen pregnant quite quickly after the miscarriage, the obstetrician put a stitch into my cervix to ensure the baby stayed put until fully developed. After nine months, the stitch was removed and the doctor thought this would stimulate labour—but no, the baby wasn't ready to make an appearance. When my waters broke, we alerted the midwife and waited until contractions began, but another ten days passed before he eventually made his entrance.

Simon's birth was uncomplicated and easy, and he slipped into the world with a gurgle and a smile in front of the open fire at home. The midwife gently placed him on my abdomen while Leo woke three-year-old Ada. She sleepily knelt by my side and touched her new little brother with great tenderness, wonder and love.

Simon was an easy and good-natured baby who flourished under our delighted adoration. From the moment he arrived, he was a tactile junkie—quite different from Ada, who resisted cuddles and preferred her independence. I wonder if the roughness of her birth influenced her ability to bond with me, though she breastfed happily until she was up and walking. She would often study the way Simon nestled in for a snuggle and then have a go, though cuddling never seemed to come easily to her.

Simon had arrived two days before my birthday in October 1979, and our little family was complete.

CHAPTER 12

Helping, fixing or serving

I'd loved my four years of naturopathic studies, yet they had left me with a desire to explore more deeply the impact our minds have on our bodies through our beliefs and attitudes. There didn't seem to be anywhere that taught about the integrated whole of a human being, and the deeper teachings of yoga held the only written knowledge that connected the mind with the body. I continued my private studies through the School of Philosophy, and through my own reading and practice of the subtle and more in-depth techniques contained in Indian writings on meditation techniques and yogic principles.

At that time, the School was quite patriarchal. This suited Leo, who saw himself very much as the head of our household—and certainly of me. We didn't socialise with anyone outside the School except family, and I fell into the role of wife and mother, being subservient to Leo's needs. All the while, I was increasingly aware of the lack of heart and compassion in the way the School's teachings were presented and lived. When a friend lost her full-term twins and was told to keep her focus in the present moment so she wouldn't drown in grief, I was dismayed even though she wasn't; she did her best to accommodate what they instructed her to do.

After his many years of attending the School, Leo too started becoming disillusioned, but his unhappiness stemmed from his inability to practise the prescribed disciplines—such as rising at 4 am—and he began to lose interest in attending the required classes. I could see he was destined to leave, and while I wasn't yet ready to do so, I knew I would have to follow him. Going to the classes required coordination and cooperation between couples, especially when children were involved.

A lot of Leo's angst came from a deep disappointment with himself: he lacked the discipline required for the various practices. We were arguing more often, and I think it was easier for him to blame me than to recognise that he'd lost interest in pursuing spiritual practice. I felt a sense of foreboding as our interests were diverging and Leo was unhappy within himself. While he held strict views about diet and any number of health-related topics, he was frustrated that he couldn't live up to his own knowledge and expectations.

***

Brenden was still dealing with his depression, and we all lurched through his good times and bad. He would sometimes be discharged from the psychiatric hospital for a few hours so we could be together as a family. He might excuse himself from the table and, before we knew it, ingest every pill in the bathroom. He made several attempts on his life, but we always got him to hospital in time. It was so painful to see him struggling when we knew the funny, creative and brilliant person he could be.

Before I was married, Ross and I had moved into our parents' home to watch over Brenden while they were overseas on one of their business trips. I was sitting on the floor arranging photographs in an album with the telephone beside me. Brenden walked past and kicked the phone 5 metres down the hallway with such quiet rage it horrified me. He was usually so placid when not depressed, and these moments of violence shocked and frightened me. Brenden was particularly manic that day, and Ross and I didn't know how to help him other than not to let him leave the house.

Unbeknown to us, Brenden called the police on another phone extension—given the one he'd kicked was beyond repair—and told them we were keeping him hostage. When sirens heralded their arrival, Brenden climbed out a window and leaped down from the front terrace above the garage. With a smile as wide as our mouths had dropped, he casually walked towards the police officer with his hand outstretched. He couldn't have been more charming as he shook the officer's hand and reassured him there had been a mis-understanding and everything was just hunky-dory.

Like a pendulum, we all swung between wanting to throttle Brenden and gather him into our arms to keep him safe.

My father adored him but had no idea how to relate to him, espe-cially when he was in the depths of his despair. Geoff finally forbade Brenden from entering my parents' home, as the ravages of mental illness destroyed his ability to make choices and subsequently his behaviour and appearance. But there were many times when Rae let Brenden in through a window, bathed his wounds from heaven knows what, fed him and gave him some money, and he went out again through the same window, and all the while my father worked in his study, totally oblivious of his comings and goings.

I returned home one day from shopping with Ada and Simon to find Brenden sprawled across the pathway to our front door, almost unconscious from alcohol and whatever else he might have taken. I brought him in, cleaned him up, fed him and put him to bed, knowing I would have to make him leave before Leo arrived. My heart shrank as I encouraged Ada not to mention to Daddy that Brenden had been in our home. I knew I was grooming her to take on the same behaviours I practised in placating Leo—these are the sins, or fears, that we pass from one generation to another, yet I didn't know a more courageous or skilful way of dealing with Leo's temper.

The stress of balancing Brenden's needs with the judgement and frustration of people like Leo was difficult to say the least. Rae and I found it hard to be the ham in the sandwich, stuck between loving Brenden and dealing with those who blamed him heartily for the results of his self-destructive decisions. They would have preferred to banish him rather than be confronted with someone they couldn't fix or understand; it was easier to point the finger at him for his choices than to see that his torment drove him to make them. I couldn't know the depths of Brenden's darkness, as I'd barely plumbed my own, but I lived with the fear of that darkness and the dreadful helplessness I felt to protect him or myself.

Protecting Ada and Simon from the ravages of Brenden's illness wasn't easy either, given his unexpected visits. I felt torn between loving him and shielding the children from his behaviour. Leo's strong disapproval of having Brenden anywhere near the house or our kids added another dimension of pressure—such control was beyond me.

Later, Rae wrote of Brenden at that time: 'Between bouts he was a natural and happy person, his sense of humour being his saving grace. But underneath was the dread of the next "attack". "Between bouts" became less and less and he'd spend endless months in hospital barely able to bear the pain of his despair and sense of inadequacy.' It was an agony to see him reduced to a drugged zombie that bore no resemblance to the funny, happy, creative, loving, gorgeous man we knew.

My family split over our inability to deal with Brenden's mental illness. Our constant anguish for him and fears of his next suicide attempt put an enormous strain on each of us, as we were all confronted with our failure to help, fix or change him. Each suicide attempt underlined the likelihood of his efforts eventually succeeding.

As time nudged towards his thirtieth birthday, I felt the awful weight of powerlessness, dread and failure. There was nothing I could do to stop him, regardless of having known about his intention for so long.

Frustrations spilled over into words better left unsaid. Driven by his own pain and distress, Geoff at times publicly blamed Rae's parenting of Brenden for his mental health issues. I'm sure it was said many more times to Rae than the twice I heard Geoff tell her, 'It's your fault. You mollycoddled him as a boy!' The agony this must have caused Rae I can only imagine; never was a mother more devoted to supporting her son in becoming the best version of himself. She constantly sought help for him, whereas Geoff simply didn't know what to do except lash out from his own sense of inadequacy. Blaming Rae was an easier path than the pain of being laid bare through introspection. And blaming Brenden was to banish him from our hearts, which surely could only lead to further disintegration—as in, lack of integration and cohesion—within the family.

None of it was easy or simple. Each of us was doing the best we knew how, given who we were, what had happened to us in our lives and what we'd made of it. Geoff's anger became the bodyguard of his anguish; for Rae, it was an insulting and painful blow.

Some relationships only survive when things are running smoothly. Many a marriage or long-established relationship has been shattered by the strain of living with a mentally ill family member. I have the greatest respect for my parents who, though they each saw the situation so differently, weathered the storms more or less together.

We were all frustrated, exhausted and often isolated as individuals within our immediate family. Extended family saw the situation differently too, and while some were able to step forward, others couldn't understand what was happening or preferred to look in another direction.

Living with a sense of impending doom wasn't easy. Brenden's words about ending his life clouded my heart, yet I still couldn't share them with anyone. And I still felt responsible for him, although keeping him safe was way beyond my control.

***

I focused as much as I could on parenting my two small children and supporting Leo. I was blessed to be a full-time mother for the first few years of the children's lives, only seeing the odd client in my practice. Ada and Simon were our delight and joy, and we bushwalked and picnicked our way through their early years. I was so grateful to be there to witness each developmental stage, and we had oceans of time to go to the beach or play in the garden.

There were odd flare-ups with Leo, so I continued to avoid touchy subjects—which, of course, isn't a good way to conduct any relationship. He was a big man, and I feared the back of his hand. It could send me across the room or put my teeth through my lip. And when those rare moments of violence occurred, I always made excuses to explain my injuries. Looking good while feeling the opposite was my well-practised art, and I could see no alternative that wouldn't bring pain to our children.

Leo was a devoted father who loved the company of his kids. They had fun together, and he was gentle and sweet with them. They came to know his fluctuating disposition as they grew older, but when they were very young they only experienced his love.

Still, there were many times when I wondered whether our

marriage would survive Leo's mercurial moods. Taking Ada and Simon from the constancy of their adoring father seemed cruel, so I persisted in training them to avoid behaviours or topics that would upset him—just as I'd been trained as a child. Was this the kind of relationship I wanted to demonstrate to my kids? I felt stuck in a trap of my own making; I couldn't extricate myself without creating a great deal of heartache for our children.

For a time after he stopped working for my parents, Leo developed a business called Friendly Herbs that supplied potted herbs through greengrocers in our district. Our back garden became a nursery, and Leo and Ada spent hours working together to pot the plants. Ada could identify by smell and sight well over thirty different herbs, and it was beautiful to see her tottering among them with her towering dad nearby. Depriving the children of such special moments seemed impossible.

***

My legs were again becoming problematic as the right knee had swung back around while the left knee was also rotating inwards. I was limping badly, and the arthritic pain kept me awake at night and often made walking difficult. I'm sure the changes in my diet and my other health-related practices made a profound and positive difference, but my legs had still deteriorated. The frequent carrying of small children and groceries hadn't helped. Neither, I imagine, had the running when I was pregnant with Ada.

By now I was often on crutches to relieve the pain. Taking the weight in my arms relieved the pressure on the arthritic joints, which was something I couldn't achieve with a walking stick—and walking sticks always seemed more permanent to me than crutches. Of course, juggling small children and crutches was a challenge, so I often just struggled on. I was loath to take any medication for the arthritis, determined to use only a natural approach due to a deep suspicion of drugs and their side effects. As a nurse I'd witnessed adverse reactions among patients, and I was also aware of the statistics around some drugs' side effects.

I returned to John McGlynn, who said there was no alternative but to repeat the surgeries for a third time, cutting my right femur and tibia then rotating each in opposite directions until my leg was realigned.

The thought of more surgery worried me, and it didn't seem to be a permanent solution. I decided to try another approach and, through friends from my naturopathic studies, I heard about a skilled Chinese herbalist in Sydney's Chinatown. He must have been a hundred, and his bent-over, smiling, toothless wife perhaps even older. They spoke no English, so I took an interpreter with me for our consultations.

The herbalist took my pulse for a long time. Finally, through the interpreter, he told me that all my problems were hormonal, that I'd never had a regular cycle—which was true—and he could straighten my leg by sorting out my hormones and giving me some exercises. I was happy to give anything a try to avoid more surgery.

I have since wondered, after gaining knowledge about the mind–body connection and the role of epigenetics, if I subconsciously altered my hormonal system as a child. Epigenetics refers to the expression of our genes being altered by the environment around our cells, which is affected by what we eat and drink, how much exercise we do, the toxins we're exposed to, our hormones, our neurotransmitters and other factors; it influences whether a gene will be expressed, enhanced, diminished or negated. Is it possible that I redirected my hormones to 'grow up quickly' so I could look after Brenden at the expense of others? No doubt it will remain a mystery—though 'mind over matter' is a commonly asserted truism.

Every day for three months, I cooked up and drank the most revolting, gelatinous concoction of dried herbs and insects simmered for hours with the cracked shin bone of a pig. Once more a vegetarian, I found this difficult, and often it was evening before I could bring myself to drink the foul-smelling, now cool, wobbly goo.

The herbalist packed my knee in black sticky muck and brown paper, and I had to bend and straighten my leg 350 times a day over a stick with a golf ball on top, inserted behind my knee.

In two months, and for the first time ever, I had a regular cycle. And, in three, my knee and leg were straight as a die! The pain from the arthritis eased too, and when I returned to see John McGlynn, he shook his head in bewilderment and encouraged me to continue whatever I was doing, as surgery was no longer needed.

What has often struck me as unscientific and strange is the closed nature of many fine doctors. I believe that medicine should sit comfortably alongside mystery; we can keep expanding our scientific knowledge and developing better ways of assisting people, while we continue to trust in the mystery—in some power beyond our current understanding. Being open to ancient healing knowledge from other cultures seemed an obvious area to explore.

John was a skilled and dedicated surgeon, and he was happy that I avoided surgery, yet he wasn't at all interested in my alternative approach. Surely doctors should be motivated to help their patients with minimally invasive treatments; unfortunately, the system isn't set up to support or encourage such an eclectic approach. The study of medicine has divided the body into bits—it's rare to find a physician who sees a patient as a whole person rather than through the lens of a single expertise. Some surgeons specialise in knees with little regard to a person's back, and yet what they do with a knee may have a profound impact on what happens in the spine. As Abraham Maslow said, 'If all you have is a hammer, everything looks like a nail.'

CHAPTER 13

The roller-coaster of life and death

When a friend introduced Brenden to meditation, his mental state improved almost immediately. Of course, Rae and I had been at him for years to try meditation, as it was a treasure to us both, but these gifts are nearly always better given from someone outside the family.

We were so happy to see him clean up his life and stabilise his health. It seemed he'd found peace and joy in the slow rhythm of a simple life at an ashram in Adelaide.

Then, for a time, he lived in a friend's shack on the banks of the Murray in far western New South Wales. I drove out to spend time with him there, surrounded by the gnarled gums that lined the river. I felt such relief to see him looking so content. There was an uncomplicated wisdom about him as he fished, meditated and collected wood. We sat by the river in companionable silence, listening to the whisperings of the ancient gums and watching egrets pick through the shallows. This remains a sacred memory.

I was too afraid of a relapse to mention his past anguish or the commitment he'd made as a child. And, of course, I was glad to enjoy the present rather than delve into what had gone before. I stayed long enough to fully relish the change in him.

As one year became two, we breathed a collective sigh of relief when Brenden's happiness and contentment seemed to consolidate. At last we could let go of our interminable worry about him. He was now beyond thirty years of age and, in my mind, he'd forgotten his commitment to take his life, even if I hadn't. My relief was deep.

We happily bade him farewell as he travelled to India to deepen his meditation by living at an ashram in the presence of his teacher.

Two months after leaving for India, he died violently by his own hand.

***

Ross called me with the news. An unuttered shriek of horror formed in my mind and body. For a moment I felt angry at Ross for delivering this blow, with no regard for the awful responsibility he'd willingly taken on by alerting people to Brenden's death.

We gathered at my parents' home in stunned and aching silence. There would be no body, no goodbyes, no packing up of possessions, no funeral, no memorial and little information about what had happened.

The story—as best we know it, having pieced it together like some wretched jigsaw—is this. Some young British tourists had found Brenden in a state of acute despair. Not knowing what to do, they took him to the gate of the British Embassy in Kathmandu. He went in but was told they were closing for the day and to return in the morning when they would surely help him. But there was no tomorrow for Brenden. That night his life became too much of a painful burden and he destroyed himself.

Geoff told us that Brenden had been cremated on a traditional funeral pyre in the capital of Kathmandu.

It was hard to come to terms with his death when one minute he'd been alive and well in India, and then he just wasn't. In some strange way, I felt that at least now he was forever safe in my heart, though knowing this brought little comfort. We have precious few photos, a letter or two, an abstract picture he drew and a beautiful cowry shell he always kept with him, which now sits with me here on my desk.

Brenden had often inhabited a world beyond our access, and as news of his death filtered through the grapevine, we received letters from strangers who loved and appreciated him. These letters often came from the 'night people' who told us wonderful stories of Brenden getting them off drugs by sleeping across their doorway or helping a woman create a home for herself and her kids away from domestic violence. He had often brought hope to others even though he found precious little for himself.

To this day, I can see a head in the crowd, a posture, a face like Brenden's, and wonder, what if it wasn't my brother who died? What if he's off living elsewhere, and someone else did those unspeakable things to himself? I know that he's dead, but reconciling the way he died has been hard. He was a peace lover, a gentle man who wouldn't hurt a fly, though his illness provoked incidents like the telephone flying down the hallway. It speaks of the anguish and despair he must have felt that he turned to such violence in ending his suffering.

As with all of the dead he is frozen in time, never a day over thirty-two.

Each family member grieves in their own way, and these are often not in synch with one another or even compatible. So it was with us. No one knew what to say.

Rae and I wanted to talk but could only do so quietly, mindful that Geoff didn't want anything said unnecessarily and certainly not publicly. Ross buried himself in busyness, doing his best to support the family and staff. We each grieved the loss of Brenden in our own private ways, though Rae and I drew closer because we struggled as much with the manner of his death as with the death itself. His suicide had been expected for so many years, but not in those last two happy ones and never with such violence. We were left to reconcile the unreality and certainty of his death.

Rae found that she could no longer meditate, even though meditation had been an integral part of her spiritual life for many years. When she closed her eyes, all she could experience were dark and menacing colours—black, grey, burnt orange, dirty green—that formed a swirling cloud between her and finding peace. She ached for peace as I did, both of us numb and unable to talk properly about our acute distress.

My uncle Peter—Rae's brother, who also worked in the family business—lowered the flag to half-mast at the office. The staff who knew Brenden were distraught. Everyone who knew Brenden, loved him. We had no language to describe our feelings.

Tears provided no refuge, and mine were stifled anyway, along with a trove of other unresolved griefs and traumas. I would cope as I always coped. There was no choice but to cope.

Leo couldn't meet me in my grief, and I couldn't blame him. Our relationship was teetering on the edge of a disastrous end, and I felt shattered. My long-held sense of responsibility for Brenden was finished. I felt that I'd failed not only him but also myself. Intellectually I knew this to be nonsense, as no one is responsible for another person's life in such circumstances, but that's how the helpless child in me felt.

✶✶✶

During this tumultuous time, we moved to a much larger home high on the hills of Manly Vale, overlooking a distant ocean. We settled in well enough, but grief came with us.

I was unable or unwilling to keep pandering to Leo's prescriptions for my existence, and I could no longer cope with some of the habits he enforced. They were only small things, like having his socks colour-coded and folded in a particular way, or his shirts hung all facing the same way while being colour-coded. Woe betide me if a blue shirt was hung among the white ones. One day, I found myself standing in front of his cupboard with a blue-checked shirt in my hand, having a panic attack because I couldn't remember whether it should go among the blue shirts or the checked ones.

If I did the laundry while he was at work, when he arrived home he would check to see if the clothes had all been ironed, folded correctly and put away. Another day, on hearing his tyres on the gravel driveway, my anxiety was overwhelming because the laundry basket still had some clothes in it. I found myself hiding clothes under a bed so there would be no evidence of what he saw as laziness.

He frequently ran his finger along skirting boards or behind furniture or the piano to ensure I was keeping everything spotless. He also checked the fridge regularly—jars needed to be stored according to type, with their labels facing out, and there were major upsets if any fruit or vegetable had wilted, let alone gone bad. Perhaps this stemmed from Leo's childhood stress around food as a precious commodity.

Whatever the reasons for his obsessions, I did my very best to have everything perfectly arranged. But the more I tried, the more he would look for what I'd missed. My self-esteem was completely tied to getting things right for Leo, and he was a hard taskmaster indeed. The only one harder on me than Leo was myself.

I had become increasingly afraid of his temper and couldn't sleep with my back to him. My fear was no doubt unfounded, but it certainly had me in its grip.

But then came a major turning point in our relationship.

One Saturday, Leo stood at the bottom of the twenty or so stairs at the back of the house, while I stood on the landing above, outside the kitchen door, with Simon on my hip and Ada by my side. I'd been preparing lunch when Leo had summoned me to the landing. While working in his office downstairs, he'd noticed an approaching thunderstorm. He stood looking up at me and, with an air of impatience, he motioned to the clouds and said, 'Your laundry on the clothesline is about to get wet.'

Perhaps I felt safer because of the distance between us and the height from which I spoke. But my reply, 'It's *our* laundry,' signalled a profound change in me.

We stared at each other, and then Leo nodded, disappeared into the laundry to retrieve a basket—and quietly took in the laundry.

CHAPTER 14

Grief and loss

Grief is a difficult beast to know and live with. Geoff and Ross threw their energies into the business, and Rae and I continued numbly with our responsibilities and chores. The only respite Rae and I enjoyed together involved a weekly meditation group, which included a discussion on spiritual teachings from *A Course in Miracles*. This group of people provided a safe harbour where we explored our life and grief from a spiritual perspective.

A few months later, Rae, Ada and I travelled to a meditation conference in Los Angeles and then on to a spiritual community, Ananda, in the Sierra Nevada mountains of California. This was a wonderful escape for Rae from Geoff and me from Leo. For the first time, we each spoke a little of what was going on in our marriages. Both of us had gone to great lengths to maintain an air of normalcy for the other, each too afraid of the consequences of speaking up. Family secrets are always destructive to someone, but neither of us had a way of articulating our distress until we were alone together.

Then, at Ananda, Rae experienced a profound moment of healing. On hearing of Brenden's recent death, our new friends there offered to host a meditation to focus on freeing his spirit, given there had been no funeral or formal acknowledgement of his passing. During this short ceremony, Rae felt the burden of grief lift from her heart. She had a strong sensation of a white dove resting in her cupped hands; she felt soft feathers and the scratch of claws as this symbolic creature flew from her hands into the light.

We returned to Australia slightly relieved of the ache of anguish, though my grief remained a crumpled heap of self-recriminations, sadness, shame and guilt.

People often don't understand the physicality of grief. I felt hollowed out or that a significant part of me had been amputated or was missing. I no longer felt capable of continuing—or certainly not as I had up until then. Life had made sense when Brenden was alive, even though it was often painful. Without him there was no sense, no compass, no way to move forward; he was the pivotal point in my life. I kept going through the motions of living, but being confronted by my sense of identity and personal values meant I came up lacking in this changed landscape of grief. My inadequacies glared back at me from everywhere I looked.

✷✷✷

While I was at Ananda, I had a strong sense that it could be good for me to return with Leo and the kids, and for me and Leo to undertake yoga and meditation teacher training there. This course was comprehensive and highly respected both in Australia and the United States, and it was only accessible as a full-time, three-month, live-in course. Care and a school would be provided for the children, and although the accommodation would be very different from our house in Australian middle-class suburbia, it would be a rustic, clean and comfortable geodesic dome set among the manzanita trees.

I discussed the idea with Leo, and we both felt it could provide a perfect opportunity to heal and improve our relationship. Perhaps by focusing on our mutual interests in a different environment, we could start afresh.

Our house sold the week we put it on the market. Six weeks after my return from the first Ananda trip, Leo and I had packed up our home, put everything into storage and set off on our adventure into a better future. Or so we thought.

Leo and I loved the course. Our days were full of the theory and practice of yoga, our meals were supplied, the children were happy and cared for, and it was a perfect environment for us all to flourish.

For the first time in a long time, I experienced moments of peace. But my laughter and the camaraderie of the other students made Leo jealous. He didn't like that there were a lot of men in the yoga course, and I was well-liked by our fellow students—as was he.

Somehow, Leo got it fixed in his mind that I'd coerced him into coming to Ananda with my sole intention being to leave him. I tried to reassure him that this wasn't true, but he chose not to believe me. Belief can trap or free us; in this instance, nothing I could do or say would change Leo's mind. Our arguments became more frequent and, given we were living in a one-room geodesic dome, I tried to shield the children from his anger. But he couldn't bear being told anything, so asking him to speak more quietly or not shout at me as it upset the children was like waving a red rag to a bull.

One afternoon during our free time, I went into town with the children to pick up some supplies. Nevada City was a forty-minute drive from the yoga teaching campus, and on our return a couple of hours later, Leo was nowhere to be seen. Everything looked normal and nothing seemed awry, so I told the children that their father must have gone for a walk, which he often did during our free time.

But Leo didn't return that night, and both children were upset. I felt uneasy—but, wanting to reassure them, I told them that perhaps Leo was staying with friends in the main village of Ananda, a few kilometres from the yoga teaching campus. I cuddled and comforted them, saying he would be back tomorrow for sure.

But Leo didn't return the next day or the next, and by then I was very concerned. Our news spread and everyone in the community was on the lookout, but there was no word of Leo.

And then I noticed that his stock market charts were gone. My heart sank. If they were gone, Leo was gone. Because his clothes were still there, it hadn't occurred to me that he had returned to Australia. He had taken what cash we had, his passport and charts, and nothing else. There was no way of contacting him, given we no longer had a home in Australia. I left messages with the only friend I thought he would contact, but there was never a word from Leo.

***

I decided to complete the yoga course, which had been fully paid for along with the costs of the children's care and education. Ananda kindly refunded the rest of Leo's fees so I had some cash for our necessities.

Stressful things often happen all at once, and a series of unexpected mishaps with Simon, who was almost four, made him even more anxious at the time that his father disappeared from his life.

I was carrying him on my hip up a muddy slope when I slipped and we both got covered in mud. Instead of laughing at our predicament, he cried inconsolably. We went to the ablutions block to clean up, and the hot water tap came off in my hand with steaming water spurting towards the ceiling. Simon sobbed louder.

The next day we were in the car when we hit black ice and slid precariously close to a sheer thousand-foot drop into the Yuba River. We hit a tree, spun around and ended up as an obstruction on a blind curve, unhurt but unable to open the car doors.

I heard a truck approaching down the hill. I prayed that its tyres would grip the road better than ours had, and that the driver would see us in time to brake. Thankfully he did see us, but instead of helping us he used his massive bumper bar to nudge our car out of his way. Perhaps he didn't know there were people inside, but he didn't check. I feared that his intention was to dispatch our vehicle over the edge, as this remote area was a little reminiscent of the film *Deliverance*.

The sound of the bumper against the car and its dreadful shuddering as we were pushed closer to the edge were terrifying. I couldn't hold and comfort Simon; he was strapped into the back seat and I hadn't had time to climb over and release him.

These events were too much for Simon, who looked at me as if to say, 'I've been left with a fuckwit! Where's my daddy?'

He started having the most awful nightmares and would wake screaming a dozen times a night. I would hold him, rocking back and forth, but he was wide-eyed, unseeing and inconsolable. It was heartbreaking, as if he didn't even recognise me.

Some of the mothers in the Ananda community recommended I take Simon to a family counsellor in Nevada City. Emily White-side was very experienced with children, and I felt it imperative to get assistance as I was way out of my depth. Emily specialised in sand-tray therapy, and Simon was given free rein in the tray while she and I talked. As I was leaving, Emily said to me, 'Wrap him in a rainbow before he goes to sleep.'

That night, I told Simon I was going to wrap him in a rainbow and connect a rainbow from his heart to mine. I did this with Ada first so he felt reassured that this was fun and not at all scary. Ada, who was seven, loved the gentle ritual I developed.

When she was all tucked up and ready for sleep, I asked her to close her eyes and imagine I was wrapping her in a cloud of red, the colour of tomatoes, cherries and letterboxes. While I did this, I ran my hand from the top of her head to the tips of her toes so she could better imagine she was being wrapped in the colour. Then I asked her to imagine orange, the colour of oranges and nasturtiums, all the while running my hand gently over her body. Next yellow, the colour of daffodils, sunshine and baby ducklings. Green, the colour of grass and fresh spring leaves. Blue, the colour of the clear blue sky and bluebirds. Indigo, the colour of the night sky behind the stars. And violet, the colour of tiny violets peeping out among their foliage. All the while, I was running my hand from the top of her head to the tips of her toes.

Then I put my hand on her heart and asked her to imagine a really strong rainbow that started in her heart and, moving my hand to my own heart, told her that this rainbow would keep us connected all through the night. I suggested she send a rainbow to Daddy and to her grandparents back in Australia, and that she could send all her love and blessings like fairy dust across the rainbow to them.

Simon watched me perform this ritual with Ada and decided he would like to be wrapped in a rainbow too. I repeated the process with him, and this time I made up a little prayer to go with what I was doing.

I wrap you in a rainbow of light, to care for you all through the night. Your guardian angel watches from above and showers you with her great love.

We also sent a rainbow to his father and grandparents.

Simon's nightmares dropped to just two that night, and the next night he had none. That was the last of his nightmares, thank heavens.

From then on, if ever I had to be away from either of the children while I was completing my course, I would put my hand on their hearts and remind them that a rainbow connected us at all times.

★★★

143

Towards the end of the course, Swami Kriyananda, the founder of the Ananda community and a former disciple of Paramahansa Yogananda (author of *Autobiography of a Yogi*), asked to see me one Sunday after the morning service. These beautiful open-air gatherings focused on meditation and devotional chanting and were open to the community of more than four hundred people.

I was curious and a little apprehensive about why Swami wanted to see me. I hadn't had anything to do with him during my teacher training course and had only seen him at a distance during the occasional gatherings for lectures or morning services.

Swami had heard about Leo's unexpected return to Australia, which had left me financially vulnerable, and he suggested that I work with him in a secretarial and housekeeping capacity. I thanked him for his kindness but said I needed to return to Australia to see if I could reconnect and perhaps resolve things with Leo. I was hopeful our time apart might help him to be open to talking things through. The children needed their father and remaining at Ananda obviously wouldn't be practical long-term. Swami gave a nod but said not to give him my answer yet and to think about his offer.

Swami was greatly loved and respected by everyone in Ananda. Although he didn't set himself up as a guru or seek people who treated him with devotion, most of the community would have given their right arm to work closely with him.

The following week, after the morning service, Swami stopped as he passed me and asked whether I had reconsidered his offer. Again, I thanked him but assured him of my approaching return to Australia. He responded by saying, 'Take a little longer to consider,' and off he went. I thought it strange that he was so insistent.

The children were feeling more settled; they enjoyed their regular routines at school and preschool, and the company of the other kids. Simon slept soundly, content that he was connected to his father through the rainbow. He and Ada had a lot of space and freedom to play and explore, as the community was spread across hundreds of acres of beautiful countryside. The only rules for living in the community were no dogs (because of the bountiful deer), no drugs and to meditate daily.

But although everyday life wasn't difficult, I remained troubled. Leo hadn't been in contact, and I felt lost, rudderless and unsure of what to do next, still quite numb with grief about Brenden, the packing up and sale of our home, and my sudden separation from my husband. Not that anyone would have known what was going on for me, as I barely knew myself and was so used to keeping my polished facade in place. I appeared content as I engaged fully with my training, a great distraction from my inner torment.

The following Sunday, Swami again asked whether I had made my decision. I repeated what I'd said before, but this time he invited me to his home to discuss why I wouldn't say yes. On overhearing this conversation, one of the parents invited Ada and Simon to return home with her for lunch and to play with her children, and another person insisted I take his car as mine had been written off in the accident.

Swami lived a fifteen-minute drive from the main community in a majestic geodesic dome overlooking the Yuba River far, far below. We settled ourselves on the deck with the distant roar of the river reverberating. Swami waited and said nothing.

Finally, I spoke up. I told him I didn't want a guru in my life and I couldn't agree blindly with everything he said. There, it was out. Having been involved with a male-dominated spiritual hierarchy in the School of Philosophy, I wasn't about to repeat the experience. Surely now he would realise I wasn't what he wanted and he'd send me away. Instead, he threw back his head and laughed heartily as he said, 'That's why I want you to work with me. I want someone with whom I can have a conversation, someone who thinks for themselves. So, now you'll work with me?'

I was floundering and stupidly said, 'I can't laugh at all your jokes, Swami. Some of them aren't even funny.'

He overlooked my rudeness and laughed even more heartily.

Wiping away tears, at last he stopped. 'That's fine. Is there anything else?'

I knew that Swami had some health issues and was very fond of rich Indian food that wasn't sensible for him. 'I can't cook what you like to eat, Swami. I'm a naturopath and the food you love isn't good for you.'

Again, he ignored my rudeness and asked what I would cook for him instead. I rattled off a few suitable dishes that were fairly plain and simple, and he said, 'That's fine. I'm happy to eat what you prepare.'

Now, Swami was a truly extraordinary man with incredible talents. Prolific in his creative pursuits, he was an accomplished musician and composer, a keen photographer, an artist, an inspiring teacher and the author of more than a hundred books. I respected him and was touched by his insistence that I work with him.

My other reasons for not accepting his offer were my need to return to Australia and Leo, as well as the fact that my children needed me. Swami's lifestyle was intensely focused and productive, and having young children underfoot wouldn't be possible.

To my astonishment, he said, 'I think your husband has made his decision,' and then more astonishingly, 'I'll get used to having children around.' I knew this wouldn't work, but before I could say another word, he asked, 'Is there anything else?'

I could think of nothing further.

'Good,' he said. 'That's settled. When can you start?'

'Tomorrow?' I hesitantly replied, and so began an amazing chapter in my life.

CHAPTER 15

Out of the frying pan

When Leo left so abruptly, I felt confused, abandoned and lost, and was unsure about what to do. I still felt an inner turmoil due to grief about Brenden, and Leo's sudden departure compounded my feelings of failure. I held a deep need to earn my right to exist and still felt very much a voyeur of other people's lives, still deeply unsure of how to live my own.

The very first morning I began my work with Swami, he informed me that an Indian saint was coming for afternoon tea and there would probably be about six people attending his auspicious visit. I cooked some banana bread and cookies, made sure there was enough milk, and found where cups, saucers and teaspoons were stored.

An hour later, Swami returned and sweetly said there may be as many as ten people for afternoon tea but definitely not more than fifteen. I happily prepared extra food, and ensured there were sufficient provisions both to eat and drink.

An hour later, Swami returned and—with a hint of humour and his characteristic sweetness—told me there could be as many as twenty people but definitely not more than twenty-five.

This continued, with Swami popping in every hour or so until he declared with certainty, 'I promise there'll be no more than fifty people for afternoon tea.' I accepted his promise, as surely a swami's promise was an iron-clad guarantee.

Later that afternoon, eighty-five people attended the afternoon tea. Perched on stairways, and in every seat and space on the floor, they sat enjoying the conversation between Swami and the saint. I looked down from the elevated kitchen in the dome at the scene before me. Somehow, everyone had a cup in hand and something to eat, yet I knew I hadn't prepared enough food for the number of people present.

Swami and the white-bearded saint in his Indian garb sat side by side, smiling sweetly at each other or talking intently. Just then, Swami caught my eye and smiled. In that instant, I realised working with him wasn't so much about housekeeping and secretarial duties as about responding flexibly and good humouredly to changing circumstances, even if they involved a broken promise. The alternative of reacting in a frustrated or grumpy manner would surely bring no joy to me or him, and it wouldn't change the fact that eighty-five people came for tea.

***

Swami regularly caused me to question my beliefs. Through his patience and perseverance with this wayward student, I could see I had collected many beliefs—about myself, life, love, God and other people—and then lived as if they were true. Swami taught me that there is no solid ground, and the only way I can have peace and good humour is for me to respond moment by moment to what 'is' rather than my version of how things 'should' be. But while it can be easy to understand another perspective, this is often not suffi-cient to change what has become second nature to us.

Most days I didn't go to Swami's residence until 10 am, when I took his mail and any messages from the community that needed his attention. I would prepare his lunch and then he'd give me some secretarial work: perhaps typing up his handwritten notes or answers to letters requesting his spiritual direction. He would often ask me to compose these answers for his perusal, correction and embellishment, and this gave me a wonderful opportunity to adapt the theory of yogic spirituality to its practice.

Swami sometimes shared the evening meal with members of the community, usually the male and female ministers who worked closely under his guidance. I would prepare the meal but leave in time to be with my children, prepare their dinner, and tuck them up for sleep and our nightly ritual of being wrapped in the rainbow.

Swami and I often shared lunch on the large deck perched far above the river, overlooking miles of mountains and forests. These were precious times when we discussed all manner of subjects, and he shared his knowledge and perspective with great generosity. I was inspired by his intellect and his ability to make profoundly complex spiritual topics easy to grasp.

I had only been cooking for Swami for a couple of weeks when he informed me that he intended to go into seclusion to meditate and fast.

The first morning of his fast, I went as usual at 10 am to Swami's home to deliver mail and messages and pick up any work. When he opened the door to my knock, I inquired whether he would like me to make him a juice. He gave me a cheeky smile and replied, 'I'd love a cup of coffee!'

'No, Swami,' came my quick reply, 'you mustn't have coffee. You're on a fast. I'll make you a fresh juice.'

He dutifully drank this while mocking 'sad eyes' at me. The next day, the same thing happened. And the next.

After the third time, a discomforting thought occurred to me. Swami had undertaken many fasts and, indeed, had also written extensively on yogic diet and fasting. Who was I to tell him how to fast? I tried to ignore the thought, but it hounded me for more than an hour and I could no longer ignore its insistence.

Each morning after my visit to Swami, he would go to his meditation room—a dark, windowless internal room—and remain there meditating for the day. When I finally understood my presumption in thinking I knew what was best for him, I almost ran from my office to his residence. The moment I knocked on his door, he opened it as if he was waiting for me.

'Can I make you a cup of coffee, Swami?' I asked.

With the sweetest of smiles, he said, 'Thank you. That would be wonderful.'

For me, this was a lesson in not presuming to know what was best for another person. It was humbling to understand my beliefs were just that, beliefs, and I had no right to inflict them upon another.

In the fifteen months I worked with him, every day Swami did something to turn my beliefs inside out and upside down. Just when I thought I understood something, he would challenge it. The training he gave me was profound.

***

Weeks flew past and then months. My father came to visit on one of his business trips, and Ada and Simon loved reconnecting with him and showing him around Ananda as well as introducing him to their friends. The children were cheerful and content with their daily activities.

I was feeling settled in Ananda with Ada and Simon, but then came a disruption. Leo was finally in touch and wanted to visit the children, whom he missed terribly. I felt trepidation about this, as

I had no idea what state he was in and whether his visit would upset or please the children, or be a confusing combination of the two.

When he arrived, the children were overjoyed to see him, but it was clear our marriage of seven and a half years was well beyond repair. Leo was still furious with me and not interested in any discussion about how things might be peacefully resolved, if not mended. He had begun divorce proceedings and cited to his lawyers that I was mixed up with a weird cult in America. They had assured him there was a good chance he would get custody of the children, a thought that sickened me as I knew the impact of his anger on me, an anger that would no doubt negatively affect the children.

He saved his bitter outbursts until I was alone with him, only to switch the moment the children were on our near horizon. He was threatening and hostile towards me, convinced that I intended to separate him permanently from his children. No amount of reassurance from me made a difference, and he wanted to take them back to Australia then and there.

Since just before Leo had arrived in late July, I'd been feeling more and more tired. I was covered in small bruises and any cut took an age to heal. In one of his heated outbursts, Leo grabbed my arm from behind; the following day, the bright red marks of his fingers were clearly delineated on my skin, and they gradually took on the blue, green and purple smudge of deep bruising—for a few days, I kept my arms covered so as not to alarm anyone. I knew it wasn't right to bruise so badly from such a minor trauma. And my cycle, though regular, was now completely exhausting as my period became much heavier than usual and went on many days longer.

I was at pains to hide from Leo that I felt so unwell, knowing he would use any weakness on my part as a weapon against me. He badgered me relentlessly to let the children return with him and threatened that he wouldn't leave without them.

I felt paralysed by the unravelling nightmare of Leo's harassment and my exhaustion. I couldn't even let my close friends at Ananda know what he was doing and saying, as he was always charming around them and I was still trying to maintain a facade of coping. Here I was again, unable to ask for help that would have been happily given, too afraid that I would expose the shame and embarrassment of my failed marriage and my fears of reprisal from Leo.

I did speak to Swami, who listened to me but didn't provide any guidance about what I should do, as he believed I needed to make my own decisions. While he would readily advise other members of the community when they sought his advice, Swami only ever recommended meditation to me as my answer.

Overwhelmed and exhausted, I finally relented to Leo's demands. I was sure he wouldn't harm the children he so loved. I never witnessed any violence from him against them, though his frustrations often bubbled over into angry outbursts.

The children, particularly Simon, were reluctant to leave me, but I reminded them that I would now be at the end of their rainbow and they could send me their love every night, just as they had been doing with their father. They were happy to be reunited with him, and I promised I would follow them home soon.

There were many tearful goodbyes as the children took leave of their teachers and friends. My heart was heavy when I packed their bags. Leo had found a house to rent in Mulgoa near where Jenny the donkey had lived with our friends, and he had already spoken to the local school about midyear admissions. He'd had a clear plan before he arrived for his visit, and I was helpless to stop him from implementing it. Perhaps it was the best solution, as I couldn't see another way forward.

CHAPTER 16

A good death

Swami had gone into seclusion for some weeks, which freed me up from most of my duties. He spent his days meditating and writing but was seeing no one, including me, except for the delivery of his mail and messages each mid-morning at an agreed time.

I used this time to focus on regaining my health, but in the following days I felt no better at all. Finally, and reluctantly, I made an appointment with a local gynaecologist, Frank Conant, to sort out why I was so weak. I put my exhaustion down to anaemia because of the heavy loss of blood from my periods.

Frank was a gentle older man, and the moment he examined me and saw the bruising, he said he didn't believe my problem was gynaecological in nature. He sent me to a clinic in Sacramento, the nearest to Ananda for a bone biopsy, which they repeated two weeks later—first from my sternum and then, when they had difficulty accessing marrow, from my pelvis.

My mother became concerned when she spoke to me during those difficult weeks as she felt that something wasn't right. Geoff had reported back to her that he was worried when he visited me; he thought that I didn't look well and had lost a lot of weight.

I maintained my facade, knowing my parents were still grieving terribly for Brenden. I didn't want to add to their burden by alarming them about my health. But my mother decided to visit, arriving a few weeks after Leo and the children had departed.

I was so relieved to see her but also terribly conflicted that I was to be a source of worry instead of support. She wanted to know what was wrong but I fobbed her off, saying I needed to attend an appointment before I could talk about anything and that I was just missing the children. Rae knows me too well and saw through my fumbling explanations, but she waited until I was ready to talk.

When I visited Frank for the results of the bone biopsies, he broke the news to me as gently as he could. I was already feeling woozy, so it was hard for me to concentrate on what he was saying. He told me that the tests confirmed I had an aggressive form of acute myeloid leukaemia. The doctors in Sacramento had suggested some experimental chemotherapy that would extend my life, perhaps by some weeks, but a remission wasn't likely and a cure was out of the question. I wouldn't be here for Christmas. If I wanted the treatment they suggested, it would need to be paid for given I wasn't an American citizen. And I remembered little more after that.

I returned to Ananda in a daze with the dreaded task of telling Rae.

✱✱✱

I've often thought my mother should be the one who gives lectures and writes books because she's had more suffering in her life than most. She has been my backbone on more occasions than I can count, and she has always been my greatest ally and friend. She has fished me out of some painful pickles, and we have always loved and cared for each other deeply. Telling her this news so soon after Brenden's death was agonising.

For just a moment when Frank gave me the prognosis, I had felt relief. I could finally go. I was exhausted by life—exhausted by grief, by pain and by myriad unresolved traumas that I'd never discussed let alone integrated. I'd spent my life trying so hard to get everything 'right' and had failed miserably. I didn't have a clue how to do a good life. Perhaps I could do a good death instead.

This feeling came and went as I struggled to come to terms with the enormity of what Frank had told me. Rae packed up my belongings, and I said goodbye to my friends, including Swami, who were all as shocked as I was. I was born twenty-one months after Brenden and now I would die twenty-one months after him.

Rae and I travelled home in a state of numb silence, barely knowing what to say to each other. Again, I moved into my parents' home, this time taking the bedroom overlooking Middle Harbour because the view was spectacular and I was destined to spend a good deal of time in bed.

***

I was loath to let Leo know of my prognosis as I knew he would certainly use it to his advantage. It was impossible to hide my illness, though. When the children came to visit me, I was often unable to get out of bed. They were used to me being active, and I ached to be the mum to them that I had always been. But I wasn't much fun, so these visits were often stressful all round. I found it difficult when the children asked my mother for a peanut-butter sandwich when I was so used to doing those things for them myself. I tried to be grateful because Rae was so willing to help, but found it hard to relinquish any sense of control or contribution.

The children were happily enrolled in Mulgoa Primary School, and Leo brought them to Mosman on weekends. We took it in turns to ferry them back and forth, but usually it was Rae—occasionally

Geoff—who returned the children to their father on Sunday after-noons, as I was too unwell to drive.

I visited our family GP, or more often he'd visit me, but I was too despairing to contemplate treatment. I felt I would rather die from the disease than die feeling sick from any treatment, given I'd been told there was no hope of a remission or a cure. The experimental treatment available in America wasn't available in Australia. Like my beloved Granny, I preferred to let nature take its course.

I was painfully aware that my spiritual aspirations were being thwarted by my trying so hard, probably too hard, to realise them. I was exhausted from living. The thought of being with Brenden, or at least free from pain and my inner turmoil, was a comfort. Life had defeated me, and I felt that all I could do was surrender to my fate.

CHAPTER 17

Finding a way through

Rae and Geoff were amazing during this time, given their hearts were no doubt overwhelmed by grief and foreboding. If I managed to shower myself sitting down, my mother would have to dry me as I didn't have the energy required for both showering and drying myself. It was a comfort knowing the children were being cared for by Leo and were happy with their daily routines. Given I became very sick and weak so quickly, and my death was on a near horizon, living with my parents was a blessing.

My days were often spent reflecting on my life while I rested in my bedroom. Around this time, I started calling my parents by their first names, rather than Mum and Dad. In thinking about my life, I wanted to fathom our family by understanding who they were and what their journey had been as people, rather than as my parents. They had both lived through the Depression and World War II, which Geoff had experienced firsthand. Rae had given up her career because of Geoff's lack of support. She had lost her father, her mother, a brother at only twenty-one and her son at thirty-two—my death would be yet another loss, but she never faltered in her loving care of me.

During my reflections, I realised two things: one, no one is perfect and there are certainly no perfect parents; and two, as parents they had always done the very best they could. Wanting them to be any different from who they were was a sure path to suffering. When I came to this understanding of their lives and motivations, it brought me compassion and a softening of the boundaries of love.

✷✷✷

For two decades, I had studied many of the great masters who purported to have the answers to some of life's most fundamental questions, and yet I wasn't at peace with myself, with my history or with my story.

I had a rich theoretical understanding of God, the Absolute or whatever holy name was used to describe the Supreme Being. For me, that unfolding creative energy was equally—and preferably—expressed as life, love or light. In my spiritual and out-of-body experiences, I had glimpsed the invisible and beneficent force that vibrates material into being. I knew this to be an indestructible, eternal, energetic force that enlivens us all—that blindingly beautiful light I encountered at seven. However, those words don't begin to adequately describe the experience of it.

I was acutely aware that only my ego persisted in believing I was separate from life, unworthy of love, beyond redemption. But knowing this didn't change it or shift my reality, and only heightened my spiritual anguish and despair. I had no trust in life, in myself, in others. I clung to the patterns I'd developed in childhood, such as my belief that I was fundamentally flawed. I felt responsible for Brenden, and for causing so much of my physical pain and disability through the harsh way I treated my body, but all the while I'd been projecting a ridiculous pretence of coping with everything.

When our local minister at St Luke's in Mosman offered me a laying on of hands, I chose to participate because I thought it might give my mother some peace. She was a regular member of their congregation and parish council, and her faith was a sustaining force for her. When the minister placed his hands on my head, I was overwhelmed with a sense of profound love, but my mind resisted receiving the gift because I was so wedded to personal condemnation. The tussle within my mind—as my belief in my unworthiness tried to surrender to the presence of love—seemed intractable.

Our suffering moulds and shapes the life force within us. Sometimes we succumb to resentment, rage, blame or self-pity—but eventually, if we are willing to sit in the presence of suffering, it can lead us home to the wisdom of simply embracing life and being an expression of its love.

Through meditation, I understood the fickle nature of my mind. As I meditated, into my mind would come the thought, 'What if I'm not here for Christmas?' Other thoughts would crowd in: 'How will my children cope? How will my parents cope? How will I cope? Who'll come to the funeral? I wonder what they'll say? Who'll be wearing my clothes in six months?' These thoughts plagued me. I could feel myself go down the emotional gurgler, over and over again.

After a time, I liberated myself from the power of this inner tumult. And, with practice and tenacity, I finally witnessed the thought, 'What if I'm not here for Christmas?' and let it go without giving it any attention. This felt like a victory over the wayward nature of my mind. My health seemed to stabilise during this time, though I was still troubled by night sweats, tiredness and terrible bone pain, particularly in my thighs.

***

On one of the children's weekend visits, Ada came and stood by my bed. I hadn't told my children the name of my illness, as I didn't want Leo to hear it, still fearing he would somehow use it to wound me further.

Ada took my hand and earnestly said, 'Mum, you're sick. If you need to meditate to get well, I think you should go back to Ananda.'

Her words felled me—I thought I had come home to die. Ada knew the people at Ananda well, and she knew I would be loved and cared for there by many friends, but returning had never occurred to me.

It was now late November 1983 and, after much discussion with my parents, I chose to go back to Ananda. I wrote letters to Ada and Simon for the future, in case I never saw them again, so they would know some of the things that were important to me. I recorded tapes so they could hear my love for them in my voice.

When we said our painful goodbyes, I was unsure if I would ever see them or my parents again.

In the weeks before my departure, the harshness of dealing with Leo's lawyers had taken a further toll on my emotional resilience. At my request, we'd sat around a table to finalise the arrangements, instead of our lawyers arguing at a costly distance. Our family's solicitor, while competent, was no match for the family law specialist Leo had employed. Too sick to care much, and against my solicitor's advice, I signed over everything to Leo: all of my possessions and assets—such as they were—and custody of our children. He'd threatened to take Ada and Simon away on a long holiday, returning after my death, unless I complied.

When I sank into my seat on the plane, it was with a heavy heart to be leaving my children and parents, but I was also relieved that I might never have to deal with Leo again.

My return to Ananda was a happy reunion. I stayed with friends who looked after my physical needs as my mother had done. I could simply rest, reflect and meditate while the fire crackled, and while

Christmas baking smells filled the house with cinnamon, nutmeg and allspice.

When strong enough, I sat or walked among the manzanita trees with their shrivelling bark rolled up into tiny scrolls. The colours of their branches and soft sage-green leaves were heightened by the contrast of fresh snow. Occasionally, while I sat meditating outside, a deer or two would step quietly by with no sense of fear. Manzanita trees grow in barren and rocky soil, and the deer blended in with them effortlessly.

These quiet moments in nature were so precious to me. I treasured the solitude as I endeavoured to merge into the landscape like the deer, quietening the heaviness in my mind and replacing it with the whispers of nature around me.

Christmas came and went. While perhaps I passed some sort of psychological hurdle, my weakness and exhaustion continued, and each day became an opportunity to slow things down to the bare minimum. At times, my connection to life felt so tenuous, so fragile, that I simply focused on following the sensations of the inward and outward breath, too weak to do anything else.

***

Swami Kriyananda and several of my friends were soon to leave for Italy, where he would teach meditation for the summer. He suggested I accompany him and his entourage. Some weeks later, when I felt able, I embarked for Frankfurt. From there, a few days later, I was driven by some of the Ananda German community to Sorrento, where a charismatic Catholic congregation had invited Swami.

I was still tired from the journey, so I was happy that my four companions in the car left me to rest while they spoke animatedly in German. I didn't know any of these people, as my transport had been arranged from Ananda, but I was more than content to relax and be looked after.

At one point, the fellow sitting beside me stopped speaking in German, turned to me and said, 'You will heal people with your voice,' before he went back to chatting with his friends. I had no idea what he was talking about and no idea if he knew I was meant to be dying, but for a moment his words nourished and gladdened my heart.

I stayed in Sorrento for some weeks, living in a little room in the home of a congregation member from the charismatic Catholic group. There was a disco above, beside and below this room, so while the days were quiet, the relentless beat of the music made it difficult to rest at night—the walls literally vibrated with noise.

My hosts were so generous and kind to me, a stranger in their midst, and I loved their laughter and animated discussions, though I spoke no Italian and they spoke little English. Sometimes I couldn't tell whether they were arguing or just speaking passionately, but given the amount of laughter that peppered their conversations, I decided it was the latter. Their culture was so different from the one I knew, where appearances were everything and what lay in the subterranean depths was better left undisturbed and certainly undescribed. Here, everything was out on the table. Meals were happy and boisterous affairs, and not knowing what was being discussed allowed me to simply marinate in my hosts' good cheer.

The charismatic community had experienced many extraordinary events, which included speaking in tongues and profound healings. However, under the direction of Padre Luigi, they wanted to internalise this energy instead of only its outward expression, which is why they had invited Swami to teach them meditation.

Swami's form of meditation, taught to him by Paramahansa Yogananda, used Kriya Yoga as a path to enlightenment. He spoke of the communion within the Christian tradition as being an outer symbol of the inner communion that results in divine experiences.

Kriya Yoga fosters and trains, through the breath, the rising of the Kundalini energy in the spine to meet and connect at the third eye, which is between and behind the eyebrows. In the ancient Sanskrit Vedas, which Swami drew from in his teachings, this is described as 'inner communion'—a spiritual awakening to the interconnectedness of life that all human beings are designed to experience. Humans are designed to spiritually awaken.

In the local church where this congregation met, I attended extraordinary services. I was familiar with the Anglican Holy Communion and other traditional rituals, but they were incredibly restrained and formal compared to this.

Swami had taught the congregation several Indian chants, and they did with them something that none of us had ever heard before. After a time, their free-flowing harmonies, backed by ten guitars, had everyone on their feet swaying or swooning in bliss. The devotion to, and love for, God was palpable. I was content to immerse myself in the music and meditate as these holy sounds reverberated in my body.

***

The congregation kindly prayed for me, and I was invited to a special service in the chapel of a magnificent home in the hills that overlooked Sorrento and the sea beyond. I had no idea what was happening most of the time, but I decided to attend the service, happy enough to be swept along in the loving energy of this group.

Before the service, we gathered together in the dining room for lunch. I was relieved not to have to participate much in the conversation, resting quietly in the atmosphere of camaraderie.

When our appetites were sated, we silently descended the stairs in single file to the beautiful chapel, richly painted with frescoes. I settled myself out of the way where I could meditate while the service unfolded around me.

I had no idea it was a special healing service for me.

As I sat there, lost in the heavenly harmonies, seven hands were suddenly upon me—on my head, shoulders, heart, back, forehead. These, I learned later, were the hands of the six church leaders and Swami.

My head fell backwards, and I was transported to a place of profound joy and peace. Brenden and countless others were present in this blissful experience, and such was its power that I couldn't move a muscle for well over four hours.

By then, everyone else had left the chapel, had another meal and were waiting to drive me back to where I was staying. I was aware of all these facts, and yet I was deep below the house in the chapel and completely unable to move. Coming back into my body felt like stepping into a cloak of cement. The light, bliss and freedom of the experience was too tantalising to resist; it took some time, in and out of the experience, before I could fully take on my body again, let alone move it.

The liberation from my body brought a reassurance that the reality of my existence wasn't dependent on being enmeshed in a physical form. And, while it makes no sense to me now, I knew in those sublime moments that we were all born of the same light, and my children would be fine whether I lived or died, as nothing could ever truly separate us. Death entailed no separation from life.

Even after I could move again, I couldn't speak for many hours.

***

I was staying a short distance from the Sorrento Cathedral, where Padre Luigi served as a priest. Each afternoon I walked over to meditate there, and while I wasn't familiar with the Catholic mass, I enjoyed the ritual of the repetitive service.

Sometimes I sat in one of the disused little chapels in order to be uninterrupted by the comings and goings of the congregation. In one of these chapels, tucked out of sight, stood an ancient bronze crucifix some 2 and a bit metres tall. It was blackened with age and lack of attention, so I asked Padre Luigi if I might be allowed to clean it. I felt that this was something I could do to repay the kindness of the congregation in allowing me so generously into their hearts, prayers and homes.

Padre Luigi needed to go through quite a rigmarole to obtain permission from higher up—all the way to the Vatican. Apparently, this was a strange request from a non-national, not to mention a pale, divorced Australian Anglican who was born Jewish, but finally permission was granted.

I had learned a great deal in the School of Philosophy about the privilege of restoring something to its natural beauty. Stripping away all that had accumulated through neglect wasn't dissimilar to what I endeavoured to do within myself: the releasing of all the beliefs that diminished me as a person and made me feel loathsome.

The School had treated cleaning as an exercise in being totally present, so I would pause and bring myself wholeheartedly into the moment before beginning to clean. This brought a reverence to the task. It wasn't about 'getting it done'—the journey was every bit as important as the destination of a shining revelation.

I stood on a stepladder to reach the top of the cross, the crown of thorns on Christ's head, and his sad and tortured face. As I listened to the toothbrush gradually removing decades of grime, I reflected on what I knew of Christ's life. There must have been times when he desired nothing more than to live an ordinary life, yet he was driven by the urge to spread the 'good news': we are not separate and isolated from love, or God, except in our own beliefs and thinking. Surely the life of a simple carpenter held some appeal to Christ, given the approach of his undignified end on the cross.

Underneath the blackened grubbiness was a deep, burnished, golden bronze. It took me several weeks to expose its full splendour. During that time, many of the women who were regular devotees at the cathedral would come in their black dresses and scarves to kneel around the foot of the crucifix. They would gently touch me and make the sign of the cross, and I was grateful for their blessings.

When my task was complete, the crucifix radiated a golden light. After a reconsecration, it was moved to have pride of place in the main cathedral. Several friends have visited since and told me they have continued to care for the crucifix, and that it still graces the front of the sanctuary.

I moved on to clean each of the small chapels lining the main cathedral and polish the little silver doors behind which the host was kept.

During the week, the cathedral was shut from midday until four o'clock, as the town closed for its siesta. Sometimes I secreted myself in a recess so I would be locked in during siesta and have the whole cathedral to myself. I relished these times—the quiet was palpable, and I could meditate, pray or clean.

One afternoon, as Padre Luigi went to retrieve the host for blessing, I witnessed the smallest hesitation in his step when he saw the brilliant sheen of the silver door gleaming at him in welcome.

Later he quietly said to me, 'There must be angels at work during our siesta,' but he never did anything to interfere with my private time in the cathedral.

∗∗∗

On the other side of town, close to the coast, stood a church where the English mass was held by a visiting Irish priest for summer tourists. I occasionally attended just to meditate; regardless of whether the mass was delivered in Italian or English, I participated in neither as I wasn't a Catholic.

One afternoon the sky was dark and threatening due to an approaching storm, and I decided to remain on the couch rather than venturing out for the evening mass. But as the time drew closer to the start of mass, I had a strong urge to go to the English-speaking service. I tried to toss the idea out of my mind, but because the urge was so insistent I finally decided to follow it and made the journey across town.

My umbrella blew inside out the moment I stepped outside, and soon the rain came down in torrents, but I continued my sodden way to the church. When I stepped inside the vestibule, I saw the Irish priest standing at the altar and speaking to an empty church. I went to the front pew, dripping, and sat down. The priest continued with the mass. Even though I'd heard it many times, I had no clear idea what the responses should be, so I made up ones that seemed familiar or appropriate. It was obvious to him, no doubt, that I wasn't a Catholic.

The wind buffeted and tugged at the roof, its metal struts and timber supports creaking in the turmoil. Thunder roared, lights flickered, and the priest finally completed the mass. He then disappeared behind the altar and reappeared a few minutes later minus his robe and in his everyday clothes. He invited me to sit somewhere quiet until the deluge had stopped or at least slowed.

I followed him to a small windowless room, and we sat together while he asked why I'd come to mass during such a fierce storm. I explained that I'd felt a strong urge and didn't really know why. Then I asked him where he was from and how long he would stay in Sorrento. He came from Belfast, he said, and he was grateful to get away for the summer season to avoid the heartache he'd witnessed at home. His duty was often to go into houses where sons, brothers and fathers wouldn't return and break this dreadful news to the women.

The lights kept flickering and then went off altogether. We sat in the dark as his story poured out. He was questioning his faith: he could no longer bear the pain of knocking on the doors of parishioners who had become casualties. How could a loving god watch while beautiful young people were killed in their prime? What sort of god wouldn't intervene to prevent such awful grief among the families left fatherless? What was the point of redemption when all life was suffering and nothing had meaning? Was everything he'd been taught some sort of sick fairytale? Perhaps Jesus had never existed and there was no heaven, just a hell here on Earth.

The priest wept and railed and sobbed his heart out while we sat in total darkness, the storm raging outside and another raging within. Finally, his story was done. The heaviness of the rain subsided and the lights flickered into life. He shook my hand without embarrassment, as if nothing had transpired between us, and we parted.

I hadn't said a word. There had been no need. I was grateful and humble to have borne witness to his suffering.

***

Being away from Ada and Simon was difficult and painful, and I often wondered when the time would be right to return to them. Swami said he was concerned about my returning to Australia too soon; he thought I would get sicker, especially if I was to try and mother the children against Leo's wishes.

Every day that I spent away from Ada and Simon, I sent them a postcard. I still have a pile of them, which my mother kept for me, and the bottom of each one says, 'I'm sending you rainbows to carry my love to you' or similar words to remind them we were always linked through the loving connection of the rainbow.

Rainbows go as far as you need them to, and my children both say it was the rainbow that kept me alive for them during that difficult time. They shared a room, and every night they sat on one of their beds together, holding hands while Ada talked Simon through the process of sending me a rainbow, then sending their love and blessings across to me like fairy dust. The rainbow was as important to me as it was to them—indeed, it was a blessing to us all.

Leo remained angry with me, and there was no point in trying to help him see reason. I knew that if I was determined to be a mother to my children, the cost would be my health and likely my life, because emotional conflict is exhausting.

My health, physical and mental, was still precarious. My energy levels fluctuated dramatically, and some glands in my neck were hard and unyielding, while others had reduced and softened. My inner turmoil and sadness hadn't abated; when I wasn't in the cathedral, I ached for a quiet space in which to rest, meditate and be alone.

I yearned for a lasting, unshakeable peace. I often experienced deep peace, but it didn't help me process my tumult of emotions. In fact, I often used meditation as a way of not feeling those emotions. I had developed many disciplines to control my mind to the point where if I didn't want to acknowledge or experience an unpleasant feeling, I could always shift my focus elsewhere.

CHAPTER 18

Escape to the country

With Swami, my friends and several of the Sorrento congregation members, I travelled to a magnificent villa high in the mountains above Lake Como near the tiny town of Veglio. The woman who owned the villa was a devotee of Swami and had gifted him the use of her home for the summer.

People were congregating from all over Europe for a series of lectures that Swami would deliver in French, German, Italian, Spanish and English—these were only five of the many languages he spoke fluently. I was unsure how I would manage the company of so many people.

We travelled to Lake Como via Assisi, and I was struck by the sweetness that imbued the picturesque hills surrounding the town. The distinctive pink stone buildings of Assisi glowed in the morning sun like jewels on the hill. We only stayed there for a couple of days, but it touched my heart and I hoped to return.

By the time we arrived at the villa and settled into our rooms, I was already feeling overwhelmed by the number of people arriving.

When I'd said to Swami that I didn't want him as my guru, he had laughed. It didn't matter to him how I chose to see him.

The deeper issue for me was his path, the path of Paramahansa Yogananda and Kriya Yoga, which I had great respect for but knew was not my path. Swami's contribution to the betterment of the world was rich and creative, and I valued his knowledge and wisdom, yet I always knew our paths would diverge at some point. The practices, chanting and philosophy, while beautiful, didn't resonate in my depths. I knew that my spiritual journey would lead me elsewhere, but I didn't have a clue about what that place might be or when it might happen.

Then, abruptly, my time with Swami came to a close.

In the dining room of the villa, he and I were sitting together at a long table with many other people. My spoon was halfway to my mouth when he said, his tone kindly but forthright, 'No one has ever asked more of me than you.' There was a deafening silence as he continued, 'I've given you everything I have. It's time for you to leave.' His words cut through the gathering and laid me bare.

I found it terribly hard to hear these words from Swami, especially as I already felt so physically and emotionally fragile. I was completely stunned—we'd never had a disagreement, and we'd always had a very respectful relationship. But although he'd spoken kindly, I found his words harsh, searing and final.

Everyone in the dining room stared at their plates and no doubt imagined that some transgression had brought on his injunction. Those who didn't know me well looked askance at me, and even those who were close to me wondered what I'd done to deserve this public humiliation. I wondered this myself as his words cut deep into my fragility, and my old and familiar feelings of not belonging anywhere surfaced painfully. I may not have accepted Swami as my guru, but clearly I'd given him a good deal of power in my life. I felt a deep sense of rejection, as if I had no place to exist.

Some months later, I interpreted those same words in the opposite way to how they landed in my heart that day. At the time,

I didn't have any idea where to go or what to do. I'd already known that his work was not my work, but the end had transpired in an unexpected moment with an abruptness I hadn't anticipated and didn't welcome!

***

I slept fitfully that night, feeling estranged from the community members whom I thought of as my extended or, at least, spiritual family.

At 6 the next morning, Swami appeared outside the meditation room where we had just completed our morning practice—in his pyjamas, slippers and dressing-gown. I can't convey how surprising this was. In all the time I'd worked with him and been in his home, I had never witnessed him attired in anything that resembled nightwear. He was always appropriately showered and dressed when in the company of people. A hush fell over the group as Swami said he had come to speak to me.

He talked to me for five or ten minutes, though it could have been much longer or shorter, and it's difficult for me to relay exactly what he said. For many years, I could only access his words—or the sense of them—in deep meditation, which might sound strange to some. It wasn't an ordinary conversation, though, and other people who were present fell into a deeply meditative space while he spoke.

The gist of what he said was deeply personal but did little to assuage my sense of rejection, grief and loss. He told me who I was, why I was alive at this time on the planet, and a little of what my work was to become. He spoke kindly but with considerable authority and assurance as if his words came from somewhere else. While his words were somewhat comforting and outlined a purpose for my life, my overwhelming sense of abandonment and confusion quashed any nourishment I might have drawn from his faith in me. The picture he painted of my purpose, when I still expected to die from leukaemia, did little to nurture hope or inspire me with confidence.

When Swami finished talking, I asked him, 'Should I return to my children?'

He thought for a moment and then said, as he had before, 'No, I think you'll become sicker if you return to Australia, as there's still too much stress and discord with your former husband. The worry of having the children caught in the middle of conflict would be detrimental to both you and them.' That was true enough, but remaining on the other side of the world without a purpose didn't seem a good option either.

'Where do I go, Swami?' I asked.

Again, he reflected for a moment and then said, 'You'll find the place.'

I found that particularly unhelpful too.

'What should I do, Swami?' I asked somewhat pathetically, and his familiar response was, 'Go and meditate.'

I tried again with, 'Where, Swami? Where do I go to meditate?'

His final answer seemed to confirm that I was very much on my own. 'You'll find the place.'

During this conversation, it was as if we had all been transported into another dimension. At its conclusion, people resumed their morning activities while Swami disappeared into his private quarters, presumably to shower and dress for the day. I was left in a weird place of not belonging. To go from the heart of a spiritual community of friends to suddenly feeling an intruder on their space was disquieting to say the least.

I slowly returned to my room to pack the bag I had unpacked a couple of days before. Given it was only the size of allowable hand luggage on an aeroplane, it didn't take long. I was too distraught to join the community for breakfast, and I was in a state of numbness when I said goodbye to several close friends knowing I might never see them again.

Just as I was leaving the main gates of the villa without a clue whether to turn left or right, Swami appeared again to say, 'There's always a home for you at Ananda.' Yet I knew my time with him and my dear friends at Ananda had come to an end.

My heart was heavy as I caught a bus down the mountain to the edge of Lake Como. By the time its full magnificence came into view, I had decided to return to the sweet balm of Assisi. I simply couldn't think of anywhere else to go. Perhaps in Assisi I could recover from the shock and shame of my exchange with Swami, which had left me feeling more lost than ever before.

CHAPTER 19

Back to the cave

It took me a couple of days to travel to Assisi, as I needed to rest on the way. I travelled by buses and trains and finally a taxi that wound its way from the station up into the beautiful walled city that gleamed a soft, heavenly pink as the sun set.

I arrived at the monastery of the Poor Clares where I found a bed until I settled upon a plan. While the monastery itself exuded a reflective peace, the busyness outside its heavy timber doors was intrusive and went on long into the night. Whenever I left the monastery, the bustle was jarring; everything around me was felt in my body, which had become supersensitive to noise, light and activity.

The next day, I retreated up Monte Subasio to the beautiful Eremo delle Carceri about 4 kilometres out of Assisi. This was the monastery where St Francis had retreated to when he wanted peace and quiet. It had been built around a series of caves where he and his followers prayed, slept and meditated.

The moment I walked in, I knew I had found my refuge. I couldn't pull myself away from the quiet of the grounds or the wall overlooking the steep gorge that plummets to the plains of Perugia.

But I had no idea if the monks accommodated tourists, as the monastery didn't look geared up for anything but day visitors.

The last rays of the sun gradually withdrew from the distant hills, and a soft evening coolness and peace settled over the mount as the tourists left for the day. Standing alone at the parapet overlooking the gorge, I turned to find an elderly priest looking quizzically at me. We both started speaking at once and then laughed.

The priest introduced himself as Padre Ilarino. He spoke no English and my Italian was rudimentary, but this didn't stop us from having a long conversation about life, love, God and music. As the colour drained from the landscape and lights began to twinkle far in the distance, I dug into my small bag for a portable cassette player and played him one of my favourite pieces of music, the slow movement of Bach's Double Violin Concerto in D minor. For me, this piece captures an exquisite beauty and poignancy. We listened in silence as the strains drifted down into the gorge.

Padre Ilarino went inside but was soon back with a cassette that he played for me. His piece was the more uplifting and jubilant 'Ode to Joy' from the last movement of Beethoven's ninth symphony. When the music finished, we stood there in the stillness of the evening as the monastery lights came on behind us and the first stars appeared.

Padre Ilarino beckoned me to follow him inside, where he showed me the alcoves carved out of the pinkish stone where St Francis and the monks had slept all those centuries before. These were coffin-shaped hollows just long enough to allow a small monk to lie—I imagine quite uncomfortably—on his back.

The priest then took me upstairs to a small accommodation area used for solitary retreats. It housed a rudimentary kitchen with a stove and sink, a bathroom and bedroom with a single bed, a table and chairs. I wasn't certain what Padre Ilarino said, but I think he was happy for me to stay, because stay I did.

I was grateful to lie down and sleep after eating some fruit. I felt in my bones that I had arrived at the place of my dreams. This monastery, far from any noise except birdsong, felt perfect for the rest, solitude and reflection I craved.

The following day, I collected my few belongings from the monastery of the Poor Clares in Assisi.

***

After I'd settled in, I descended to the cave where St Francis and his followers had prayed and meditated centuries before. Many paths wind around the steep gorge to various caves that have formed naturally or in some cases have been enlarged by the monks who inhabited them.

The Grotto of St Francis is accessed from the main courtyard via two tiny chapels leading to an awkward and steep flight of stairs carved out of the pinkish stone. Just before the stairs swing around to the right to enter the cave, an open carved window overlooks the beautiful gorge. Outside this window, the tree still stands where, eight hundred years ago, St Francis preached to the birds to go to the four corners of the Earth and spread the good news of the gospel.

The cave itself is very small, perhaps 2 metres long and little more than a metre wide. There is a fenced area where St Francis sometimes slept and meditated, and monks and pilgrims often leave flowers there along with a candle. To the right of the Grotto's entrance is a space the perfect size for one person to sit cross-legged with their back comfortably cradled by the cave. It was here I sat on that first morning and then every day for several months. All I needed was a cushion for my bony bottom.

I had always been a fan of St Francis. I loved his wild search for God and his great love of all creation. He'd had little regard for the strictures and structures of the Church, determined to experience

God through raw and passionate endeavours that included enforced suffering, deprivation and gratitude for all things.

The walls of the Grotto are infused with his spirit of inquiry, and when I first sat with my back to the cave, I felt I would either die or find peace there. Francis too had come to this place determined to find union with God. I felt in good company.

As I sat to meditate on the first morning, I could no longer keep tears at bay, something I had accomplished up until then. I was terrified of weeping—I thought that if I started, I might never stop, or that I would shatter into a million fragments and never again feel whole. But Swami's words were the catalyst for a deep catharsis, and in this sanctuary at the heart of Monte Subasio, my floodgates opened. Over the next few weeks I wept, wailed, shuddered and shook my way through countless past traumas.

I had always done my best to avoid the raw and cathartic sobbing that can accompany trauma. And I had used any number of tactics to avoid knowing myself in my depths through the lonesome exploration of my inner landscape. Yet the pathway to healing and peace often requires traversing the regions of grief, despair and sorrow without looking for distractions.

That first day was gone before I knew it, and once more Padre Ilarino appeared at my side. He helped me to my feet and led me upstairs. I entered the beautiful but simple dining room with a long, worn timber table and a wooden bench that had supported a thousand cloaked monks. Crusty white bread, a meat stew with vegetables and a goblet of wine awaited me. I stared at what Padre Ilarino had prepared, as he stood nearby with his fingers interlaced over his round little Franciscan belly. Franciscans, I was to discover, are not only exceedingly fond of their food but also believe that each course must be accompanied by a different wine.

I had barely eaten meat for fifteen years except during my

year in New Zealand. And any naturopath knows and enthusiastically proclaims, 'The whiter the bread, the sooner you're dead.' And wine? I had barely touched alcohol, coffee or even tea for the same amount of time. In that precious moment, I realised I knew zip about anything. For all my studies, for all my efforts, I knew absolutely nothing worth knowing. The uncomfortable process of dismantling my beliefs had well and truly begun.

I was humbled to realise that it was more healing to be grateful for what Padre Ilarino had lovingly prepared for me, a stranger, than to adhere to beliefs that no longer served me. While I found this first meal difficult to chew, let alone swallow, Padre Ilarino stood by to ensure I ate. Perhaps he was worried about the pale, skinny, divorced Anglican, holed up in his sacred Catholic cave, and he was determined to make me eat! My dying in the cherished cave would not be tolerated. He wouldn't allow me to indulge in the many deprivations that St Francis had engaged in, which included fasting, the wearing of rough rope belts against the skin, and having bare feet in the snow.

✷✷✷

And so my life took on a rhythm. Each day I spent up to eighteen hours in the cave, meditating, weeping, and praying for relief from my turmoil and anguish. I wept for Brenden and my helplessness to help him. I wept for the little girl ravaged by guilt, pain and isolation. I wept for the voiceless part of myself unable to call out or ask for help. The more I looked for faults and failings in myself, the more I found, and I often felt useless and dispensable to the world. Such was my despair, I even felt that my children might be better off without me. The only relief came from nature, music, yoga, prayer and meditation.

As terrified as I was of the gaping black hole within me, I began to suspect that life and healing would be found by embracing this darkness. Brenden had plunged headlong into the black hole, never to resurface, but it seemed that light and peace lay paradoxically close to its darkness. Perhaps I would find the light I so craved by welcoming the darkness that clouded my heart.

In meditation, I clearly perceived the coping mechanisms that I had created to feel in control of my life. Who was I, if not this collection of beliefs and attitudes? And yet they were the very things I needed to release. My trust in life was tenuous, as the belief that I needed to earn my right to exist was all pervading. Letting go of my perceived control was quite terrifying. I had become completely selfish through my total absorption in my own chaotic, unmanaged and judgemental thinking.

When so consumed with my own misery and self-loathing, I could barely make eye contact with anyone. During this time, friends from Sorrento travelled over three hours to visit me and, because I felt so low and loathsome, I couldn't bear to meet with them. I had described myself previously to them as a 'rotten miserable worm that doesn't deserve to exist'. These dear friends left a pile of 'worm food' outside the cave next to a little pen drawing of a worm with a halo above its head and flanked by two angels. This picture still sits on my desk.

Occasionally I drew pictures of food for Padre Ilarino or the monks to purchase for me in town, such as a sketch of a pear tree x 6 or a chicken sitting on a nest of eggs x 6. These kindly monks provided for my needs so I didn't need to leave the quiet sanctuary of the monastery, and Padre Ilarino continued to prepare the evening meal for me. And whenever a monk went into Assisi, he would post off a wad of the postcards I wrote each day to Ada and Simon and purchase more.

Sometimes after the evening meal, Padre Ilarino and I would sit and talk in the sanctuary of the surrounding woods, especially in the long twilights after tourists left for the day. These were strange conversations: he spoke non-stop in Italian, I spoke in English, and we were never sure if the other understood our meaning. But it didn't matter, as there seemed to be an invisible energy flowing between and connecting us, and I relished our time together. It was easier somehow to pour out my story knowing that he didn't understand much of what I was saying. Sometimes we don't know what we think until we hear what we say, so these long conversations were often revelatory to me—if not to poor Padre Ilarino, who at least didn't seem to mind enduring them.

I would also sit alone in the woods from time to time. One day, I was eating grapes amid the trees while marinating in a wretched self-pity I couldn't shake. A beautiful blue and black butterfly landed on my knee, so I squeezed a drop of grape juice for this lovely visitor before I quickly returned to my self-inflicted pity party.

To my surprise, an identical butterfly landed on my other knee. Again, I squeezed a drop of grape juice for this beautiful creature. Then it suddenly struck me: 'I'm good for something. I'm a good place for butterflies to land on!' Such was my low state at the time, it took some extraordinary events to help me see things differently.

***

While the Eremo delle Carceri opened early in the morning and closed around seven in the evening, most people arrived after 10 am and were gone by 5 pm. Signs that read *Silenzio* were scattered here and there in the monastery grounds, but total silence was hard for tourists to maintain, so I would hear their laughter and chatter as they descended the stairs towards the cave in which I was meditating.

Many visitors never noticed me in the corner; those who did must have wondered at my presence. Some would arrive eagerly, skipping downstairs on young sturdy legs, barely noticing anything as they passed through the cave. Others would slow their step and stop talking as they entered this sacred space. Occasionally a person or two would join me in silent prayer or meditation, moving on quietly when done.

As time passed and I found more peace, some people would stay an hour or two, and we would soak in the quiet together; these were often people who had softly and reverentially descended the stairs as if they could feel the sanctity of the cave before their arrival. Very rarely, a person with their own burden would join me in the weeping.

Through all of this I kept my eyes closed, as I didn't want to intrude on anyone else's experience of the cave any more than I wanted them to interfere with mine.

***

One special day remains clear in my memory—the day I realised there was nothing and no one to blame for how I felt. Disappointing as this was, it was a mighty revelation as I so often blamed events, people or myself for my misery.

I could still be sitting there now, a dusty little pile of bones in the corner of the cave, moaning about my childhood, blaming myself for being inadequate and loathsome, resenting how easy it seemed for other people, blaming myself for the rape and for Brenden's death, regretting the years of pain, loneliness and hospitalisations, chastising some fundamental flaw within myself, railing at the suffering in the world, tired of existential and physical pain and sickness, sad that I might die and leave my children motherless and my parents suffering the loss of a second child.

But I realised that nothing of how I felt would make an iota of difference to the facts. The fact was, this was my life, my one precious life to live. Those traumas and tragedies *had* happened.

The weeping had led me to a place of deep acceptance and certainty that it isn't our traumas and tragedies but the view we take of them that determines the quality—and perhaps even the quantity and direction—of our lives. Once I reached this place, my perspective changed dramatically. I realised that my suffering was within myself, and while I couldn't change the events of my life, I could certainly change how I chose to see them.

Until we truly awaken, we are governed by the unconscious commentary that constantly judges, criticises, blames, compares, rehashes the past or projects scenarios into the future. Once my tears were shed, I was more easily able to connect with the wonder of experiencing each moment without so much clutter from the past. Life became simpler as I more consciously chose to take care of my physical, mental, emotional and spiritual wellbeing. No longer preoccupied and overwhelmed by a busy unconscious mind, I could make better use of my conscious thoughts.

When I was present and my mind was quiet, I was able to access deeper qualities within myself. My insight, compassion, wisdom, humour and intuition worked seamlessly, and I knew moment by moment what to do, how to be, what to say. During meditation, I stopped building on beliefs or judgements that distracted me; instead, I challenged them to see if they were useful—and I became more willing to release the ones detrimental to my growth towards a larger version of myself.

Most of us don't know that we can make these choices. We so easily become helpless victims of our reactions, not recognising that while we may not have control over life's dramas, disappointments and tragedies, we can have control over how we respond to them. We have the potential to shift from feeling like a helpless victim to being an active co-creator of how our life is experienced. We can choose to see the glass half full or half empty. The perception is entirely up to us.

***

There was no space for yoga postures in the cave, but I incorporated and practised yogic principles as well as breathing exercises or pranayama. As I became stronger, I spent the mornings upstairs in my accommodation space where the sun streamed in, doing some gentle yoga postures or asanas. Swami's way of teaching yoga linked affirmations with postures, and I incorporated these into my daily practice.

His words to me had lost their sting and, indeed, I began to see them in a very different light. He'd said that no one had ever demanded more from him than me. Instead of seeing this as another terrible flaw in myself, I realised that, given he was a spiritual teacher, as his student I had sought his teachings—and this I had done with diligence and tenacity.

Swami had also said that he'd given me everything he had. I now saw this quite differently too. If he'd given me everything he had, then that was both considerable and more than enough. He had a wealth of knowledge, insight and real wisdom that he had generously shared with me. He'd said it was time for me to go, and he was right.

I was amazed at how the same words could be interpreted so differently; it was simply dependent on how I chose to receive them. If I heard them through the filter of self-loathing, they only added to my shame. If I heard them without judgement, there was no malice in them. And, indeed, they acknowledged the many gifts he'd given me.

***

As I let go of this resentment, the leaves began to turn, heralding the approaching quiet and rest of winter. I started feeling ready to re-enter the world. There was a peace in my heart and almost a spring in my step, and I ached to be with my children once more.

My time at the Eremo delle Carceri had been profoundly healing, not only for my body but also, far more importantly, for my mind.

I no longer worried about whether I would survive or succumb to leukaemia. All I wanted was to be with Ada and Simon, and to bring to them—and to my life in general—the peace I had discovered in the Grotto.

At my departure, Padre Ilarino wept and gave me his blessing. He had taken me in as a stranger, and though our conversations were many and varied, and rarely understood by the other, we parted as dear friends. After all, perhaps it's not so difficult to find peace when no one speaks your language! It's in our relationships that we rub up against each other's prickly, twitchy bits.

Leaving my quiet sanctuary wasn't easy. Stepping through the threshold at the entrance to the Eremo meant crossing from a safe, contained environment out into the hubbub of the world, but I knew I was ready to make the journey back to Australia.

My trip down Monte Subasio felt so different from my ascent those many months before. I felt humble and grateful that so much had been given to me so generously and without expectation. I wasn't free of my self-doubts, judgements or fears, but they no longer dominated my mind. I had a much greater capacity to witness my thoughts rather than react to them as a helpless victim.

My preference, of course, was to live. But now I had found an unshakeable peace that I knew wouldn't be destroyed by dying. The peace that passes all understanding was the gift I received in the cave. I fully expected to die and had arranged everything for my departure: my will, my funeral, and the letters and tapes for my children. I was ready to die or to live, but at no time did I feel as if I was fighting for my life. My focus was only on finding peace with my past, peace with myself, peace with life.

Like everyone, I only had a brief moment to grow and blossom upon the Earth, and then I would leave. I wasn't warming up for the big event. Life is found in each moment, and it's up to me whether

I squander it through fear, worry, greed, anger and resentment, or I let go and trust in the moment.

I had discovered the great joy of living like a tourist. When we travel, we drink in the moment: its sights, smells, tastes and sounds. We travel with fresh and heightened senses. Then we return home, where humdrum routine can numb us, and we sacrifice the moment to our anxieties and responsibilities as if worrying makes a difference. But we are all tourists, just passing through.

When the time came, I wanted to be on my deathbed with a soft smile born of an assurance in my heart that I had lived a useful life, free of regrets—and, hopefully, a life that brought a little love into the world. This sounded like a great way to both live and die.

CHAPTER 20

Home again

My parents had supported me financially throughout this time, because I had signed over all my assets to Leo before I left Australia. I was penniless, and they were more than happy for me to move into their home yet again.

Rae had been looking after Simon one day a week while Leo went to the stock exchange and Ada was in school. Rae often cared for the children on weekends too, which gave Leo a break from the responsibility of being a full-time parent. I was so grateful to her for the love and care she extended to my children during the time of my illness. I had missed so much of their formative years and was eager to rekindle our familial ease of frequent contact and connection.

On my return, I wasn't very robust but much better than when I had left Australia almost a year before. Blood tests showed that I had a high number of baby red blood cells but no sign of leukaemia. When these results were sent to the United States for Frank Conant to share with the doctors in Sacramento who had made the original diagnosis, their only response was that I'd had an unexpected remission that wouldn't last more than a few days, perhaps weeks, at most.

I found this challenging, as I had packed up the whole of my life and reduced my possessions to what could be carried in hand luggage. Everything else I'd once owned now belonged to Leo. I was living in the land of uncertainty—how much to unpack from the suitcase and start living? I knew I could now achieve a good death but was still unclear about how to construct a good life, especially given the unpredictability of my health.

However, one of the greatest blessings of nearly dying was that I now knew happiness wasn't derived from possessions. I had largely lost any desire for 'things'. They counted for little in the scheme of happiness and, as the German saying goes, 'The last shirt has no pockets.'

On the other hand, my happiness was certainly derived from seeing Ada and Simon. The children and I clung to one another in delight when they visited on weekends. We enjoyed exploring parts of Sydney and simply being together. Simon had started at the same school as Ada and, of course, they'd both grown so much since I had last seen them. Their company felt like a balm to me. I had no words to describe my inner landscape or the path that had led me to a different experience of myself and my life. But although uncertainty paralysed me from taking action, and nothing stood out as an obvious way forward, I was happy, humble and grateful to still be alive. The joy of being reunited with my children and parents was more than enough for the moment.

***

After about three months, as my health continued to improve, Rae took me by surprise when she said, 'Have you thought of working, dear?'

This moment was emblazoned on my memory as we drove across the Harbour Bridge. My mother's question posed the possibility of me actually *living*.

How could I start my life again if my reprieve from leukaemia was only temporary? It was a long time since I'd worked in an office, and the idea of returning to the book-publishing business, while generously on offer, held no appeal to me.

So my answer to Rae startled her as much as it did me. All I could say was, 'I just want to be paid for being me.'

I knew what I didn't want, but I still had no clue about what I did want. I didn't want to say 'yes' to things when my body shrieked 'no', but I could see nothing to say 'yes' to. Not knowing my direction was uncomfortable, as we all like to feel motivated, to have a purpose to our step and, if possible, to feel inspired by what we do.

My stay at the Eremo had been a little like a convalescence. It had given me time and space to reflect, and I'd released a mountain of grief, frustration, trauma and despair. I'd found a pathway home to myself. Now I continued to nourish my body, mind and spirit while I waited for a sign—or my intuition—to guide me forward in creating a meaningful life, for however long I might have it. I didn't want to just fill in time until I died, no matter how soon or far off my death might be.

The disquieting stimulus of my mother's question prompted me to call Marcus Blackmore—the businessman at the helm of his family company, Blackmores, well-known in Australia for their vitamin and herb products—whom I had met during my days at the naturopathic college. I explained my predicament to him: 'I am qualified as a naturopath, a herbalist, a homeopath, a massage therapist, and a yoga and meditation teacher. I was meant to die from leukaemia, but I'm still here in what my doctors described as "an unexpected remission", which they said won't last. I don't know what to do, Marcus. I don't want to wait around until I die.'

Marcus didn't seem to hesitate in his response. 'Don't focus on what your doctors have said. Go into naturopathic practice.'

A Mosman GP was looking for a naturopath to work in his clinic, and Marcus offered to introduce us.

The idea of becoming a naturopath didn't light my fire, but I still felt a flicker of both fear and interest. Embarking upon a career seemed a bold decision, given the uncertainty of my health. But after the intensity of serious illness and emotional catharsis, being a naturopath seemed rather tame—though I didn't tell Marcus about my misgivings. At least if I went into practice, I told myself, I could increase my independence and earn an income. My tenuous hope of taking custody of my children would only manifest if I created a home and offered them an education.

After speaking with my parents, who were happy to financially help me into a practice, I met with the GP, Emmanuel Varipatis, to discuss the possibility of working together. Emmanuel was supportive of me taking on only as much as I felt I could manage, and so began my life's work. I just didn't know it at the time.

PART 3

In search of meaning

CHAPTER 21

Behind closed doors

Early in 1985 I joined Emmanuel's practice, which was conducted from a small federation timber cottage in the heart of Spit Junction. It was close to public transport and near to my parents' home, where I continued to live until I could establish my independence.

The cottage had a homely atmosphere, and my clinic room was large and comfortable with a huge sash window that let fresh air and sunshine in. It was a thrill to create a safe and comfortable space for whoever might come to see me, and I felt a flicker of excitement when my business cards arrived.

Each decision towards establishing a practice felt monumental. Was there even a point in getting business cards printed when I might only use them for a short while? What seemed like simple choices were seasoned with my constant uncertainty—these small activities and preparations felt like a symbolic investment in life. I fluctuated between asking myself, 'What's the point of starting anything when I'm going to die anyway?' and a hopeful twinge that maybe I could keep living. My decision to live like a tourist meant I was trying to focus only on today, the moment, what was immediately before me. Business cards and a practice contained a belief in a future.

I was weary of reflecting on my story of catharsis and healing, and I decided it was time to put this aside and focus on being of service to others. In Italy, I had been loved and cared for when I'd held little love or care for myself. As a naturopath, I would endeavour to see the beauty and courage in people who, like me, gave life their best shot even though their inner world may well be at odds with their outer appearance.

Although I love the sublime beauty of nature, the invisible world has always been far more interesting to me than the physical. We can so easily be seduced by appearances while making no inquiry about what lies beneath. People often say to one another, 'You look well,' which can convey the message that they don't want to hear how the other feels. Assuming someone is happy because they look alright runs the risk of ignoring their more private experience. I prefer to ask people, 'Do you feel as good as you look?' as I know our outer appearance often belies our inner reality.

∗∗∗

Feeling both excited and apprehensive about commencing my practice, I started off with just a couple of mornings each week. Emmanuel understood my predicament and was supportive of my efforts in beginning this new adventure, and he referred a couple of his patients to me for dietary or other advice.

Within the first two weeks, a woman with breast cancer came to see me, and a man with AIDS came the day after that. Both Jenny and John had been told they wouldn't see Christmas, which was what I'd been told almost seventeen months before.

I felt that I was meeting fellow travellers in the transit lounge of their lives. I was eager to hear about their experiences, as so much of what they described mirrored aspects of my own journey. They were often far more articulate than me in describing their inner worlds. My journey had been very private and solitary; behind closed doors, I was moved by people's willingness to let me into their innermost thoughts and emotional journeys, as well as various secrets they'd sometimes held for many years.

My question for Jenny and then for John has remained at the foundation of my work: 'What is it that stands in the way of you being at peace?'

Jenny couldn't switch her mind off at night, as her worries about her health and future overtook her when she wasn't distracted with the busyness of her days.

I talked her through a relaxation technique to focus her attention on the breath. She felt the benefit of deepening the breath and increasing her oxygen intake and, with practice, she felt that she could calm her busy, busy mind. I offered to make a personalised tape to talk her off to sleep at night and another to use during the day for relaxation and meditation, and she eagerly took up my offer.

I also prescribed herbs that would help settle her agitation, and I encouraged her to develop a nightly ritual that would train her mind to wind down for sleep an hour before bedtime. This ritual included taking a warm bath or shower to wash away any stress from the day; burning aromatherapy oil to help her develop an association between that particular scent and sleep; sleeping in natural fibres for her nightwear and sheets; and ensuring her bedroom was clean and orderly so the space would feel restful. I suggested she limit sugar in her diet as she ate far too much of it—most of us eat too much sugar, which is very detrimental to our health and increases restlessness in some people. Jenny also needed to exercise earlier in the day rather than in the evening.

Jenny was happy to use these practical strategies to manage her mind more effectively and find the rest she needed as she underwent her treatment. A week later, she returned to discuss her diet and to get her meditation practice checked. Already she was sleeping well, and feeling much calmer and more in control of her choices.

Meanwhile, John's answer to my question, 'What is it that stands in the way of you being at peace?' was that diarrhoea was making his life miserable. It was stressful for him to leave the house because he always needed to be in close proximity to a bathroom. He was being treated for cryptosporidiosis, a common parasitic infection in people with a compromised immune system.

We discussed his diet and found that several foods, such as orange juice, dairy products and fried fatty foods, were likely exacerbating the problem. By eliminating these foods, and with the addition of slippery elm powder and homeopathics, John no longer experienced the urgency and could leave the house with greater confidence.

He also learned to meditate to better manage his stress. He improved his nutrition, including coconut smoothies, so his body could more quickly assimilate foods, which were still destined to pass through his system more rapidly because of the tenacious parasite.

Jenny and John found that these strategies empowered them to make a positive difference and improved the quality and perhaps the quantity of their lives—Jenny was here for two more Christmases, and John another five. Common sense tells us that if a woman can sleep soundly rather than tossing and turning with a chaotic, mad-monkey mind, or a man can hang on to his food long enough to extract and assimilate nourishment, both people will fare better.

I realised that being of some small service to a fellow human being is perhaps the greatest joy known to us. It leaves us feeling grateful that we were present to bear witness to their suffering, and humble if we have been able to offer comfort, insight or even a moment of peace. Once my patients were more physically comfortable or benefiting from the calmness that meditation brought, our conversations became deeper as I continued to inquire about aspects of their lives where peace was lacking.

Patients with serious health issues often protect their loved ones by not discussing their fears and uncertainties with them. These patients are usually happier to speak to someone not emotionally enmeshed in their life. I was unafraid of bearing witness to their despair or self-loathing or condemnation, and their hopes, fears, dreams or tears. Everything they described helped both of us to bring light to the deeper layers of our shared existence.

***

Word quickly spread about my particular interest in assisting people with serious health issues. Patients told other patients about me while having their treatment in hospitals or clinics, and their doctors saw the benefits that they received and started referring patients to me.

In the early years I always wrote to a person's doctor, letting them know what we had discussed and to encourage contact if he or she had any questions. I hoped my letters would reassure the doctor of my intention to assist their patient in a collaborative and complementary way. While I never received a response, doctors could see that I was supportive of their patient's medical treatment—that I wasn't offering an alternative to their treatment and that I kept my focus on areas outside of their expertise.

Naturopaths aren't allowed to treat cancer in Australia. This didn't matter, as I wasn't interested in treating cancer or AIDS (and not a lot was known about AIDS at the time, other than that it was caused by a virus and transmitted through blood or bodily fluids). My focus has never been on stopping people from dying; it is solely on helping people to live—and to live as well as possible, given the complexities of their circumstances. I'm always more interested in understanding the person in front of me rather than their disease. What's their story and how do they feel about their story?

Every day I listened to my patients describe their poor self-esteem or the effects of past traumas. In that sense, my story was no different to theirs—we were all struggling to find peace in the midst of our difficulties, to find a pathway through some unspeakable suffering or to make meaning of our lives after unexpected trauma or illness. While people often appeared to scrub up well, when I scratched the surface I found stories of despair, loneliness, grief, shame, anguish, loss, trauma, abandonment, childhood sexual, emotional or physical abuse, low self-esteem and rejection. Through their lips, I heard my own story told, over and over again.

Of course, while it's great to have a story, we don't have to *be* the story. Our stories break us open to the hidden depths of human strength, compassion, resilience and understanding. A story may break our heart, yet through courage and our willingness to share the journey, we find our spirit. The invisible world of the human spirit is capable of containing the story without being defined by it, and this is inspiring, heartwarming and uplifting. If we are to find peace, we need to see beyond the story to the spirit that enlivens and connects us all.

I wouldn't change one bit of my story now. Each trauma has led me to a greater understanding of myself and an enlarged capacity to be present to each precious moment, even though many of the events may be painful to experience. As one young girl, Kate Critchlow, told me at the tender age of nine when she was facing her own mortality, 'Sometimes hearts have to break before they heal.' Her words later became the impetus and title for my book *Sometimes Hearts Have to Break*. They were wise counsel for me, as I felt my own heart break again and again while I listened to people's stories.

Kate had drawn me a picture of Garfield the cat, and in the bubble of his thoughts were three hearts. She told me that she had drawn two pictures but she'd put them on her windowsill and the wind had blown the other one away. When I asked, 'What was in the other picture, Kate?' she replied, 'It was exactly the same as this one, but the hearts in the bubble of Garfield's thoughts were all shattered down the middle.' Somewhat shocked, I gently offered, 'Perhaps the wind is telling you, you don't need to have broken hearts.' Kate responded by shaking her head and telling me, 'No, Petrea, you don't understand. Sometimes hearts have to break before they heal.'

Just before she died, Kate reached out to squeeze her parents' hands and said, 'I want you to love each other the way you've loved me.' Such wisdom from children reverberates deeply, as they can so easily articulate a truth we all recognise.

Before any consultation, lecture or residential program, my habit has always been to simply remember my humanity while holding the intention, 'May I be used for the good.'

This intention allows a sacred space in which healing may begin or continue. I can happily offer myself up in the spirit of being of service to this person no matter the crime, no matter the pain, no matter the rage, fear, panic, despair or hopelessness. If I don't pretend to know what's best for someone and am willing to hear their story without expectation or judgement, this allows them to discover their own best answer.

I may not know the characters in their story, I may not have been diagnosed with the same disease, I may not have suffered in the way they're suffering, but there is no experience I cannot share with them, no terror I cannot understand, no anguish I cannot care about, no grief I cannot witness. It is enough to be fully attentive and hold the space for whatever needs to be expressed—rage, fear, their regrets or their weeping.

When a person feels deeply heard in an atmosphere that feels safe and non-judgemental, there is no shame, no wound, no secret, no suffering that cannot be shared and witnessed. We are all fragile and vulnerable. We are all strong beyond our knowing—it is in our willingness to be vulnerable and present to one another's suffering that our strength and humanity are discovered. Not everything can be fixed or changed. What makes suffering bearable is when others share the journey with us, easing our sense of isolation. It is a comfort to know that others have walked the path and left a legacy of both survival and love.

***

Within a few months, most of the people I saw had a life-threatening illness, mostly cancer and HIV/AIDS. I found my work to be wonderfully rewarding: my own unarticulated experiences were being described by my patients, and my knowledge and skills in naturopathy and meditation teaching were of such benefit to them.

A wheelchair-bound woman, Bella, came to see me from interstate. She and her husband hired a private jet to make the journey to consult with me, so they obviously had some relatively high expectations of my assistance. Bella sat weary and crumpled in the wheelchair as her husband pushed her into my office then left us to sit in the waiting room.

It turned out that these wealthy people had been to many alternative healing clinics all over the world for cancer treatments. Bella's days were dictated by a strict regimen of juicing, a precise method of meditation, the taking of dozens of supplements, along with a very restrictive diet of organic produce. At the time she visited me her doctors told her she had just four to six weeks to live.

As Bella described her daily routine to me, I presented a calm facade while quietly panicking on the inside. She knew far more about alternative and complementary therapies than I probably ever would, and I wondered what I could possibly say to her that would be of any benefit.

Finally, I noticed my preoccupation with my panicked mind and my lack of attentive listening. I brought myself into the present moment by coming to my senses: being aware of the shape and weight of my body, the pressure of the chair supporting my body, the touch and texture of my clothing, and the air against my skin. This helped me to simply be in the room with Bella and focus intently on being present to what she was saying. As I did this, I heard the heavy drone of the bees in the flowering wisteria outside my window and caught a whiff of its divine scent. I was aware of the sunlight streaming in and the distant hum of traffic. A quiet came over my mind, and the atmosphere in the room palpably changed, as if this moment had become more sacred.

To my surprise and no doubt to Bella's, I said, 'Forget about your diet and juicing. Eat what you like, but go into the children's hospital and read to the children in the burns unit.'

Well, Bella dissolved into tears, as did I.

I thought it an appalling thing to say to someone with only a few weeks to live. My tears stopped not long before hers, and then her story flooded out between the occasional heart-rending sob.

Bella had ached to have children throughout her life, but her husband didn't want them. So the idea of reading to children in the burns unit, of doing something with and for children in her last weeks, sounded perfect to her. I was surprised and relieved that she not only wasn't offended but had found my suggestion helpful.

I must have taken courage from this, because I then said to Bella, 'Forget your meditation practice but listen to the slow movement of the Double Violin Concerto in D minor by Bach twice a day, as if you've never heard it before.' It was a favourite piece of music of mine, but I had no idea of the relevance to her.

Again, Bella dissolved into tears and wept for what seemed a long time. My eyes were moist too as I witnessed her heartache.

Finally, when I passed her tissues and she stopped shuddering with sobs, she whispered, 'I love the violin. I played it up until the day of my marriage. My husband hates the violin, and I've never played it since.' She loved the idea of listening to this particular piece of music because it was the very piece she'd been studying when she stopped playing all those years ago.

By the conclusion of our time together, Bella sat more upright in her chair and was feeling much calmer. She even had a hint of colour in her cheeks. I saw her greet her husband by telling him that she now had a clear direction, and she left the cottage feeling happy and motivated to put into practice the ideas we'd discussed.

At first I found conversations like this surprising, even unnerving. They didn't seem to have much to do with naturopathy, meditation training or complementary therapies. However, it seemed that when people were hungry for assistance, and when my mind was quiet and I was deeply attentive to the person and their story, whatever was helpful to them arose in this healing space. I came to value the insights that these conversations sometimes brought with them, and I became more trusting of such intuitive nudges to ask seemingly unrelated questions or say unexpected things. I began to understand the benefits of the healing potential that complete attention engenders.

Six months later, I received a beautiful postcard from Bella that described her deep sense of fulfilment about the time she was spending with children in the burns unit. Scrawled across the bottom was: 'PS. Tumours still there but not bothering me.'

Twelve months later, I received another card from her, this one saying that she was organising other women to read to the burns unit children.

Bella died eighteen months after our initial consultation from a brain haemorrhage while sitting on her swing in her beloved garden. Her doctors believed that the chemotherapy had weakened her blood vessels, hence the haemorrhage. At the time of her death, she was free of cancer. Perhaps the resolution of her grief freed up the necessary energy that could more productively be utilised for her healing? Bella's experience was not isolated. As people found greater peace in their lives, often their physical health improved. Or, if their death was the outcome, they were enabled to let go lightly of life, which helped both the patient and their family to take leave of one another lovingly.

CHAPTER 22

The peace that passes all understanding

Within my first year of going into practice, I had two patients whom I thought would benefit greatly from meeting each other.

Diane had a pituitary gland tumour that, while not malignant, affected her hormone levels and created pressure in her brain. Her doctors strongly recommended that she never have children, as the hormones involved in pregnancy were likely to exacerbate her condition to the point where it would become life-threatening. Diane was feisty and articulate, and she described her inner emotional world with clarity, insight and forthrightness.

Josh, on the other hand, had a lymphoma, was dreadfully shy and didn't appear to have emotions. Our appointments were peppered with long silences as he struggled to answer my questions. I wondered why he persisted in driving four hours to see me when it was clearly such a struggle for him to put his thoughts and feelings into words.

Josh was tall, fair-haired and lanky, and as his lymphoma had progressed he'd became painfully thin except for the hard lumps that distended his neck, making it difficult for him to swallow or turn his head. This slowed his response times further, the symptom seeming to match his disposition. His prognosis was poor, and his doctors thought his remission from lymphoma was tenuous and temporary. He didn't know how he felt about facing the end of his life, yet he was keen to be in the company of other people who lived with serious health issues.

Like me, Josh and Diane were both in their early thirties, and they were interested in meeting each other. At our first support group, we established four guidelines to ensure that our group was a safe space in which we could utter the unutterable and feel supported and heard. The guidelines were confidentiality, attentive and active listening, non-judgement, and staying with our experience rather than our theories.

This was the first of many support groups—the first such groups in Sydney. They were without an agenda and weren't deliberately educational, in that we didn't choose a topic around which to focus our discussions. A well-facilitated support group provides a non-judgemental, nurturing, supportive atmosphere that allows people to find their own best answers while others listen compassionately and, when appropriate, share their experiences.

The four guidelines I established with Josh and Diane have never changed over the decades—they capture the essentials for hosting a safe group environment.

***

In the first year of my practice, I volunteered at St Vincent's Hospital in Darlinghurst to massage people with AIDS. Having just been through a profound illness, I couldn't imagine how it must feel to experience that while people were too fearful to touch you—at that time, meals were left outside patients' closed doors for them to retrieve. It took about six months to get the hospital's administration to approve my volunteer service, as it seemed they were worried about what I would do with patients behind closed doors! I assured them that my intentions were pure.

The first patient I massaged was just seventeen. Tony had only had two sexual encounters and was unsure if he was gay. As I massaged his body, he wept quietly, the puddle on his pillow expanding. When I asked him whether he wanted to talk, he said, 'No one has ever touched me like that before. I've only ever been touched when someone wants something from me.'

Tears filled my eyes as Tony's story broke my heart. He had been thrown out of home at fifteen because he thought he might be gay. He was full of rage against his family and despair at their judgement and subsequent rejection of him. He refused to let them know he was sick and had no intention of telling them his prognosis or where he now lived. He'd been told to expect to die within eighteen months.

I had recently started a support group at the Albion Street Clinic for people with HIV/AIDS, based on the four guidelines of the groups I facilitated in my clinic. I encouraged Tony to attend this group so he could safely express his feelings and gain support from other men who understood his confusion and suffering. He took my advice and became a regular member of the group for several years. Through participating in it, he found his peace and healing.

When I visited him in hospital to say our goodbyes, I walked into the same room where we had met four years previously. His mother was massaging his feet, his father was holding his hand and his sister was reading quietly in the corner. I massaged his distended belly until he beckoned me close and, taking off his oxygen mask, whispered, 'It's been an honour and a privilege knowing you. Thank you for teaching me about love. These have been the best four years of my life.'

While it is sad that Tony died at twenty-one, he died healed of everything that had ever stopped him from being at peace. Perhaps without AIDS, he and his family might never have healed their split.

He had found the peace that passes all understanding—and, para-doxically, AIDS became the catalyst by which he found this deeper healing.

When people speak of a 'cure', they are speaking of the body. Healing is about peace. I've known many people who have died healed of fear, anxiety or angst, and I've known others who have been cured of their disease but are still very much in need of healing.

✶✶✶

The support groups proved very popular and gradually increased in number to meet the demand. I was approached by a surgeon and two other health professionals interested in providing a nurturing environment for their patients, and the four of us started another support group at Waverley Hospital that ran over three months.

Kay Moechtar and her partner, Wendie Batho, attended this group. Kay had a rapidly progressing form of advanced breast cancer at diagnosis, and she'd been told by her doctors that her life would probably be limited to a couple of years.

She had given birth to three beautiful children who were now young teenagers, and she and Wendie raised them together along with their father, who would often visit and was considered very much a part of their family.

Kay was a regular member of the weekly meditation and support groups, where she aired her concerns within its safe confines and explored the awful reality of leaving her children before they'd reached adulthood. She grappled with the seeming irreconcilability of giving birth to children and not staying alive to raise them to maturity. This was an agony with which I and other parents were familiar.

Neither Kay nor I could have known it then, but our lives were inextricably woven into one fabric from our first meeting, a story that unfolds later.

CHAPTER 23

Stepping out

My practice had expanded to five days a week within the first year, and I was predominantly seeing people with cancer, HIV/AIDS, motor neuron disease (MND), multiple sclerosis (MS) and other life-threatening or inhibiting illnesses. I was still enjoying my work immensely and learning every day how better to be of assistance to the courageous people who came to see me.

My nursing studies, while incomplete, had given me a good understanding of the medical approach to treating these diseases. Usually there was no conflict between traditional medicine and my practice of naturopathy and more gentle ways of supporting health, along with my yoga and meditation teaching. Very occasionally, though, my advice would contradict the medical instructions a patient had been given, and this was always stressful for everyone involved.

Marilyn was a regular member of our support groups, and I saw her from time to time as a patient for dietary advice. Towards the end of her life, she was hospitalised with a bowel blockage after her ovarian cancer spread throughout her abdomen. Bowel blockages are incredibly painful, and sometimes the only resolution is surgery. However, Marilyn's blockage resolved itself after she spent five weeks in hospital with a nasogastric tube, her bowel resting while she was fed intravenous fluids.

Just before she was discharged, Marilyn rang me to check the dietary advice she'd been given. The dietician had told her that because she hadn't eaten for five weeks, it was important for her to eat highly nutritious foods to rebuild her weight; the foods suggested included plenty of cheese, bread, milk smoothies and cooked eggs. I shuddered when Marilyn told me this—given the potential for her bowel to block again, filling her digestive system with constipating foods like cheese seemed ludicrous, especially as she was also on high doses of constipating pain killers. Cheese was known as 'bung' in World War II because of its effects.

I gave Marilyn a very different eating regimen, then rang the dietician to let her know of my involvement and to ask why she had suggested those foods. She politely explained that Marilyn needed to build herself up physically after being without proper food for five weeks, so she had suggested highly nutritious foods accordingly.

But when I questioned the addition of cheese and bread to Marilyn's diet plan and suggested that these foods were likely to be highly constipating, especially given the high level of pain medication she was taking, the dietician snapped and said, 'It doesn't matter what she eats. She'll be back here soon with another blockage anyway!'

I found this attitude very distressing. Until then, I'd thought that anyone who had ever witnessed someone with a bowel blockage would do whatever possible to avoid a recurrence.

As it turned out, Marilyn never returned to hospital and never had another bowel blockage. By introducing slippery elm powder and non-constipating foods to her diet, eaten in small amounts and often, Marilyn remained comfortably at home surrounded by her much-loved family and cats until she died there peacefully, six weeks later.

For the most part, I offered a complementary approach rather than an alternative one, and this helped smooth the way for collaboration with the medical profession. My reputation meant that I was always welcome to visit patients in hospitals or hospices.

***

While deeply grateful for the generous support of my parents—who continued to share their home with me and provide financial support—I felt ready to take on the responsibility of first purchasing a car and then creating a home for myself.

I fluctuated between making bold decisions as if life was mine to live, then apprehension about my precarious health. I was regularly reminded through my patients that remissions can end abruptly and death often follows. The patients I found particularly challenging were those who had the same kind of leukaemia as me; sometimes these people had been in remission for months or even many years. It was always sobering to be reminded of the fragility of life.

Taking on the financial burden of paying rent was a minor challenge, but still a concern—a third of my practice was pro bono, as I understood the ravages of illness on both bodies and bank accounts. I soon found a tiny two-bedroom flat in Waverton and decided to work from home to conserve my finances. I moved in with a knife, a fork, a doona and a pillow and slept on the floor until I could afford a bed.

I continued to live like a tourist, seeing the world afresh while living on borrowed time, and I held no desire to accumulate possessions. But, of course, my flat needed basic furnishings. My parents loaned me a timber and marble coffee table, a desk and a chair. Ross was soon to move to the United States with his American wife, Dianne, so he generously loaned me his beautiful burgundy leather armchair and footstool, which our parents had gifted him for his twenty-first.

These borrowed items remain with me to this day. Ross's chair has had thousands of patients bless both it and me with their stories—and, though my remission is now sure and Ross is living in Australia, it still graces my office. I have offered to return it on several occasions, but he is content that his chair has found a home with me.

***

My interactions with Leo had become more civil and then warmer as the pain of our marriage and divorce receded into our histories. Ada and Simon were visiting my flat on weekends, with Leo and I taking turns to ferry them between Sydney and Mulgoa.

My personal life had stabilised, while my work was new, challenging and exciting—and sometimes downright scary. I found that working from home had some special benefits and just the odd risk.

Patients preferred the relaxed and homely environment as well as the confidentiality that my flat offered. Before long, my practice wasn't only full, I was also booked up weeks in advance with appointments. On the odd occasion, I felt vulnerable or at risk by myself with a mentally distressed or unwell patient.

One such was Peter, whose fuller story appears in my book *Sometimes Hearts Have to Break*. Peter arrived at my door with a face like a thunderclap, his black satchel in hand. I felt ill at ease just walking down the hallway to my consulting room with Peter following behind. After we'd gone through the usual details of his name, address and phone number, I asked, 'Why are you here?'

Peter, an electrician, carefully lifted a contraption out of his satchel that he later explained was a means by which he planned to electrocute himself after overdosing on sleeping pills. He then threw the remaining contents of his satchel at me, leaping to his feet and screaming, 'I'm fucking dying and these aren't fucking helping me and now I have to come to a fuckwit woman, for help!' as hundreds of pills of every size, shape and colour flew at me and across my office.

I have no idea what possessed me, given my history with angry men, but as he collapsed back into Ross's chair, I knelt in front of him and said, putting my hands on his knees, 'You must be terribly frightened.'

At this, Peter crumpled and sobbed and sobbed his heart out. All his friends and lovers were dead. His doctor was dead. He had nursed many men through their last days of dying from AIDS. Who was going to be there for *him* now *they* were all gone?

Such were the stories that unfolded within the safe confines of Ross's chair and my office.

***

After some months, towards the end of 1986, I could afford a larger flat in nearby Waverton with fewer stairs for unwell patients to climb.

This move meant that Ada could come and live with me. She was increasingly unhappy about living with Leo, and it broke my heart to see her so reluctant to return to him after our weekends together. Weekends just weren't long enough—we missed the daily routines and shared experiences that living together affords. There was also a small sunroom for Simon to sleep in on his weekend visits. Our life together began with him as a frequent visitor, while occasionally Ada would go to Mulgoa for the weekend.

Leo was happy to relinquish his care of Ada, as he was beginning to have some health issues and felt she would benefit by being closer to me. He was far more friendly to me now, probably because he could see the benefits in having me as an ally rather than treating me as the enemy. This brought greater flexibility to our discussions about the children and more collaborative solutions when we needed them.

Given that she would now live with me, Ada asked me if she could change her name. I agreed wholeheartedly, and she happily settled down with a baby-name book. She narrowed it down to Kate, Clare or Helen, settling upon Kate. I don't think any of us ever slipped by calling her Ada again! It was a delight—she finally had a name that she—and everyone except Leo—felt happy about. After about three months, she said, 'The thing is Mum, if you're really a "Kate" then you just can't be an "Ada"', and I understood exactly what she meant.

I approached Queenwood Girls School, where I'd attended for a year, and pleaded with them to take Kate in Year 6 so she wouldn't have to change schools again between primary and high school. She had already attended several schools, and I was keen for her education to be completed in one. My parents generously paid her school fees.

Kate left for school at seven-thirty in the morning, so I saw my first client of the day as soon as she went and would consult with patients until about seven in the evening. After school, Kate would focus on her homework, and then the two of us ate dinner together. I relished the ease of living with my daughter after such a long time, and Simon's presence on alternate weekends was a delightful bonus.

✳✳✳

My practice continued to increase until I was booked out six weeks ahead. People kept calling to say that they'd been told they only had four weeks to live, so I would see them on weekends. This was also when I visited people in their homes, hospitals or hospices if they were too sick to travel.

There was no time for life outside of being a parent, and I wanted to raise my children for as long as was possible while doing what I could to be of service to people who came to me for assistance.

It had been liberating to simplify my life down to the bare essentials, but I'd come a long way since my possessions fitted in hand luggage. I had gradually accumulated a fulfilling career, more contact with my kids and everything I needed to support family life. I'd even bought one piece of furniture that was more symbolic than essential.

While I didn't *need* a beautiful antique Japanese blanket box, it felt like an investment in a future—meaning that my confidence in my future was growing. I loved that the box had a long history and no doubt a tale to match; now we would have a shared story. It took pride of place for a while and still sits in my living room.

***

I had only been in practice for a couple of years when I was asked to speak in public about my experience of facing my own mortality and working with people facing theirs. I was nervous about giving a public presentation, especially on such a personal and difficult experience—but I didn't expect to have a panic attack.

There were four speakers at the event, and we were all seated on the stage with about three hundred people in the audience, mostly medical practitioners and other health professionals. The auditorium had no windows. Standing for long periods has never been easy for me, as my legs become painful and swollen. But asking for a stool would have involved admitting I had a problem with my legs and bring unwanted attention to me; so, of course, I didn't ask.

I was the first speaker. As I went to the lectern, my heart was pounding. I took hold of the lectern's sides to steady myself as heat rose in my face and my breathlessness and internal shakiness increased. I reached for a glass of water and spilt its contents down the front of my clothing. Without uttering one coherent word, I returned to my seat on the stage looking, and feeling, like a

My parents, Rae and Geoff.

Me as a toddler.

With my brothers Ross and Brenden and our pet dachshund, Brynner.

Our family holiday in Europe.

Brenden feeding a lamb at my godmother's property near Kilmarnock in New South Wales.

Me nursing a koala.

Celebrating my thirteenth birthday with Rae and Geoff.

Fellow trainee nurse Zibby Kellett and I enjoying toffee apples in a break.

My older brother Brenden, 20, and me, 18.

Brenden, 31, at Wentworth, New South Wales, 1982.

With my children Simon and Kate at my brother Ross's wedding.

With Ross and his wife Dianne, Rae and Geoff, 1986. Simon can be seen peering out from behind the sofa.

Being interviewed on television during a lecture tour of the United States for my first book, *Quest for Life*, in 1996.

Wendie and me.

With Padre Ilarino, who loved and cared for me at Eremo delle Carceri monastery near Assisi.

My corner of the Grotto of St Francis where I meditated.

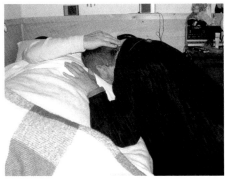

Padre Ilarino's last blessing.

With Wendie on the set of *This Is Your Life*, being presented with the album by Mike Munro.

Family portrait on the set of *This Is Your Life*: Kate, Ross, Simon and Geoff standing behind Wendie, me and Rae.

The launch of my book, *Your Life Matters*, The Briars, 2004.

Gong Blessing Ceremony, Quest for Life Centre, 2007.

The Quest for Life Centre, Bundanoon. ROBYN FAGAN

The Ruth Cracknell Garden at the Centre. ROBYN FAGAN

Receiving a 'For Purpose and Social Enterprise Award', Telstra Business Women's Awards, 2016.

With Marcus Blackmore and Wendie at the Blackmores Sydney Running Festival, 2013.

Walking Kate down the aisle, 2013.

With Simon, Edinburgh, 2008.

Happy times with Geoff and Rae.

Besotted with my granddaughters, Olivia and baby Izabella.

With Wendie, Bled, Slovenia, 2015.

Fundraising tour to Italy and Slovenia, 2015.

With Richard Glover in the 702 ABC studio, Sydney.

With Wendie, Assisi, 2015.

wet idiot. I then had to sit while the other three speakers eloquently delivered their speeches! I don't remember a word they said as I was so consumed with the shame of having performed so poorly.

The next time I was asked to speak at an event, without hesitation I said, 'Yes'. I refuse to go to my grave living with all the fears, limitations and anxieties that I accumulated as a young person. I don't want to be defined by past traumas, and I want to grow and flourish regardless of the things that might have caused me to shrink.

CHAPTER 24

A growing confidence

Other than my immediate family, everyone I knew had a life-threatening illness. Occasionally the children and I would socialise with my clients, particularly if they had kids around the same age. I felt a deep sense of gratitude for the purpose my life was taking on. Every day above ground left me humble and grateful for the opportunity to interact with such courageous people.

When I asked them what stood in the way of them being at peace, people revealed extraordinary stories of suffering, of dashed dreams, of tortuous self-loathing, of broken-heartedness, of family secrets, of grief, shame, guilt, resentment, regret, abuse and remorse. Our explorations went to the very heart of our shared existence as we addressed the questions: Who am I? What am I doing on the planet? Am I living the life I came here to live? If not, why not and what am I going to do about it?

These were the very questions I had contemplated all my life. How do we live a life of purpose? How do we identify our purpose? Does each of us have a preordained purpose or do we choose it?

While living in Sorrento, I had asked Padre Luigi these questions. His response was simple: 'Be where you can love the best.'

At the time, I'd drawn little comfort from his words as they only added to my confusion, but I had come to value this uncomplicated wisdom.

Most of us want to feel happy and useful; that our lives contribute to the wellbeing or happiness of another; that our presence has nourished another human being; or that we have expressed our creativity to invent or create something of beauty or benefit to others. This isn't about a life in neon lights—it's in our small gestures of kindness, in the way we live our values, in the giving of time with a listening heart.

Love is in the detail. It is demonstrated in the way we set a table, season a meal, stroke a brow, hold a hand, stand up when the world would have us sit, sit when the world would have us move to violence. It is about living a life true to our purpose and as an expression of the creative loving power of the universe. Not 'my way' but 'Life's way'—a way that supports and enhances Life—even if you call Life by another name, such as God. The challenge is to align ourselves with the wise, compassionate, intuitive, humorous and spontaneous essence that lies beyond the story of our lives.

The people I saw in my practice and through the support and meditation groups helped me to find the words to describe the journey of healing that I had undertaken and they had now embarked upon. I remain indebted to them. Without them, I would never have found the words that have, in turn, benefited others.

I continue to learn from people willing to share this precious inner journey, because it involves courage, relentless honesty and a deep commitment to heal from the notion that we are somehow separate from love—which is our essential nature.

✳✳✳

The downside to the success of my practice was that my flat was becoming cramped. An increasing number of people attended the weekly support and meditation groups, sitting on every available piece of furniture and on every inch of floor space. A frail person might arrive, and someone slightly less frail would give up their seat to ensure they would be as comfortable as possible.

It was humbling and heartwarming to see people demonstrate such selflessness and compassion. But it was also becoming obvious that my furniture wasn't always suitable for people who were unwell. I felt for them enduring this additional discomfort as, for instance, some people needed to lie down for the duration of the group, or sit in a chair with a straight back and with arms to support them getting in and out.

I did what I could to accommodate all of these people, who clearly weren't deterred by the cramped conditions, but I also yearned to provide a better environment for our support and meditation groups.

After the three-month course at Waverley Hospital, about twenty-five women and men, including Kay Moechtar, had become regular members of the Monday morning support group at my flat. Most of them had cancer, but there was also a sprinkling of both gay and straight people with HIV or AIDS. Regardless of the cause of each person's disease, they were all facing their mortality with courage, honesty and good grace. There is an extraordinary dynamic when people gather to listen intently to each other speak the truth of their current experience without judgement or interruption.

Together we traversed the powerful landscape of all human emotions—abuse and shame, grief and loss, hope and humour, sorrow and despair, compassion and laughter, anguish and hopelessness, love and connection, guilt and blame, faith and self-loathing, resentment, anxiety and panic. And in this supportive space, it was easy for us all to venture vicariously into the emotional spaces being described.

While listening to someone tell their story, we can explore our own deep place of emotion. It's incredibly empowering and illuminating to hear someone articulate what we are feeling before we've found the words to describe it to ourselves. This helps us understand that we are not alone with our complex and fluctuating feelings. And, of course, the moment we articulate the feeling, we discover that we're already more than it is, as we have captured it in words. The energy of the feeling is released, and we find relief in the mutual knowledge that we are in company that empathises and understands. To discover that our experience isn't unique leaves us comforted and less isolated.

***

Many years ago, a man with AIDS demanded of me that I write about 'black holes'. He shouted his instruction at me, a habit with him: 'Nobody talks of the inner darkness—the agonising, isolating madness that engulfs and consumes. You know about black holes, so for god's sake write about them!'

The first thing this gentleman had said to me, with considerable volume and passion—before hello, before he'd sat down, and only just after I'd closed my consultation room door—was this, 'I've arranged my public schedule to kill myself in November, but I'll be damned if I'll die before I've learned how to love!' He was a public figure, and in the 1980s the stigma of AIDS hung over many a man and woman as an unbearable shame.

Suicide was a common topic of conversation in the weekly support groups I conducted at Albion Street for ten years, from the beginning of the epidemic in Australia. At that time, the grim reaper regularly appeared on our screens as bowling balls knocked men, women and children off their feet. Judgement, rage, grief and fear were rife in the community, and there were many unknowns as friends, lovers and doctors died from this insidious disease.

It is often in the unexplored darkness of our inner world that the light is discovered. The public figure and I shared many conversations about his self-loathing and the harsh judgements he inflicted on himself, and finally tears of sadness for the small boy who had felt so unloved and misunderstood by his mother and so wounded by life. Many people mistook his arrogance as a belief in his own importance. His bravado concealed the self-doubt that infused his every waking moment and, now that he was facing his mortality, served only to sharpen his resolve to find healing and peace.

Because of this, he frequently attended support groups in my home, hoping that anonymity would be respected there. In facilitating these groups, I was a bit like a mother lion protecting her cubs, as anonymity and confidentiality lie at the heart of honest disclosure. It is an added and unnecessary agony when a person's public profile is acknowledged at a time when they are desperate to explore their inner darkness and vulnerabilities.

In these weekly groups, the public figure forged a formidable relationship with another member, a nun called Maryanne. They were an unlikely duo: she spoke quietly with hands folded neatly in her lap, while his gestures were large, his presence dominant, his voice deep and passionate as he unpacked his trepidations. But sometimes Maryanne would articulate how he felt before he'd come near being able to understand his experience or describe it to himself, let alone others. He found it unnerving and uncanny that Maryanne could accurately describe his inner landscape before he could find his own words. She had led a sheltered life after entering a convent at sixteen, while his life had been a wild and sometimes dangerous exploration of the world.

Yet they became fast friends and, towards the end of their lives, I ferried them between hospices for visits. Sometimes they just sat in silence, basking in each other's company, and at others they shared some new insight from their journey to the edge of life. Watching them sit together, holding hands, remains a sweet memory.

***

The meditation groups were also very important and helpful. My gratitude for the practice of meditation is immense—the ability to witness thoughts, feelings and sensations without being overwhelmed by them is a treasure beyond all others. Many of my patients and support group members came to appreciate this too. The Tuesday evening meditation group sometimes had fifty or more people attending. The attendees became dear to one another and easily welcomed new members into their midst. In time, we developed rituals to address our grief at the loss of members who had grown dear to us all. Meditating in a group always engendered a deeper experience of transformative states than in people's individual practice. They relished the profound peace and stillness their practice afforded them and the rare opportunity of being in deep silence together.

One of the members, Rob, had a melanoma which had spread throughout his body when he first started attending the meditation group. The initial and extensive surgery to remove the melanoma in his neck had resulted in most of one side of his neck being removed. He then had one lung removed and later, a third of his remaining lung removed. By the time he started attending the meditation groups the melanoma had spread to many other areas of his body.

Rob, whose daughter was only eighteen months of age at the time, had been told his life would end within two or three months. Rob drove with a friend from the other side of the city to attend every meditation group on Tuesday evenings for the next six years. He mostly lay on the floor underneath my dining room table and snored his way through each practice. Rob was adamant that he wasn't asleep; 'I go somewhere', he would say. A guided practice can take a person into a profoundly deep and restful state, and he loved the deep quiet and stillness he experienced. I maintained contact with Rob for over twenty years and he remained free of melanoma and lived long enough to see his daughter grow to adulthood. He claimed that meditation vastly improved his quality of life and, along with many other lifestyle changes, perhaps his quantity of life too.

By this time in my life, I no longer took my thoughts or feelings so personally, so seriously, and focused on cultivating a sense of compassion and kindness towards suffering, whether it was my own or someone else's. My mind's unconscious inner chatter had stopped. I was grateful for the uninvited, unexpected questions or suggestions that popped out of my mind's quietness when I was with a patient or in a support group.

I was frequently called upon to see people that no one else had been able to help; people who were suicidal or deeply despairing, bed-bound or depressed. One woman, Lizzie, had been in a distant and unreachable place ever since she had returned from an overseas exchange student placement. During her year overseas, she had been unwittingly caught up in a satanic cult and since her return, Lizzie had stopped speaking altogether. Her distressed parents cared for her at home but they were at their wits' end because nothing and no one seemed able to assist their once vibrant and academically brilliant daughter. My visits to an increasingly dishevelled Lizzie were always challenging as she would just stare unseeingly at me or her surroundings. I wondered whether my presence or words had any impact upon her but her parents remained grateful for my visits. The inner calm and stability afforded through meditation allowed me to offer compassion and support to this family though I could only trust that my words to her, and to her parents, brought some small comfort. I found it painful to be in the presence of someone I couldn't help but I also knew from long experience that not every-thing can be fixed or made better.

When facilitating groups or in more intimate conversations, I gained great fulfilment through helping people understand them-selves better, and to challenge and more deeply explore their fears and anxieties. It is easier to venture into the caverns of anguish in good company. Laughter was a frequent visitor to our conversa-tions, and I was in awe of how people could be sharing anguish and tears in one moment and then crack a joke in the next. These encounters left me feeling humble and grateful to play even a small part in the most intimate areas of people's unfolding journeys. The resilience and capacity of the human spirit to embrace its challenges remains a constant inspiration and wonder to me.

CHAPTER 25

A full house

Each week, Kate and I shared our home with up to a hundred people with life-threatening illnesses, not only through the support and meditation groups but also through my private consultations. I continued to learn so much through working with so many people living at the edge of life. While many vastly improved their quality of life, many also went on to die and it was hard to love and lose these wonderful people.

I developed rituals of healing and remembrance for the support and meditation group members when much-loved participants died. Each death provided us with an opportunity to consider the shaky ground on which we all live. We wept and laughed together as we shared the precious journey of healing and loss.

Several times a year, I conducted weekend retreats in the Southern Highlands for members of the various groups. These were incredibly inspiring and wonderful opportunities for people with HIV/AIDS and cancer to share their insights, laughter and tears. Costs were kept to a minimum so that as many people as possible could be present, and there were often fifty people in attendance. Children were frequently present at these weekends too, as many of the participants were young parents.

I organised the catering, purchased and transported the food, sorted out the sleeping arrangements (taking people's physical needs into account), arranged the car-pooling to get everyone to the venue, and facilitated the programs. We all prepared meals together through a roster that depended on people's level of wellness, and those who felt most confident in the kitchen would oversee the preparation.

On the Saturday evening, we conducted a very special ceremony to allow everyone present to honour and acknowledge people we loved who had died, and to reflect on our own mortality.

In the centre of our circle was a small fire on a table surrounded with flowers and dozens of unlit tealights. I would lead a meditation where we calmed and centred ourselves, and then we would visualise those we loved who had died. We inwardly reflected upon the qualities that each of these people possessed and what it was that endeared them to us—their humour, tenacity, wisdom, insight or other qualities. We took some moments to tell them, silently in our minds, whatever lay in our hearts. We listened for what they would say to us in response; then we visualised them dissolving into light.

When participants felt ready, they would venture into the centre of the circle, using the fire to light a tealight in acknowledgement of the person they were honouring, and place it among the flowers. Afterwards we sat in darkness and silence aside from the crackling of the fire and its dancing flames, and the dozens of tealights flickering among the flowers. Each participant's face was deeply reflective.

During the ceremony, any children present would always be entranced and respectful. Finally, at the end, they would light sparklers from the fire and deliver one to each person in the circle as a symbol of our continuing journeys. The joy, love and wonder on the children's faces and the sputtering stars of light from the sparklers left us all in a space of connection and brought us fully

225

into the present moment where life was unfolding beautifully. The ceremony felt deeply sacred to each person in the circle and the children felt it too.

Our willingness to come together like this was profoundly healing. The ceremony melted isolation, as shared silence is such a gift. And it often made difficult conversations possible after they had been hovering unsaid in the space between couples. A willingness to acknowledge people who had died enabled painful and challenging words to finally find utterance.

***

Another feature of these weekends was the horseriding. Some people who were quite unwell still chose to go riding, so suitable steeds were found for them. The owners of the property were well-experienced with riders of all abilities and disabilities, and they displayed great compassion for the people attending.

Many of the riders needed assistance into the saddle, and most had never ridden a horse before. The joy on their faces was beautiful to behold as they set off to ride through the eucalypt forests. On their return an hour or so later, they would be sitting a little straighter and their faces would be deeply contented.

Such activities were a sharp contrast to their lives at home. They returned from these weekends braver and feeling more enabled to tackle their challenges, having discovered more strengths and capabilities within themselves.

Participants would also develop a stronger sense of community. The care that they showed to one another was always so moving— perhaps someone unwell would give up their day bed or seat to someone sicker, assist them to their feet, or fetch a cushion, a glass of water or a blanket.

***

Craig was an opal miner from Lightning Ridge. He rang me from Royal Prince Alfred Hospital on a Friday afternoon as we were preparing to leave for the weekend retreat. Craig said he'd just been told by his oncologist that he had six weeks to live due to the extensive spread of his melanoma. His face and jaw were distended with the tumour, so eating was difficult and painful.

I offered to pick him up and take him with us for the retreat. Given he didn't have family or friends in Sydney, he accepted happily. It turned out that Craig thought all 'poofters deserved to die', so being a member of the retreat was quite confronting for him, but he stayed. Some of the people with HIV/AIDS were excellent cooks, and they and others prepared food for him that he could manage to eat without too much pain.

On his return to Sydney, I arranged for Craig to move into a hospice. He wasn't well enough to live independently, and a return to Lightning Ridge would have been unwise given its remoteness and his short prognosis. I visited him regularly in the hospice, and his mother moved in with me and my children as she knew no one in Sydney and needed a base close to her son.

Each week, Craig travelled by taxi to attend the support groups at my home, which was close by. He found that many of the lads with HIV and AIDS were just like him—and, like him, they were all facing their mortality in their early twenties.

After attending several weekend retreats in the ensuing months, Craig was determined to attend the next one. But, by now, his pelvis was in three separate pieces due to the melanoma's progress through his bones. There was no way we could transport him to the Southern Highlands by car as even the short taxi ride to my home was painful and a challenge for him. However, Craig was determined to attend, as these weekend retreats were very important to him. It can be hard to find people comfortable in your presence when you're experiencing profound pain and physical distress, and he knew he would be in good company. Black humour was often present at these gatherings, along with touching moments when anguish could be expressed, heard, witnessed and held in the hearts of those present.

Good friends of mine, John and Mary Butters, arranged for the pilot of the AGL helicopter to transport Craig from a park near the hospice to the property where the retreat would be held south of Sydney.

Forty people stood in a paddock waiting for Craig's arrival. After the helicopter touched down, his friends with HIV gently lifted him into a wheelchair that they carefully carried to the main room where we would gather.

Moments when we connect with our common humanity, leaving aside our prejudices and judgements, are profoundly healing. We see the other as our self, and we experience the love and compassion that connects us all in a deeper and more honest place beyond our usual pretences and prejudices. While curing is focused on the body, healing is about the heart and losing our sense of separateness and isolation.

My own fragile mortality still hovered in the background of my life, though the fear of going out of remission occupied my mind far less. I expected that this would happen at some stage, but in the meantime my wonderful companions gave me courage and strength that I likewise gave them. We didn't feel alone with our grief and concerns as we all felt we had friends for life.

CHAPTER 26

Difficult work

Another wonderful activity that I instigated in the late eighties was to take people with life-threatening illnesses, dressed as clowns, to cheer up children at the Camperdown Children's Hospital. The CLOWN Project stood for Compassion and Love Offered When Needed. Gore Hill Technical College students made beautiful costumes to fit a variety of clown sizes.

Each week, people who were frail, people with amputations, people on crutches or in wheelchairs got dressed as clowns and visited several wards where children were seriously ill. They had many activities to share with children, including donated books and toys. The clowns' own frailties meant they connected gently and compassionately with the kids.

One little girl was from Indonesia with only her aunty accompanying her. No one else spoke her language. The nurses said she was withdrawn and fearful of her surroundings.

When one of our clowns spoke Bahasa to her, her eyes were like saucers. She had never seen a clown before, let alone one speaking her language. He gently got her confidence, and it was beautiful to see her soften and relax as he told her a story in her own language. She ended up laughing with joy.

The CLOWN Project provided such a beautiful opportunity, with both the clowns and the children benefiting from these visits. The clowns loved that they could provide comfort to children instead of being the ones perceived by others as needing support. This provided a liberation from feeling like a sick person, to feeling grateful to have helped someone else.

***

Occasionally I moved in with families when a child was dying. This was particularly heartbreaking; no parent ever expects their children to predecease them. I learned so much from these children—once pain was relieved, they had an extraordinary capacity to let go of the painful parts of their journey, and then full-heartedly focus on the love and lightness they felt.

Nine-year-old Charlie was my first great teacher in the heart-rending journey of a child dying. (His story is another that I told in *Sometimes Hearts Have to Break*.)

Just before I met Charlie, I was invited to work with Dr Jerry Jampolsky in Sausalito, California. Jerry is a wonderful child and adult psychiatrist who works extensively with patients of all ages living with cancer and HIV/AIDS, and in many other arenas of difficulty and conflict around the world. At the time, he conducted support groups for children and worked with visualisation and other techniques to bring them healing and peace as they journeyed towards their death.

When I first met Charlie, I told him that I was travelling to the United States to work with Jerry in several weeks' time. Charlie asked, 'Why are you going?' I explained that there might be many children like him I'd be asked to work with, and that Jerry had a lot more experience than me; I had questions I wanted to ask him, and I expected him to train me so that I could help more children.

Charlie closed his eyes for a while and then said, 'I think you'd better go and get your questions answered.'

As the weeks progressed, it was obvious I might be in the States with Jerry when Charlie died. I had become very close to him and each member of his family.

The day dawned when I was due to fly to the States.

I visited Charlie on my way to the airport and, sitting by his bed while he slept, I realised I was going to America to ask Jerry all the questions to which Charlie had the answers. It would be a lot more fun to work with Jerry but, three hours before I was due to fly, I cancelled my trip and moved in with Charlie and his family.

The next couple of weeks were incredibly hard. I had never been with anyone who experienced as much pain as Charlie. Living with his family on that difficult, raw and tender journey was unforgettable. It didn't change the awful fact of Charlie's death, but it changed the way the family made that unwanted and tragic journey. We made it together and have remained firm friends ever since.

Anastasia was another child I worked with. At twelve years old, she was paralysed from the neck down. She asked her mother to leave us alone because she wanted to tell me something. Then she asked me to turn her head so she could look directly into my eyes. Hers were clear and sparkling. She was afraid it might upset her mother to hear her say to me, 'Petrea, if this is dying, it feels wonderful. I feel like I'm being born into light.'

Another girl, Jenny, was just seven years old and had a little brother of four who was an energetic handful. Jenny had her leg amputated below the knee due to an osteosarcoma. She asked her mother to take her little brother from the room so we could talk. As soon as they left, Jenny hopped over and sat on my lap. Wrapping her arms around my neck, she looked straight into my eyes and said, 'Petrea, I know I'm dying, but who's going to help Mummy look after my little brother?'

These moments were full of heartbreaking poignancy, and I was amazed by the innate compassion shown by children. They also have a remarkable capacity to embrace their deaths so long as they're given a safe and honest environment in which to ask their questions or share their insights. I didn't need to have their answers, and I learned the value of simply saying, 'Great question. I don't know,' and then offering whatever small comfort I could.

It was such a privilege to be invited into people's homes and lives at these profoundly difficult and painful times.

✳✳✳

Life was full and rewarding, with every day and evening taken up by my work and being with my children. However, while I felt deeply involved and engaged, I was also becoming exhausted. My boundaries were too elastic, and my evenings often involved phone calls with people in distress. The number of suffering people seemed unending, and my work with children could be very challenging.

Then eight patients died, all in the same week—people whom I had come to love. There simply wasn't sufficient time for me to take on the enormity of their loss, while also, in some cases, visiting and comforting their families or conducting their funerals.

Through my work, I was privileged to share intimate journeys that confronted me with every judgement I could hold about myself or another. Judgement separates: that is its purpose. The heart of yoga is union, the healing of all separation so we merge with the eternal, the loving, the indestructible essence of love that lies beyond judgement and dwells within each of us. Surely no other work could have provided such an extraordinary opportunity for me to release myself from all judgement. However, I was becoming overwhelmed by grief with no end in sight. I didn't want to just survive doing this work. I knew it was my vocation, my privilege and purpose, and I wanted to thrive and flourish through being in service to the people who came to see me.

Around this time, one of the regular support group members, Pamela, generously gave me a set of keys to her holiday apartment in Mooloolaba, Queensland. She saw I was working virtually non-stop and becoming worn out.

And so, while Kate stayed with my parents, I drove to Queensland and settled myself in for a good two-week rest in paradise. The Pacific Ocean sparkled invitingly in front of the unit, while the Mooloolah River flowed past smoothly on the last leg of its journey before emptying itself into the sea.

The first night I turned on the television only to view an ABC story on AIDS in the prison system—and I dissolved into sobs. Who would be there for them?

I couldn't control the tears as I wept for the agonising stories I heard every day. Why does it have to hurt so much to be human? Why do parents lose their children? What's the sense in so much pain, suffering and loss? What is the point of it all? I cried myself to sleep on the floor, only to awaken to more sobbing. I barely made it out the door during those two weeks, and I drew only small comfort from the wisdom of Kate Critchlow's words, 'Sometimes hearts have to break before they heal.'

On the long drive home from Queensland, I asked myself some tough questions and came to some realisations.

Why did I need to be needed by all the people who clamoured to see me? I was booked out six weeks ahead, and I didn't like the tension of having to squeeze someone in who probably wouldn't live long enough to slot neatly into my diary. I realised I had repeated an old and ingrained pattern—laid deep in my neuronal pathways and habitually activated by my subconscious—of putting others' needs ahead of my own. This time, I had made seriously ill people more important than me from a sense of survivor guilt: their needs became more important than mine because I'd somehow cheated death.

I also realised that I needed to find someone who would listen to me as keenly as I endeavoured to listen to everyone else. Someone who would 'get me' and be a regular touchstone in my work. How fortunate I was to find a fabulous psychiatrist, Phil Palmisano, on my return home. I asked for an appointment to see if Phil would be willing to provide me with supervision in my work; he kindly agreed to do this and, even more kindly, only ever bulk-billed me. Phil was a great listener, of course, but he also offered sage counsel seasoned with a wonderful sense of humour. We treasured each other's stories, and he shared much of himself over time.

Given my tenuous remission, we joked that he might not need to see me for too long—I then saw him every week for nine years. Tuesday morning at eleven was my dedicated time with him. Nothing was off limits in our discussions, which ranged over personal, historical, professional and current issues. As our years together unfolded, our sessions became a touchstone in my life.

As we'd agreed, Phil and I regularly focused on my professional world, and we often discussed the importance of separating my issues from those of the people I worked with. If patients or support group members wanted to talk about suicide or euthanasia, I needed to be very clear that I wasn't trying to rescue Brenden over and over again. I had to focus on helping to provide people with a non-judgemental space to explore their options.

While suicide was a frequently raised topic, especially in the Albion Street groups during those early years, it was very rarely chosen in the end. Many people kept the means to end their life safely hidden somewhere easily accessible and that seemed sufficient to allay their fears. Often a support group member would claim that when he got to be thin and unwell, he would exercise his right to end his suffering—a few years later, when he became thin and unwell, peace was in his eyes and a smile was readily found upon his lips; he had found his peace and was in no rush to depart.

***

During my journey home from Queensland, I also decided to drive Kate to school each morning, instead of her travelling by bus. This allowed us to spend precious time together.

After dropping Kate off, I would walk the length of Balmoral Beach with the intention of hearing every wave come to the shore. I would then have a fresh juice and short black coffee before I saw my first patient of the day.

Meditation was still an essential daily practice, but this exercise in mindfulness was *my* time. Having attended to myself, I was ready for everyone else.

CHAPTER 27

Broadening
my horizons

On my return home from Queensland, I wasn't particularly surprised to find messages aplenty on my answering machine.

However, one stood out from the general inquiries for appointments: a message from the Department of Corrective Services. When I returned the call, a woman asked if she could visit me at home to discuss 'a matter'. I was curious and agreed.

We sat in my lounge room with tea while she described in some detail the behaviour of the HIV-positive prisoners in Long Bay Gaol—which, at that time, was far from exemplary.

The twelve prisoners were kept in an isolation unit within a maximum-security gaol; none of the other prisoners wanted to be anywhere near them, such was the fear of the virus. The only spasmodic contact between the two groups of prisoners were the tennis balls whacked over the walls to bring in drugs and related paraphernalia.

The HIV-positive prisoners were being disruptive because they wanted the same services and rights that people with HIV received outside the gaol system. They had set fire to their unit and flushed clothing down the toilets to block up the system. The naughtier they became, the more locked up they were. The more locked up they were, the naughtier they became, to the point where wardens were refusing to work in their compound. There had been one suicide. There had also been threats against the wardens of syringes filled with infected blood.

These twelve prisoners were a relatively incompatible group in terms of their crimes, which ranged from petty theft to bank robbing, drug trafficking, rape and manslaughter. They were a mixture of IV drug users and gay men. It seemed the only thing they had in common was HIV.

My visitor went on to ask if I would consider working with the prisoners to settle them down, with a view to then integrating them into the mainstream gaol where no one wanted them—and, if so, what my hourly charge would be.

Well, I thought that this would certainly stretch my skills.

I told her I couldn't promise any success. I wasn't a psychologist and had never worked in a gaol. But I'd be happy to do what I could to help, and my usual fee was $35 an hour. She thanked me for my time and asked me to think about it a little more deeply. She would return in a week for my answer, and she added that I might want to review the fee.

My heart went out to these men who were in confinement at the very time when they no doubt most ached to be with loved ones. No wonder they were angry and, of course, most of them had little emotional literacy or ability to express their feelings in healthy and acceptable ways; no doubt it felt far more powerful for them to punch someone or set fire to something than to say, 'I'm really scared I'm going to die in prison away from my family and friends.' Working with these men would undoubtedly broaden my horizons.

My visitor returned a week later and asked for my decision. I reiterated that I was happy to take on the challenge and my fee remained the same. She suggested a much higher hourly rate, and I graciously accepted her offer, knowing that this would help mightily given the amount of work I did on a pro bono or voluntary basis. I figured it was the universe's way of supporting me. Little did I know this was danger money.

***

There were ten gates to unlock and relock by the officer who escorted me on my journey to the isolation unit deep within the maximum-security gaol. On arrival, I would leave my belongings in a locker at reception and enter the unit empty-handed.

Once I'd settled in and got to know everyone, I sought permission to cook with the men, and I gave two reasons for my request. First, if we were cooking together we would be shoulder to shoulder rather than eye to eye; because the main people who eyeballed them were police officers and wardens, I knew it would be difficult for us to form a trusting bond unless we were shoulder to shoulder. While we cooked together we could discuss safe sex, death, dying, drug use, relationship issues, grief, self-respect, health and their precarious future. Second, it would help me to educate them about their need to take better care of their health—most of them lived on sugar, white bread, sweets, instant coffee and cigarettes.

Corrective Services was happy for me to go ahead with this plan, and they agreed to pay for all the food I needed. The only proviso was that we weren't allowed to cook with anything that could be fermented into alcohol. From then on, I regularly took bags of food into the isolation unit.

I'd developed one of my favourite recipes, pumpkin pie, when my children were young and vegetarian. It combines steamed pumpkin with onions, cottage cheese, mixed herbs, honey, eggs and butter, and it's baked in the oven without a pie crust. Of course, cutting up pumpkin with a flimsy plastic knife in gaol was enough to stimulate any human being into a murderous frenzy. Checking first that they weren't being observed by the wardens, the prisoners slid a panel away in the back of the kitchen cupboard and retrieved a 20-centimetre knife that did the job in no time at all! Once the pumpkin was peeled, the knife was cleaned and returned to its secret location.

***

One prisoner was probably a psychopath—he had no regard for anyone. I always made sure I wasn't alone in his company. He would happily masturbate while talking about his grandmother's funeral; when I called him on his behaviour, he would just smirk and continue until I walked away. I eventually wrote a report stating that he should never be integrated into the mainstream gaol, but after I'd finished working at Long Bay he was taken out of the isolation unit for economic reasons. Not long afterwards, he infected a warden with a syringe of his own blood; sadly, the warden subsequently died. In time, so did the prisoner, after he'd been transferred to Goulburn gaol where I can only imagine the treatment he received from the wardens.

But I never felt threatened by him or any of the other prisoners. At worst, they might have held me hostage to achieve some political end, but I knew they wouldn't hurt me. They appreciated the fact I came into the gaol to help them. When I shared my own story, they felt safe to share their fears and struggles. Preparing meals, talking and eating together allowed us to quickly form a deep bond of trust.

In addition to cooking and eating together, we held twice-weekly support and meditation groups. This helped them feel that they had access to the same services offered to HIV sufferers outside of prison. They particularly loved my guided visualisation practices, perhaps imagining that they were far away on a tropical island, with palm trees swaying and the warmth of the sand between their toes.

***

I had only been working at Long Bay for a couple of months when two of the prisoners set upon the other ten and beat them up. Now ten prisoners were allowed out of their cells into the recreational area while the two perpetrators remained locked up, or vice versa. This made it more difficult for me to defuse the situation, let alone resolve the issue of the massive expense of their isolated incarceration.

One of the most extraordinary miracles I have ever witnessed happened a few weeks after this fight.

The men were all adamant that they wanted their weekly support group, but I didn't have time to conduct two groups. Finally, it was resolved. The two recalcitrant prisoners would be on one side of the bars, while the other ten would be on the other side with me. We were still able to form a circle.

One man asked whether I was conducting their group in precisely the same way as I facilitated the support group at the Albion Street Clinic. I responded, 'Yes, it's almost exactly the same as that group.'

'What do you mean by *almost*?' he asked.

I explained that we usually closed our eyes and did a focus to centre ourselves before we each had an opportunity to talk. Another man immediately snapped, 'I'm not shutting my eyes 'round those bastards,' even though the bars separated them.

But slowly, each prisoner closed his eyes.

I was just about to begin talking them through a brief practice of 'coming to our senses' when the first man asked again, 'Is this exactly the same as you do it at Albion Street?' There was silence for a moment, before I replied, 'This is almost exactly the same as we do it there.' And, of course, he immediately responded with, 'Why almost?'

My heart was pounding. I said, 'Well, at Albion Street we join hands to come together as a group before we start,' as I reached out to the hands on either side of me.

It was one of those moments when I dared not breathe as the miracle unfolded. With eyes still closed, they reached out to one another, through the bars, to form an uninterrupted circle. Such precious moments are never forgotten.

During this group session, when it came time for the two unruly prisoners to talk, they softened. First one and then the other apologised for their behaviour and the disruption they had caused, and they asked if the other prisoners would allow them to once more mingle as one group. Such emotional vulnerability was rare and touching, and the other prisoners responded with grunts, nods and agreement.

***

There's one story I'd like to share because it powerfully illustrates a great lesson to me. But it's not an easy story to read, and if sexual abuse of children is particularly distressing to you then you might want to skip to the next chapter. Some of this story also appears in *Sometimes Hearts Have to Break* but it bears repeating.

Bruce was the least popular prisoner among the group as he was known as a rock spider—the name they gave to a child molester. He always seemed shy to me though also a gentleman. He read voraciously on a wide range of topics and usually kept to himself. He would participate in the support and meditation groups but make little contribution. His individual sessions with me often broached deep and personal matters sometimes stimulated by the other prisoners' discussions within the support groups. Bruce was always well-mannered, often making me a cup of tea when I arrived or fetching a chair for me.

Bruce had a healthy T cell count (these cells are the part of the immune system attacked by HIV). Most of the other prisoners had health issues associated with a very low T cell count, but Bruce seemed in excellent physical health.

Bruce occasionally mentioned his paedophilia as he described being 'taken over by this illness', which caused him to follow and, if he could, molest young boys.

One day, Bruce suddenly collapsed on the ground and was subsequently diagnosed with a tumour wrapped around his spinal cord, which caused instant and complete paralysis. Six weeks later he was dead.

Five weeks after Bruce's collapse, I visited the prisoners in the gaol as per usual. As I approached the isolation unit I could hear the pandemonium unfolding inside and saw broken glass on the footpath. When I entered the warden's office I was greeted enthusiastically by the officers on duty as the prisoners had, since their release from their cells that morning, been on a destructive rampage. There was a fire alight in Bruce's cell and the wardens refused to enter the space while the prisoners were so angry. They assured me, should I choose to enter the space where the prisoners were on rampage, that I would be safe so long as I stayed within their view. This wasn't of great comfort to me!

One thing that really frightened the wardens was the spilt blood of these prisoners. They refused to clean up blood and, given one of the men had punched his fist through a window embedded with wire and was bleeding profusely, there was no way they would enter the room the prisoners were in the process of destroying.

The men were throwing furniture and had broken the pool cues to inflict damage on the fridge and other immovable furniture.

The pool table had been upended and broken furniture was strewn around the recreation room.

I paced up and down with the prisoners as they shouted abuse or curses at Bruce who lay dying, under guard, in the nearby Prince Henry Hospital. They wished him a slow and painful, paralysing death. The news of his death on a near horizon had precipitated this angry outburst.

The prisoners also talked about the boys Bruce had molested, most of whom were aged between ten and thirteen years of age. My son Simon was ten at the time and though I'm sure that most of the stories the prisoners repeated to me were born of their imagination rather than fact, I found it difficult to keep my own anger and disgust in check.

Gradually, as we paced together and I listened to their awful stories about Bruce, the prisoners began to settle down. It was a challenge to diffuse the situation, as one man's anger would reduce just as another's reached boiling point. I 'parked' my feelings of anger and disgust for later appraisal. In those challenging hours of settling the prisoners down to the point where each one returned to his cell and was locked in, adding my upset to theirs would hardly be helpful.

The prisoner who was still bleeding profusely left a trail of blood spatters everywhere he went. As he finally settled down I was able to attend to his wounds, wrapping a towel around his hand until the gaol doctor could be summoned to better attend to him. I then removed all traces of blood from the floors, wall and other surfaces he'd manage to affect while on his rampage.

I went from the gaol to the hospital to visit Bruce, but I found it very difficult to be anywhere near him. My judgement of him at that time precluded me from being with him and I only stayed for a few minutes. I was amazed at the depth of the feelings of loathing I felt. So much for compassion and being of service!

On the drive home from Prince Henry Hospital I felt exhausted and confused and wondered why. (Now, as I write this, I think it's extraordinary that I wondered at my exhaustion!)

I retreated to my office to meditate and reflect on the events of the day. The inmates, I realised, had only been expressing their fears. They, after all, had far fewer T cells than Bruce. But they couldn't just say, 'I feel afraid because what has happened to Bruce could happen to me.' They lacked an awareness of their feelings as well as an ability to articulate them. They also wanted to seem macho and powerful—a willingness to be vulnerable is definitely not a high priority for any incarcerated man.

The men had rationalised what had happened to Bruce—a sudden, painful, paralysing death—in terms of *his* crimes as a way of reassuring themselves that *their* crimes didn't warrant such a punishment. My second realisation was even more enlightening.

When I had visited Bruce, he had been sitting slumped and pale, in a large armchair. He was very ill and frail. I had been sitting with a paedophile. Having come straight from the gaol to the hospital, I had brought my judgements, prejudices, anger and assumptions with me. I couldn't see past them to the frail and sick man I was visiting. Instead, I'd seen something that didn't actually exist in our moments together, except within my own mind; in my interactions with Bruce, *I* kept him trapped as a child molester because that was whom I chose to see and relate to.

I was grateful to have the opportunity of visiting Bruce one more time a week later. Before I entered his hospital room, I paused for a moment to bring myself into the present. When judgement has the potential to cloud my mind I would often imagine I was contained within the body of Jesus, Buddha, St Francis or some other being who sees the world with less judgement than me. I took some long, slow, deep breaths and, after greeting the guard at his door, entered the quiet of Bruce's room.

He was sitting in a big chair propped up with pillows. I pulled up another chair and took on his much slower breathing pattern in order to slow myself down and be in Bruce's time zone rather than the busier one of the outside world. It was obvious he was very close to dying but finally he lifted his head, and he asked whether he could tell me something he had never disclosed to anyone. Of course I agreed. Bruce talked for almost two hours about his childhood, the years when this 'sickness' would overcome him, what he had done to children and how he felt about his imminent death.

He began by recounting his miserable childhood where he was brutally abused, molested and regularly raped by his alcoholic father. His father often brought home his drinking mates from the pub. They too abused and raped Bruce and he suffered regular beatings in order to ensure his silence about what was happening to him at home. He tried to escape by hiding in the garden shed or the outhouse but his father would always find him, and it was easier to be found than to endure the beatings he would receive when he tried to run away. The Department of Community Services had often returned him to his father's care and he was too terrified to tell them the truth of what was happening at home. Bruce had run away for good when he was eleven and lived on the streets, avoiding the police. As angry as I had felt a week earlier at the thought of his violations against children, I now felt compassion for that poor child who knew no better than to escape the violence and abuse.

Bruce stopped several times to rest or to say, 'I've never told anyone this before. Is it alright for me to keep talking?' Each time I assured him I was interested to hear more.

Bruce shared the heart-rending story of his life up to his being in prison, his sudden deterioration and now, his dying. To my complete shock, he then looked directly into my eyes and said, 'But, Petrea, I've become a Christian and I've asked forgiveness for what I did to young boys, and I *have* accepted it.'

245

I sat in stunned silence. I heard myself think, *How dare you accept forgiveness for what you have done to children.* I found it extraordinary to realise I wanted Bruce to suffer for all eternity and never find peace.

I refrained from saying out loud the cruel words of my judgement and brought myself back to listening. The anger and recriminations I so easily could have dumped upon Bruce were no more or less than those I held against myself. Anger is so often just the body-guard of sadness, fear, anguish or grief.

While I felt disgusted by Bruce's crimes against innocent children, I believed his appalling choice to follow and molest boys was born of his own awful suffering. His courage in telling me his story made me aware of the remnants of my own self-loathing, which had reverberated throughout my life, and gave me an opportunity to witness and release myself from such judgement. It is second nature for us to judge others but these judgements only separate us from one another. If we release the judgement, we find a deeper sense of connection with the other person and our compassion is a natural response. It is possible to love the being while abhorring the actions of that person.

It must have taken great courage to utter the words, 'I have asked for forgiveness, and I have accepted it,' given Bruce had received nothing but condemnation and hatred from people. Like us all, he yearned for unconditional love and acceptance and I imagine he had never experienced it until he shared his painful story.

When I said my goodbyes to Bruce, I hugged him gently and thanked him for sharing his story with me. It was a privilege to bear witness to his outpouring and I was deeply grateful for, and humbled in the presence of, his courage. He died peacefully a few minutes after we parted. I like to think that by sharing his story and having it witnessed without judgement, he found his peace and healing. Perhaps now he could leave behind any desire to have power over someone else, for his own gratification. I hope so.

Bruce's story was hard to hear and tested the bounds of my compassion. He died in the right place, in gaol and under guard. His actions are beyond forgiving but it is possible to find forgiveness and compassion for the wounded being while not tolerating his despicable behaviour. As a child molester, he needed to be kept away from young people; gaol was exactly the right place for him. Forgiving the person does not imply any acceptance of his actions. Compassion allowed me to see the wounded child who grew into the man capable of inflicting on others the pain he experienced himself. This insight doesn't excuse Bruce's behaviour; but through extending a compassionate listening in which he found healing is perhaps to create the possibility of a better future for all of us.

An atmosphere of acceptance and unconditional love allows both myself and the person to whom I'm listening to feel comforted and connected. Whenever I let go of judgement a space is created for the unexpected to arise or a different perspective to be understood. The essence of forgiveness requires us to leave judgement aside. Then we see the person or situation afresh, without preconceptions, assumptions or expectations.

CHAPTER 28

On the move again

In 1988, I was asked by three separate publishers to write a guide-book for people living with life-threatening illnesses. I felt quite daunted, given I'd left school having produced only rudimentary pieces. I rang a journalist friend who'd written some articles about me, and she kindly offered to guide me in my literary pursuit.

I enjoyed the writing process. After years of working closely with thousands of seriously ill people, I found it relatively easy to document the practical aspects of living well when dealing with serious illness and how best to create an environment for healing and peace. My life was providing me with so many new and inter-esting challenges and, while mindful of how precarious life can be, I felt very much alive and engaged. Other books followed; each time, the writing process became easier.

Books weren't my only creative outlet. After advice from Ross, I had been producing something else that I hoped would be of use to many people.

Ross has always been a wonderful support to me, even while living on and off in the United States for many years. After Brenden's death, we realised we didn't know each other very well, considering the time I had spent in hospital, his and my travels, and the fact that each of us had a relationship with Brenden but a more tenuous one with each other.

Since I had begun my work with people living at the edge of life, Ross often didn't understand why I exposed myself to so much grief and pain, but he always stood by and supported me. On one of my early visits to him in California, he suggested I'd been teaching meditation for long enough to make recordings of the practices that could be helpful to a wider audience. On little yellow sticky notes Ross penned the financial advantages of making these practices more widely available. He gave me the confidence to believe in myself.

A couple of days later, I travelled up to the Sierra Nevada to visit with friends living at Ananda. On my first morning there, I was woken by the sound of a friend playing the silver flute. I thought Gopal's music would be the perfect backing for the relaxation and sleep practices I was ready to record. There were recording studios at Ananda, and within forty-eight hours we had put down and mixed two practices called *Sleep* and *Relaxation*. Both are still available today, and *Relaxation* is still, after thirty years, the third most popular of my recorded practices.

Ross was delighted when I returned with the tapes. Thanks to him, I went home to Australia with the first of what were to become a dozen popular meditation practices for helping people with chronic pain, self-esteem, healing or forgiveness issues, or who wanted to learn to meditate, relax or fall asleep.

***

The boost to my income from the sale of my books and meditation practices enabled me to take on a larger home. The widower of a patient generously made this large, four-bedroom Federation home in Crows Nest available to me at a very reasonable rent.

This meant I now had a spacious consultation room along with a large sunroom where the meditation and support groups could convene, as well as three bedrooms, enough to house Simon, Kate and myself. The house was also more accessible—the few stairs to the Waverton flat had been difficult for unwell people to navigate.

Around this time, Leo was dealing with his own health issue, which meant he could no longer care for Simon. When Leo made this decision, I was in the United States visiting Ross and my Ananda friends, but Leo couldn't wait for my return a week later and left Simon with my mother, who was also caring for Kate.

When I returned, the three of us were finally reunited as a single-parent family, and life settled into a new rhythm. My practice was full, I had increasing numbers of speaking engagements, and two hundred people now attended support and meditation groups in our home each week.

My children developed an amazing capacity to be present with unwell people. We frequently discussed how it felt for them to be surrounded by so many people with life-threatening illnesses; they told me that, for the most part, it gave them a heightened sense of understanding and compassion for people who were struggling with a variety of challenges. I admired my children's capacity to see past the physical illness and connect with the 'being' of a person rather than be worried by appearances or challenging sounds, behaviours or occasionally smells.

Undoubtedly, it was difficult at times for Kate and Simon as I was often preoccupied with work and the phone would frequently ring—indeed, the telephone number in the back of my published books was for the one by my bed. People would call at all hours when they were feeling desperate.

Kate was known to disconnect the phone during dinner; I often wouldn't discover this fact until much later, after we had enjoyed a rare undisturbed evening together. Kate was also known to say, 'You have to be dying around here to get any attention,' which I am sure was the case on more than a couple of occasions. At other times, unbeknown to me, she would take it upon herself to have long and in-depth phone conversations with people, and they often commented later that my 'secretary' had spent an inordinate amount of time offering them sage counsel.

***

On several occasions, young people with cancer stayed with us, and Kate and Simon would take them out for various activities. These experiences were challenging but also enjoyable for my children, giving them a deeper appreciation of life and its fragility.

At one time, two of my patients with AIDS were a couple with two small children, one of whom was also infected with the virus and subsequently much smaller than his younger sister. As the parents became sicker, it was difficult for them to care for their very active little children. Kate was about fifteen, and she loved children and was fabulous with them. We discussed the possibility of us having the children on weekends to give the parents a break, and Kate took on the major responsibility of looking after the little ones. She took them to the zoo, on ferry trips and to the park; she played games with them, bathed them, made clothes for them and generally cared for them as if they were her own. I so admired her capacity to take such loving care of other people's children.

It was, of course, tremendously beneficial for the parents, who could rest and recover during the weekends instead of having to keep up with their children's high energy levels.

Sadly, both parents died within a month of each other and, because the children were being adopted by friends of the family, we never saw them again. I recently heard through a mutual acquaintance that both children continue to flourish now as young adults.

***

There were a couple of instances when people moved in with us—after I'd discussed this with the children—so I could care for them.

Oliver had a terrible depression that would hold him in its tenacious grip, and occasionally he would sleep in our sunroom so that he would be safe from harming himself. I knew him well, having seen him weekly for eight years for massage and counselling. He had experienced a terrible childhood as a 'different' boy in a one-teacher school in the country. For six years, this teacher told him he was hopeless and would never amount to anything because he was interested in poetry and music rather than sport. The daily chiding undermined his confidence, and it was a lifelong struggle for him to make any increase in his sense of self-worth.

Oliver owned a music shop and traded two CDs each week for our appointment. In this way, he greatly expanded my appreciation of music as my repertoire grew. When he attended a weekend program with me, I acquired all of Mozart's piano sonatas!

Soon after Oliver moved out, a long-time support group member, Julia, moved in when she needed care but wasn't sick enough to be in a hospice or hospital.

Her three young adult children were weary of preparing for her death only to have her continue living—they'd had to galvanise themselves, over and over again, to cope with her imminent death. Each time Julia's doctor had said she would soon die, they'd been wonderful in caring for her; however, after six years of this, they wanted to study, to travel, to get on with their lives.

So, after a family discussion, Julia moved in with us. I slept in the lounge room while she had my bedroom; this meant she could share her porridge with our pet dog, Bonnie, if she didn't feel well enough to eat it herself and it was a far happier environment for her than being confined to a hospital or hospice bed.

***

Several times while Simon was visiting his father for the weekend, Kate and I moved in with a family when a young mother was dying.

Kate would spend time with the children, while I'd care for the woman and help her husband, children and extended family to say and do the things that allowed them all to gently take their leave— incredibly poignant moments where tender words or actions were enabled.

Peter, just four years old, looked at his mother's face just after she'd died. He said, 'Yep, she's definitely gone. The light's no longer in her eyes.' Then, running to the mantelpiece, he retrieved a family photo and brought it to his father and me. 'This is how I remember her. See the light in her eyes?'

Several weeks later when I visited the family, Peter asked me a question. Sitting on my lap, he said, 'Petrea, you know the light that was in Mum's eyes?'

'Yes, Peter,' I replied.

'How did the light get out of her body?'

'Hmm, that's a great question. I don't know. I've heard that it leaves through the top of the head, but I don't know,' I said, hoping my fumbled response would be sufficient to assuage his curiosity.

'Petrea?' he asked.

'Yes, Peter?' I responded, unsure of what was coming next.

'Now that she's light, does she need to go through doorways or windows or can she just go straight through the wall?'

'That's a great question, Peter. I don't know, but you know how you can feel her in your heart?' I said hopefully.

'Yes,' he responded emphatically.

'Well, I think she can be anywhere, whenever you think of her.'

Peter jumped off my lap and ran outside, seemingly happy with our conversation.

It struck me that we all have so much assistance in bringing life into the world but so little when taking our leave. I thought of this work as midwifery for the dying. Someone who is comfortable with the practicalities of caring for a dying person—and who also brings compassion, vulnerability and lightness into an often painful and difficult situation—can make a profound and positive difference to how a family experiences the loss of a loved one.

I've been blessed to accompany many, many people to the edge of their life and to have been present when they died. It is clear to me that someone 'leaves' at that final moment and I am convinced that we are more than our mortal remains. I have often explained to children that death is like the story of the balloon. What makes a balloon beautiful is the air inside of it. The air is invisible but when it leaves, all we are left with is a piece of coloured rubber. The spirit is like the air in the balloon. The spirit is what shines out of a person's eyes and is felt in the warmth of their hugs; it is the love that has endeared that person to us. When it disengages from the body, it cannot be seen, but it can be felt. The more substantial part of a person lies beyond the form of the physical body.

So often when I have been with a person nearing death, I have noticed that everyone around them is focused on the body. And yet, it is clear to me that their spirit is elsewhere. Frequently people's bodies seem almost to be on 'automatic pilot' where their breathing and heart rate are regular but they are unresponsive to any outside stimulus. It is especially at these times that I feel people are 'else-where', doing whatever it is that might need to be completed before they die—or in the case of Rachel, live.

Rachel was in such a state while in hospital awaiting a lung transplant from a disease called fibrosing alveolitis. The machines were keeping her alive but her oxygen levels had plummeted and, given the sudden deterioration in her health, she was not expected to survive the day. Her husband Barry and her two young sons had been summoned to her bedside.

Fibrosing alveolitis is a disease which causes a progressive thickening of the air sac walls in the lungs, making it increasingly difficult to breathe. Rachel was on a respirator, as there was no cure for her condition.

While it was a tragic and sad gathering that day, Rachel suddenly found herself above her body, looking down on it and her family gathered around her. She experienced a profound sense of peace and knew, in that moment, that everything was going to be alright. On returning to her body, she began to improve. Over the coming days, she meditated as much as possible.

Unbeknown to me, Rachel used my meditation practices during this time and they became her lifeline. We met some months later, when she brought me a magnificent bunch of flowers to thank me for being a comforting voice in the turmoil of critical illness. The moment I spoke to her she dissolved into tears, as my voice had been her friend and companion during those days and weeks of her return to health and her full recovery from fibrosing alveolitis. Rachel's life was transformed from that moment and since her own recovery she has radiated the presence of peace and calmness to many patients through her nursing and other activities.

PART 4

A home for the bewildered

CHAPTER 29

Hope and hesitancy

In the Eremo, Padre Ilarino had provided me with a safe haven in which I'd found a pathway to peace, and I was motived to create this sense of safety for others. I'd often thought of establishing a charitable foundation to further this vision I held for my work.

My hesitation in moving forward with the idea was based on the uncertainty of my health. An organisation seemed like such a responsibility to take on—what if I established such a venture and inspired others with a vision for a more compassionate way of caring for people, only to go out of remission and leave others to clean up my mess? But months had turned into years and I was still alive. Indeed, time seemed to be flying past. I couldn't get my head above the parapet to see a clear path into the future because I was so occupied with the responsibilities of single parenthood and my work.

After a support group meeting, Pamela—the woman who'd once given me the keys to her Mooloolaba apartment—said to me, 'I'm leaving you some money when I die. I want you to take a holiday, hire a secretary or start that bloody foundation you're always talking about.'

Pamela's words gave me the impetus to create the Quest for Life Foundation, a registered charity devoted to empowering people with the necessary education, skills and support to create healing, resilience and peace in their lives, regardless of the challenges they are facing.

Many wonderful people came together to help ensure that the Foundation's legal and financial framework was in place; most of these people were patients, members of support and meditation groups, or they had been touched by someone I'd helped. When Quest was finally established, I called Pamela's recently bereaved widower and told him that her words had given me the courage to establish the Foundation regardless of my own precarious health. Though Pamela never formally included the gift in her will, he knew she had wanted to leave $35,000 to me—and so he sent a cheque for $38,000, acknowledging the interest he believed would have accrued, and the Quest for Life Foundation had its first bequest.

***

In its first few years, Quest paid for a telephone line and some secretarial support, but my focus remained largely on providing services for people rather than fundraising or growing the vision I held in my heart. I didn't feel I had either the skills or time to actively further the goals of the Foundation, and I was only just managing financially, so it survived on occasional donations or small bequests. Although I had been taking better care of myself, I was still often overwhelmed by the needs of the people who filled my life and our home—and, at the same time, I yearned to provide a better environment for them. Our home had become a safe harbour, but so much more could be offered to people living with significant challenges. However, while I dreamed of having a more appropriate and substantial place for people to stay, I was still hampered by a lack of time and financial support, as well as my uncertain health. I shared my vision of this place with our board, but the enormity of the project seemed daunting for all of us, so nothing concrete was put in place.

At least Quest was getting more organised. The Foundation employed an administrator, Geoffrey Colwill, who coordinated the support and meditation groups, set up the accounting procedures, and began a database of people who attended groups and retreats. With two hundred people passing through our sunroom each week, and so many of them and others attending regular weekend retreats, we needed to develop policies and procedures to ensure that people who availed themselves of our services were cared for appropriately.

Geoffrey brought a rigour to the accounting and governance procedures of a tax-deductible charity that was essential for it to grow and flourish. He also understood the necessity of keeping compassion and genuine care and support at the forefront of all the Foundation's activities, as he personally knew many people who were suffering.

Around this time, a prominent journalist, David Leser, wrote an article about my work for *Good Weekend* aptly called 'Midwife for the Dying'. David spent weeks with me while he worked on this article; he attended support groups and one of the weekend retreats I conducted in the Southern Highlands. He was so moved by my work, he asked whether he could serve on the board of the Quest for Life Foundation, which he did for several years; he has remained a dear friend.

***

During the next few years, I continued my counselling work with people who faced an increasing range of illnesses, both physical and mental. Word of mouth was always the main way that people heard about the groups or became my patients.

I continued to see people in their homes, hospices or hospitals. I also started another voluntary massage program, this time at the Sacred Heart Hospice in Darlinghurst.

In time, other health professionals approached me to be trained as massage therapists for people nearing the end of their life. Other professionals wanted to learn the skills of group facilitation. The money from these trainings allowed Quest to provide more services for the increasing number of people who sought our assistance.

CHAPTER 30

More flesh and bones

Walking was again becoming difficult and painful, and my right leg was now bowing outwards. My limp, while not as pronounced as it was when I was younger, was still noticeable. I was also plagued with what I called 'ants': a deep, crawling restlessness that extended from my hips to my lower legs.

When a leg is in its correct alignment, a straight line can be drawn from the hip, through the middle of the knee and down through the ankle. That straight line didn't pass anywhere near my knee—it was already well outside my body.

John McGlynn had long retired, so I needed to find another orthopaedic surgeon. I 'interviewed' a few of them, wanting to find one I felt I could work with to get as many years out of my legs as possible. I wanted to find someone skilled but with a sense of humour, who could advise me without being cavalier in his or her approach.

One surgeon told me that not only did my leg need straightening immediately, but I also needed a knee replacement. He could do both at the same time. This was more than I was expecting, and when he insisted on my having another bone biopsy first, I was confused. Bone biopsies are not fun: I'd had two, one from my sternum and another from my pelvis, and they were very painful. When I asked him why, he simply said, 'We need to establish a new prognosis for your leukaemia.' When I looked puzzled, he continued, 'There's no point in giving you a new knee if you're only going to get a few years' wear out of it.' I didn't feel we'd be a good fit, so I continued my search for a surgeon I could work with.

I liked Jim O'Brien the moment I met him. I explained my long and complex history, and he respected and listened to my story. He believed I had somehow transmuted pain signals into 'ants'. When the ants became unbearably uncomfortable, pain medication certainly helped me to sleep and function.

Jim told me that the structural issues would need surgery because once the line of alignment is outside the body, gravity will ensure it progresses rapidly towards collapse. We decided against a knee replacement.

The surgery involved a third tibial osteotomy. But instead of rotating the lower leg as John had done twice before, Jim took a wedge from the outside of the tibia to collapse the bowing into a straighter line, and then the bones were screwed into place.

***

Before this surgery, I needed all the usual blood tests and X-rays. When I visited my GP to get the results, they were all fine—except for the HIV result, which hadn't been finalised. The GP said he would chase it up, and I rang the next week for the results. They still weren't back from the pathology lab, so they assured me again that they would chase them up. A third phone call the following week finally stimulated action.

The night before the surgery was scheduled, thirty people were in my sunroom waiting for the evening meditation class to begin, when the phone rang. It was the GP.

He started by saying, 'Are you sitting down?'

If ever you have heard the 'serious doctor voice' then you surely recognise it.

The GP went on to say, 'I'm terribly sorry, but your HIV test has come back positive.' He knew I had worked with prisoners and hundreds of other men, women and children with HIV. His first suggestion was that he would send someone immediately to collect more blood. I asked him to wait until after the meditation class, and he arranged for a nurse to arrive at 9.30 when the group had dispersed.

Around this time, there was media coverage about the possibility that some strains of the virus could pass directly through the skin and cause infection. I had certainly had the blood, sweat and tears of dozens of infected people on my skin. In the space of the two-minute conversation with the GP, I considered the fact that Simon had been having a lot of mouth ulcers recently. The question loomed, 'Have I already passed the virus on to my son?'

As for me, by the time I was off the phone I had adjusted to the possibility that I was infected. 'If I need to deal with HIV, so be it.' I've had several shocks throughout my life, and I must give credit to the power of meditation to help me remain calm and present, but even I was surprised by how quickly I adjusted to this news.

Generally, there's meant to be counselling before and after the provision of a positive diagnosis of HIV, so people have time to come to terms with it. The diagnosis is never meant to be given over the telephone—I've known of people who committed suicide on finding out they were HIV-positive. And while HIV testing is meant to be conducted under an anonymous coded system to protect a person's confidentiality, it later turned out that my name had been on the blood sample throughout the testing procedure.

When my secretary arrived and I told her the news, she was more traumatised than me. I poured her a Scotch and went into the sunroom to teach meditation. As I entered the room, everyone smiled at me. I had the weirdest sensation, as if I had the letters 'HIV' written across my forehead. I'd heard many people with the virus say this over the years; it was as if everyone could see their shame. I reassured myself that I was probably a bit in shock after all, and I began to teach the class. 'Relax your ankles,' I'd say, then think, *I wonder if they'll still come for meditation once they know I have the virus.* 'Feel your thighs soften and spread against the chair,' I'd say, then think, *Will they still hug me when they know?* And so the class passed.

The nurse dutifully arrived later that evening and took more blood. I'd phoned a friend who was an AIDS specialist as soon as the meditation class dispersed, and he assured me that he would follow through on the rapid processing of the second blood test. He also reassured me that the first sample could easily have tipped off a false positive because of strange proteins in my blood after leukaemia.

I also called the nearby hospital where I was due to have the tibial osteotomy the following morning. My surgery was postponed until the results were certain. Orthopaedic surgery is a messy business, and if a person is infected with HIV or Hepatitis C then safety precautions for theatre staff are significantly increased.

✳✳✳

Given I had scheduled a week off from work for the surgery and there was nothing in my diary, Rae and I spent a few days away together until the results were known and the surgery could be rescheduled.

My friend called me the following morning to assure me that my HIV test was negative—and that when the original sample had gone through a more definitive test, it had also ruled out my being HIV-positive. He believed that because the phial of blood had remained in the GP's refrigerator for three weeks before being tested, this was enough to have tipped off the original false positive.

The GP was mortified that he'd given me the information over the phone, that my name had been on the phial throughout the entire testing process, and that they had been more than tardy in getting the original sample tested. I'm sure that everyone involved thought I would sue them for these breaches of protocol.

While I wasn't concerned about financial gain, I was keen to ensure that no one else would have this experience—most people wouldn't adapt as quickly as I had. I decided to contact the Medical Complaints Unit so the whole sequence of events and breaches could be properly investigated. There was a thorough review of the case, and both the clinic and the pathology company were required to make several changes to their collection processes so that my experience couldn't be repeated.

∗∗∗

I went ahead with the tibial osteotomy the following week. To my surprise, the pain was considerable and unrelenting after the surgery: my whole leg, from the hip down, was agonisingly painful. The fact I was experiencing more pain than the staff thought I 'should' was upsetting to me, as I too felt that I *should* be managing better. After all, I was meant to be some sort of 'expert' on managing pain.

However, I couldn't help still being desperate for the fourth hourly medication. And, after ten days post-op, the pain wasn't abating. The old and familiar pattern of not wanting to be a bother still ran deep: I was being a 'good' patient by not causing anyone a problem and only speaking up when the next pain relief was due.

At 2 am I rang the buzzer to request the next scheduled round. When the nurse came, she asked if I could wait awhile as she had several post-op patients in need of attention. Of course, I said that this wouldn't be a problem. But an hour later when she hadn't returned, I was whimpering with the pain and felt again like a little kid who couldn't make her needs known.

It wasn't until I was reduced to this vulnerable state that I realised the pain was from sciatica rather than the osteotomy. When the nurse did finally return, she found me crying with pain. I was then able to explain the situation. Her response was, 'No wonder you're in pain!' Once alerted, the nurses organised physiotherapy to relieve the pain, and things began to improve.

It was during this hospitalisation that I had a panic attack. Confined to my bed, trapped in my pain-ridden body inside a hermetically sealed room, I felt claustrophobic and overwhelmed by the lack of fresh air. One of the night nurses kindly wheeled my bed to an outside atrium where I gulped in the delicious coolness of the real, unconditioned air and savoured the blissful touch of a breeze on my skin.

CHAPTER 31

Who'd have thought?

1992

While I was still recovering from my tibial osteotomy, I reconnected with Wendie Batho at a lecture by a Tibetan monk, my friend Sogyal Rinpoche, in Sydney's Town Hall. I had recently launched Sogyal's *Tibetan Book of Living and Dying*, and he had returned to Sydney for a series of lectures.

Wendie's partner Kay had died earlier that year. Like many of my patients, Kay had become a dear friend, and while I didn't know Wendie very well, I had visited them at home a couple of times and knew their three beautiful teenage children. The whole family always struck me as being very loving and close, as indeed they were.

After Sogyal's lecture, Wendie asked if she could thank me for the care I had extended to Kay and the family by taking me to dinner.

I rarely socialised with family members after a patient died. I knew so many people living at the edge of life, and I had little time for socialising. Family members often continued to attend the support and meditation groups, and I usually attended the funeral of their loved one; indeed, I conducted dozens of funerals myself. But I was reluctant to socialise.

This time, though, something moved me to say yes. We made the arrangement for a few weeks later when I would be out of the leg brace though still on crutches.

Wendie picked me up, as I was unable to drive, and we had a wonderful evening. She understood my life because she had often been in my home for the support or meditation groups, and she and Kay had attended several weekend retreats with me in the Southern Highlands. She was still living with the tumult of grief and the exhaustion of caring for someone she loved deeply. Our conversation was peppered with laughter and tears, and we formed an instant bond of friendship. For the first time, I felt I was with someone who truly 'got' me.

As a way of thanking me, because she knew about my love of music, Wendie offered me season tickets to the opera. She also wanted to give me a weekend away in Terrigal. I was touched by her consideration, given she knew how busy I was.

Neither of us could have predicted that by the time this precious weekend in Terrigal eventuated, we would be a couple. Our weekend away became a celebration of the deepening love between us.

✳✳✳

It's a great blessing to be with someone who gets you. While many people wondered at the long hours I spent with unwell people, Wendie understood my motivations and passion for the work I felt was my purpose. She too had worked with considerable passion in education, which was her vocation as well as her career.

Wendie had spent the early part of her adult life working as head of a girls' school in Keravat, New Guinea, after performing what she called a 'family-ectomy'. Her upbringing wasn't a happy one: she was raised mainly by grandparents who, long before her, had done a particularly abysmal job of raising her father. As she was shunted between relatives living in Greenacre, Rose Bay and Palm Beach, much of her childhood was quite solitary against plush and not-so-plush backgrounds. Wendie had adapted to the shifting circumstances of wealth and human frailties that surrounded her.

It had never occurred to me to love a woman, but loving Wendie was natural and easy. Those of us lucky enough to know her, let alone be loved by her, find a fiercely loyal, funny, intelligent character who embraces life with gusto. Some people find her manner too direct, as she lacks my natural hesitation to deliver difficult news. But I have learned so much from her in this regard because she has often accused me, quite rightly, that when I need to give difficult feedback to someone, they are likely to leave our meeting with a pay rise and a pat on the back.

Like me, Wendie does what it takes to bring her dreams to fruition, and when we fell in love we thought we'd be mad not to give our relationship a go.

I had never fancied people because of their physical bodies. I was always more interested in what lay behind appearances and knew from an early age that facades could be deceptive—after all, I was an expert at cultivating them.

✳✳✳

Wendie had only been volunteering for a few weeks at the Quest for Life Foundation before she surprised me with a comment. We were in the room where my books and meditation tapes were stored when she said to me, 'You know, Petrea, you might not die, and you don't actually have a life.'

Wendie has a wonderful ability to articulate what many people think but would never utter out loud. Her words came as a shock, but she'd just recognised, long before I did, that I didn't have any life outside of my work except for parental responsibilities.

On reflection, I saw that my dedication to easing the suffering of others was fuelled by an urgency to do as much as I could before I died. My principle focus was to be here to see my children educated and manage on their own without me, and to do the work that felt both challenging and rewarding.

Wendie's comments opened the discussion about how we might create a life together. Some of her friends were concerned that she was repeating a pattern because she was with someone who might also die. Other friends secretly—and not so secretly—thought that she had shifted her feelings from grief to falling in love with me as her counsellor. However, I'd never been her counsellor and that wasn't the nature of our relationship. We just loved each other with a deep and unshakeable love which, like a good vintage, has matured and increased with age.

Wendie wept daily during our first two years together, because loving someone doesn't preclude grieving another love. I respected Wendie's grief. I'd known Kay well, and a person's grief is testament to the depth of their love.

Kay's children knew she had loved me, and they welcomed me into their family. They were happy that Wendie had found someone to love, as she is a woman with a great deal of it to give, and I count myself extremely fortunate to be the beneficiary of such unbounding support and care. Kay's children, and now their children, are as much loved as my own, and we feel so lucky to have been woven together into one delightful fabric of our extended family.

One of the many things I admire about Wendie is her tremendous capacity to love other people's children. She'd cared for—and along with Kay, paid for—the education and raising of Kay's three children, and she loved them as her own. Wendie then took on the love and care of Kate and Simon. Between the two of us, we now have eight grandchildren, all of whom we adore.

***

At first, my love for Wendie came as quite a shock not only to myself but also—and especially—to my parents and children.

Kate didn't initially take to Wendie's presence in our home given, as she rightly said, 'My mother turned into a lesbian just before my HSC!'

Before long, though, both children grew very fond of Wendie and confided in her many things they wouldn't dare tell me.

Simon was particularly happy when she pulled him aside for a private chat about the fact she was, at the time, a school principal. He had never been interested in his schooling and really, as Wendie said, 'It is rather expensive childminding.' He is an extremely bright and intelligent person but, like me, he found school tedious and his interests lay elsewhere. My falling in love with a school princi-pal had been daunting for him, so he was mightily relieved when Wendie told him she would never mention school to him unless he raised the subject. From then on, they were great friends.

When I told Ross about my love for Wendie, his immediate and heartfelt response was delight. He was unreservedly happy that I had found someone to love and who loved me in return. The fact I loved a woman was neither here nor there for him, and he shared my happiness with his lovely wife, Dianne.

But Geoff wasn't happy about my relationship with a woman. In fact, he immediately resigned from the board of the Quest for Life Foundation. He was always concerned about how things appeared to others; at that time, he still put public appearances before family and couldn't bear to have any association with something that might bring criticism or judgement. The fact that I was a 42-year-old woman free to make my own decisions was irrelevant. While Rae accepted our relationship without fanfare and was supportive, she had little influence over Geoff's entrenched views.

Geoff summoned me to my parents' penthouse in Mosman for a meeting. When I arrived, the atmosphere was more than frosty.

Rae was out of sight in another part of the house, while Geoff sat in the lounge room, ostensibly reading a magazine. He didn't put it down when I arrived, so I sat and waited until he was ready to speak. Finally, he put it aside and said, 'I cannot believe you have a woman sleeping in your home under the same roof as your children.' An awkward silence followed, until I said, 'I'm sorry you feel that way, Geoff, but Wendie is a wonderful person and I love her.' My words did nothing to assuage his anger. All he said was, 'Well, I'm appalled you've made this choice.' And that was the end of our conversation—Geoff once more picked up the magazine and buried his head in its shaking pages.

I called Ross, who was living in the States at the time, and described the difficulty that Geoff was having in coming to terms with Wendie's and my love for each other. Ross called Geoff and underlined to him the importance of this loving relationship, arguing that it was something to celebrate.

To his great credit and unbeknown to me, a few days later my father telephoned Wendie and invited her to lunch. She was extremely apprehensive about this meeting, knowing of Geoff's strong disapproval. But she arrived at their home dressed in her finest silk suit, complete with stockings and high heels, and with an armful of irises, as she knew they were Rae's favourite flower.

My father greeted her rather formally at the door, and the three of them drove down in relative silence to the Spit, where they settled at their table overlooking Middle Harbour. Wendie nervously waited while the pleasantries were attended to—Geoff ordering a Scotch, Rae a brandy and dry, and Wendie a mineral water! Anyone who knows Wendie would laugh at that, because of her fondness for wine, but she was on her very best behaviour.

Wendie was expecting a strongly worded suggestion that she be a friend to me but no more. Instead, once drinks were in place,

Geoff raised his glass and said, 'We love our daughter and want only the best for her. If Petrea loves you, then we love you, so welcome to the family!'

After that, Wendie was warmly embraced into our family, and she readily admits that Geoff was the best father she ever had.

CHAPTER 32

Leo's lump

The saga with my legs continued. While I could walk quite well, living with chronic pain was and is tiring. My knees swelled easily when I stood for long periods, as I did when lecturing or delivering workshops, and I couldn't walk very well on uneven ground—sand, grass or European cobblestones were all very difficult. The slightest tilt in the joint meant I had raw bone on raw bone, because all the cartilage had been removed from my right knee during three arthroscopies. There had been many times when I stood up, perhaps in a restaurant after a meal, only to have to sit down again and wait until the cartilage relocated itself so I could put weight on the joint.

My orthopaedic surgeon, Jim O'Brien, couldn't understand how I could walk at all given the state of the joints and the raw patches of bone on bone, but the pain levels I experienced weren't unmanageable and I was very careful with the way I walked, turned and generally used my legs. The great blessing—on a good day!—is that my legs have taught me to remain focused in the present moment and made the valuable practice of 'coming to my senses' a constant in my life.

Leo had often helped at times when I'd needed to have surgery or be away from the children for any reason; he'd simply move into our home to take care of them. His hostility towards me had completely disappeared, and he'd become a frequent visitor on weekends. He still had many idiosyncrasies and fixed ideas, but most were tolerable given the short amounts of time we spent together. He came to love Wendie's company, and the children were happy that we all did our best to get along with one another.

Leo had little money—having lived for some years on the funds I'd signed over to him when I had leukaemia—and because he lived outside of Sydney, the only way he could have regular contact with the children was if he stayed in our home. He often slept over when Wendie and I went away for the weekend.

Leo knew very few people and, while he was likeable in many ways, his eccentricities tested most long-term friendships. This meant he had no support network except us to help him when he suffered from his own health issues.

***

Leo had a lump—a fibrous histiocytoma between his shoulder-blades. Histiocytomas aren't generally malignant unless left unattended, but Leo was unquestionably a quirky character who held unusual and rather extreme ideas about health and healing.

His histiocytoma started off as a relatively small lump that he had removed three times. When it grew again after the third surgery, he decided that doctors didn't know what they were doing, and he determined he would treat himself through nutrition and fasting. The problem was, Leo was rarely consistent. There were times when he would eat nothing but apples for a month, and the lump would disappear; then he would eat chips and burgers, and the lump would reappear. This went on for quite some time, with the lump coming and going depending on the strictness of his eating regimen.

However, a time came when the lump was no longer fluctuating in size. It grew and grew—until he had to wear it in a sling because it was so heavy. He looked like a weird version of the Hunchback of Notre Dame. I harassed him to go back to the doctors and have it removed, but he was determined to rid himself of it 'naturally'. Although it must have been incredibly uncomfortable, Leo rarely complained about it and his life began to revolve around this wretched alien clinging to his back.

The histiocytoma was growing rapidly, fed by a network of hundreds if not thousands of blood vessels wrapped around his chest like webbing. The tumour extended from the top of his shoulders to below his waist and outwards on either side to his armpits. This extraordinary tumour is best not described in further detail.

I finally convinced him to see a neurosurgeon at St Vincent's Hospital because, by this time, the lump weighed more than six kilograms. It was literally like a soccer ball hanging between his shoulderblades.

Before our appointment, I wrote to the neurosurgeon. I knew that if he gave the slightest indication of judgement about Leo and his eccentric ways, my ex-husband would walk out of the consultation and refuse to return. I was very keen for him to get the lump attended to once and for all. Though we had been divorced for years and there had been many testing times with Leo, I continued to care for him and felt sorry for having caused him so much emotional pain. And there simply wasn't anyone else who would look out for him, let alone help him.

The surgeon was particularly sympathetic and overly solicitous towards Leo as we walked in together and sat down. It was to be one of the funniest conversations I have ever witnessed.

To assess if he had the facts correctly noted, the surgeon recounted Leo's story. 'So, Leo, you've had a lump on your back and you've had it removed?'

'Yes, that's correct,' replied Leo with characteristic gusto.

The neurosurgeon continued, 'And, Leo, the lump came back and you had it removed again?'

'Yes, that's correct,' replied Leo, again with his usual unflagging enthusiasm.

'And, Leo, the lump came back a third time and again you had it removed?' asked the neurosurgeon, being as gentle as humanly possible.

'Yes, that's correct,' replied Leo with emphasis.

Then the surgeon hesitantly said, with a kindly look on his face, 'And now it's back, Leo, would you say it's a very large lump?'

Given the doctor's approach, Leo may as well have been a small frightened child rather than a difficult and exceedingly eccentric man in his late fifties.

Without further conversation, he turned around and lifted his shirt to reveal the soccer ball-sized tumour hanging off his back.

'Oh yes, Leo, I see it,' the surgeon said in the most even of tones as I successfully suppressed my hilarity.

No medical professional had ever seen such a grotesque monstrosity. In a developing country, no one would survive so long with such a tumour; in Australia, no sane human being would have left it unattended. The surgeon excused himself for a moment as he rushed out the door to see if he could find another doctor in the building with whom to share this extraordinary case. Alas, he returned frustrated and dejected because no one else was available to witness this singular medical phenomenon. He said that Leo would definitely benefit from having the tumour removed but, given its size and location, he would need a combination of surgeons.

Leo said he'd think about it, but I could already tell he had no intention of pursuing a surgical option. He had clearly humoured me by attending the appointment while remaining firmly wedded to his bizarre beliefs.

***

Even though the lump was rapidly growing, a few weeks later Leo flew to visit Sai Baba in India. He hoped that the Indian saint would help him, possibly even cure him.

Leo was 195 centimetres tall and flew scrunched up in economy class. How he underwent the long flight doubled over with the weight of the tumour on his back, I'll never know. I am sure his fellow passengers found it to be one of the longest and strangest journeys they ever made.

From India, Leo recounted to me how he'd sat on the floor of a shower stall while an artery haemorrhaged from the tumour. His body went into peripheral shutdown: his blood only circulated between the heart and brain to keep him alive while the rest of his body survived on minimal blood flow. He sat in the shower for two or three days until he could get one finger moving, then two, and gradually he brought his body back to life. It is truly extraordinary what the human body is capable of surviving. This happened several times.

When I suggested to him that his dying in India would be painful and difficult for his teenage children, he joked about not bringing his body back to Australia and laughingly said, 'Just float me down the Ganges.' I tried to reassure the children while being realistic about the possibility, even likelihood, of their father dying from blood loss before he made it back to Australia. There would be no point in my going to India to bring him home—if I knew one thing about Leo, it was his relentless determination to do things his way.

In India, all people looked with disdain upon Leo. He later told me that he was considered the lowest of the low because of the monstrosity clinging to his back. I imagine most Indian people wondered why a man who could easily have surgery in his home country would be living in theirs. And, indeed, what dreadful karma was he living out with his alien companion?

Leo rang me before his return flight, saying he'd haemorrhaged again and was exhausted from washing the hotel's bed sheets—I could only imagine the scene. He just wanted to sleep, but I knew he was teetering on the edge of life and encouraged him to get on the flight home. We would be there when he arrived.

★★★

The following morning, Wendie and I were among those waiting at the airport to greet the arrivals. I had determined in my mind that Leo would go from the airport directly to the hospice—if he still refused to go into hospital—as I could no longer look after him and felt it was unfair of him to expose our children to such unnecessary trauma.

As Wendie and I waited, we noticed anxious men running around with walkie-talkies. I nudged Wen and said, 'Do you reckon they're looking for us?'

Without hesitation, the men quickly escorted Wendie and me behind the scenes—and there was Leo, sitting in a wheelchair on a pile of newspapers with blood and plasma dripping through them to the floor. He had survived the trip only to collapse in customs due to further haemorrhaging. He was unbearably skinny and his skin was a greyish-blue. His icy cold hand descended on mine as he declared in his broad Dutch accent, 'Ah, Petrea! It's so good to see you!'

The simple fact was, whether I liked it or not, Leo had always loved me in his own strange way, and he was home.

An ambulance had been summoned, of course, but most international flights arrive during morning peak hour. As an attendant pushed the wheelchair at a fast trot towards the terminal entrance to get Leo to the ambulance as quickly as possible, he said to me, 'Is he going to die?' and all I could honestly say was, 'It's possible.'

An hour later, Wendie and I were again reunited with Leo in the emergency department of St Vincent's Hospital. He was lying on his side. The nurses were nonplussed, not having a clue what to do with him. His haemoglobin was 3.8 instead of in the normal range of 13 to 17, and they couldn't get a blood pressure reading. After so many years of living with this growing mass, his body had adapted in extraordinary and creative ways, allowing him to survive.

I had rung St Vincent's Hospital and Sacred Heart Hospice the week before Leo's arrival to warn them of his impending return with this massive tumour; I was frustrated but understood why they didn't believe me when I tried to describe its size and the magnitude of the challenge about to descend upon them.

The tumour had become very unpleasant, with a few sinuses several centimetres deep. Leo had packed it, heaven knows how, in plastic and towels soaked in diluted lavender oil under the sling to make the trip home. The nurses couldn't cope with the smell, and it was left to me to gently unpack the tumour and get him into a bath.

The only part of Leo that never faltered for a moment was his mouth. He was as weak as a wobbly kitten, but he talked non-stop about how pleased he was to be home with me. I reminded him that we were in hospital, and I stressed that he wasn't coming home to the children until the lump was removed.

Leo taught me a great lesson during this hospital ordeal. When he was finally ensconced in a warm bath, he decided he wanted to shave. I went off in search of a mirror but there wasn't one to be found anywhere in the ward. I returned to him apologetic that

I couldn't find a mirror, then he vigorously pointed to something in the corner of the bathroom, saying repeatedly, 'Get me that. Get me that! Get me that!' with increasing agitation. I finally figured out what he was wanting: a dusty, broken aluminium paper-towel cover, on the floor in the corner.

I stood holding this cover up for him to catch a glimpse of his unshaven face in its dingy reflection. This comical scene was fortunately a private moment, and I wondered what on earth the staff would think if they walked in. Surely they would wonder who was the madder of the two of us.

That is when a beautiful, life-saving mantra occurred to me: 'No one does Leo better than Leo does. There's Leo doing Leo now. If I want Leo to be any different from who Leo is, I'm going to suffer. There's Leo, doing Leo now.'

I softened and smiled. Leo had always been relentlessly and consistently himself. My wanting him to be any different would be a sure path to my own misery. In that moment, I understood why I loved him despite his irritating foibles, outbursts and challenging idiosyncrasies.

***

Before subjecting him to surgery, the doctors tried to increase Leo's haemoglobin through blood transfusions, but every time they slightly increased his blood pressure, the tumour haemorrhaged. They finally decided to take him to theatre as he was.

The likelihood of him surviving the surgery, given his lack of blood pressure and his perilously low haemoglobin, was minimal. There were literally hundreds of blood vessels to be cauterised. Leo was quite cavalier about whether he lived or died. He said his farewells to his children, Wendie and me before being taken to the operating theatre.

The surgeon and his team were truly heroic and remarkable. Nine hours later, Leo was lumpless: the 8.8-kilogram tumour was gone, and a bare rectangular patch of exposed flesh remained.

I am sure that people find this story hard to believe. I would too, but for the fact Leo took us on the long, miserable journey with him. And I have photographs, although the tumour only weighed about 6 kilograms when they were taken. The hospital staff certainly took detailed photographs, given no doctor had ever seen anything like it or would again. Without a doubt, Leo was a singular character who taught me to never ever give up on a person as the human body is capable of amazing feats of resilience.

It is hard to say whether Leo had a classifiable mental disorder. He exhibited so many odd behaviours, such as declaring to the doctors who had come to witness this extraordinary medical phenomenon, 'I did this for humankind, to show what the human body is capable of.' This was in keeping with the way Leo had experimented throughout his life with diets, fasts and water treatments such as sitz baths, though now his ideas were more extreme. The seeds of paranoia were there too in his mistrust of the medical system, and these seeds sprouted and developed as he aged.

Four days after the surgery, Leo returned to theatre for skin grafts taken from his thighs and applied to his rectangle of bare flesh. There were grave concerns about the skin adhering to bare bone, and the surgeon decided to go ahead only on the condition that Leo agreed to radiotherapy once the grafts had fully healed. However, on the fourth day post-op, Leo discharged himself from hospital having decided that doctors knew little about treating skin grafts. He never returned for radiotherapy.

It was aggravating that Leo wouldn't comply with medical advice; however, it was typical of him and to be expected.

***

I approached the owners of the Southern Highlands property where we conducted retreats. They had become good friends of mine over the years, and I asked if they could help Leo by giving him some work and a place to stay. They created a low-stress job for him on their property where he lived in a caravan.

Leo gradually recovered his health and strength. He stayed on the property for some years, creating gardens and doing simple chores.

Kate and Simon would visit him there. I so admired the love and care that they always extended to their father. He often lectured them mercilessly or talked incessantly about his health and his strange philosophies around healing. Regardless, Kate and Simon continued to love him and remain in contact with him.

CHAPTER 33

Our tree change

I had worked hard to repay my parents for the financial support they'd given me, as well as to house and feed my children; Leo had never financially contributed to their welfare except during the years when I was unwell. My income was derived from my practice along with the sale of my books and recordings, which usually just covered the rent and food for me and the children, given the amount of my pro bono work.

But as Wendie and I created a life together, we decided to purchase a house with the meagre funds we had, most of which came from her superannuation. Her heart was no longer in the education system as she too had found the journey through illness and the loss of someone she loved to be a profound and life-changing one.

Every weekend the two of us searched up and down the coast and hinterland to play out the fantasy of how we might create a life outside Sydney, as purchasing a home there was well beyond our means.

Finally, we settled in Bundanoon when we found a small and secluded house set in a beautiful garden on a battleaxe block. While walking around the garden, we were in awe of a magnificent gum tree whose roots were nourished by a natural spring forming a pool at its feet. I said to Wendie, 'This is it.' We'd instantaneously fallen in love with the tree and knew this was the place even before we entered the house.

Kate had recently moved out of home into college at the University of New South Wales, while Simon was completing Year 9. He wasn't overly keen to move to the country, because he was happy at his school in Sydney, Glenaeon. He was only slightly relieved to find another Rudolf Steiner school in nearby Bowral, and as soon as he was able he secured an apprenticeship to follow in his father's footsteps as a chef.

***

Wendie and I decided our home would become our private space—I would no longer work from the house. After having two hundred people in the sunroom each week for years, the idea of home being a sanctuary was very appealing.

We were also unsure if my work would continue, given we had no idea how many people would make the two-hour drive to Bundanoon from Sydney. Wendie was toying with the idea of becoming a real estate agent as we thought about how to reinvent ourselves in the beautiful country of the Southern Highlands.

The real estate agent who'd sold us our house had an adult daughter in remission from a lymphoma. She was finding it difficult to re-engage with her life due to the constant fear of recurrence—a common and understandable fear that I knew only too well. The agent asked whether I would counsel her and, while I replied that I would be happy to see her, I also told him that I needed to find professional rooms in town first.

The following day, before we'd even made the move to Bundanoon, the agent phoned to say he'd found me rooms, and he asked when I would see his daughter. So, I rented half a house in town from an elderly gentleman who lived at the hotel. Before long, my practice resumed; I saw a constant stream of people living with all kinds of difficulties, including depression, grief, loss, family conflicts, anxiety, cancer, chronic illnesses, motor neurone disease, multiple sclerosis, trauma and despair.

***

By now, Wendie and I had a very close relationship with my parents, who were still living in Mosman. On one of their visits to our new home, we showed them a nearby house that we believed they would love living in. Within six months of our relocation, they too had moved to the village, and we were delighted they were so close to us.

Over time, Geoff shared some of his experiences from the war. Some were wonderful, funny or sobering, but there were also stories of shame, pain, terror and distress—and, as he wept more openly, he softened.

Geoff's journey to find his peace was long and difficult, and it was wonderful to witness the integration of long-buried traumas in this later part of his life. He still needed to control Rae, but to his children and grandchildren he was kind and generous with his time and in many other ways. He certainly became a loving, loyal and staunch supporter of me personally and of the Quest for Life Foundation to which he and Rae regularly donated. He made a huge contribution to the world of publishing and to many charitable organisations throughout his life. He had much to be proud of—his family foremost, as we had weathered many a storm together.

Geoff frequently gave me sound advice around a variety of financial and other business matters. He loved being the patriarch of the family, and he enjoyed being called upon for counsel.

His fondness for Wendie was obvious, and they enjoyed dozens of robust discussions around political, economic and social topics. My father had certainly met his match, as Wendie is a voracious consumer of information about global affairs. While their political differences were sometimes considerable, they both shifted their stance through having these discussions.

It was lovely to enjoy more time with family, and weekends were mostly reserved for such gatherings. For the first time, my life had expanded well beyond my practice, which now existed more or less within the confines of business hours.

***

Within a few months, Wendie and I decided to conduct Quest's first residential program at a motel in Bundanoon.

Over the past decade I had conducted dozens of retreats and educational programs in the Southern Highlands, and now it was wonderful to have Wendie's support in co-facilitating these powerful opportunities for education, support and healing. She had years of experience within the education system at all levels, including university lecturing, consulting and group facilitation.

Forty-seven women with breast cancer attended that first weekend program. We went on to conduct a dozen residential programs each year for men and women living with the challenges of cancer, grief or mental health issues.

At the same time, I was being invited to speak at an increasing number of events. In the busiest of these years, I delivered seventy speeches—six in one week! I've always preferred to speak without notes or a digital presentation. It wasn't until I was invited to give a speech at the National Press Club in Canberra that I became nervous and went with back-up notes; it went well enough, but speaking directly to my audience is still my preference. There's an aliveness and vulnerability in such talks, when speakers voice the truth of their own experience.

Wendie and I relished the privacy of our garden and home life and, along with Simon and our three dogs, we settled into a routine. Wendie complained from time to time, 'I'm used to *having* a secretary, not *being* a secretary!' but other than that life was happy, and we were busy with family, my practice, my speaking engagements and the residential programs.

CHAPTER 34

Healing journeys

Wendie and I enjoy travelling, especially in Asia and, as the children matured and moved on with their lives, we had many wonderful adventures in countries including New Zealand, Italy, Slovenia, the United States, Canada, Vietnam, Nepal, Cambodia, Thailand, Malaysia and Indonesia. Perhaps our favourite has always been India. The assault on our senses, the shifting contrasts and the deep underlying spirituality of this ancient land and its people is a delight to us both.

In 1996 my first book, *Quest for Life*, was published for the US market. Wendie and I embarked upon a lecture tour throughout the States with our good friend Roma Newton. My US publisher arranged the schedule, and we completed thirty-two presentations or television interviews in thirty days across a dozen states. Wendie and Roma were kept busy selling books and meditation practices at each event; because Americans have such enthusiasm for consumption, they would often purchase every one of the dozen practices I'd recorded.

That year I was also invited to participate in a conference, *The Four Faces of Woman*, at Mount Abu, a hill station in Rajasthan,

India. Two hundred women from more than one hundred countries came together to discuss aspects of being a woman—the eternal, the traditional, the modern and the Shakti face, the face of innate power.

The Australian contingent were an enthusiastic group who promptly bonded. Sister Angela from the Franciscan monastery at Stroud was there, along with many other fabulous women for whom spirituality was important. Australians have always had a robust rather than pious view of spirituality, and as most participants dressed in white and became more reverential, the Australian contingent dressed more colourfully and enjoyed a good deal of laughter and conversation.

After the conference finished, and because of our interest in health and wellbeing, Wendie and I travelled with a local doctor into the surrounding desert to visit a man with tuberculosis and his wife. After travelling for half an hour on a desolate dirt road, we left the car and trekked for a kilometre or so down a well-trodden track winding through a gully and up the other side into a scrubby landscape. This couple lived there in the simplest dwelling we'd ever seen, a one-room mud and stick hut. They greeted us with much smiling and bowing at the entrance. The man, his smile wide and toothless, moved slowly, bent over with frailty, his ribs clearly visible in his tiny frame.

As we entered their hut, I was struck by its cleanliness. The dirt floor had been brushed spotlessly clean with a bunch of sticks bound together by long grass strands. In one corner were three or four metal plates, two cups, a couple of bowls and two saucepans scrubbed clean and neatly stacked. A flimsy piece of faded and frayed cotton was the bed cover on a woven mat of sticks. Hanging from a strut in the roof were several small hessian sacks that I imagined might contain rice or other staples.

Outside, near another woven stick bed, an open fire occasionally smoked, signalling that it could be stirred into life whenever needed. Timber was unavailable—the only vegetation were scrubby desert bushes and the very rare stunted tree—so fuel was derived from a pile of dried-out cow pats stacked neatly in the corner.

These people appeared to have no other possessions, yet they smiled broadly as they welcomed us so warmly into their humble home. We gently declined the woman's generous offer of tea and were struck that, given we couldn't see any food, she should offer us anything at all.

The doctor briefly examined the man. After a fleeting visit full of friendly gestures and a good deal of nodding, bowing and smiling, we returned to the car immersed in our own thoughts. Everything this couple possessed would have filled a medium-sized cardboard box. There are so very many ways to live a life, but the universal need we share is for connection and love. Our surroundings don't define the ease or difficulty with which we discover the simplicity of what really matters.

***

After the conference, Wendie and I travelled on to Kathmandu as I was keen to visit the city where Brenden had ended his life. I wanted to walk the streets, smell the air, absorb the atmosphere of the city where he had made that fateful decision.

I was surprised by my tumult as the plane began its descent among the Himalayan mountains to land in the saucer-shaped valley that encloses Kathmandu. An aching lump of emotion swelled in my throat when the plane circled for landing. I reached for Wendie's hand but couldn't explain to myself, let alone her, the tsunami of grief engulfing me.

For some time, I had lectured and written about grief. I had counselled hundreds of people through their grief. I had wept for dozens of much-loved people over the many years of my practice.

I had wept about Brenden frequently, had planted numerous trees in his memory, had talked and laughed about him on countless occasions, but nothing prepared me for the gut-wrenching sobbing to come. Perhaps the looming presence of the mighty Himalayan mountains helped elicit such powerful emotions. Wendie gently took over as we made our way through customs and on to our hotel.

I had written to the British Embassy before we'd left Australia, alerting them to our impending visit. We knew Brenden had gone to them for assistance in the afternoon before the night when he ended his life. There were so many unknowns about his death, and I was keen to see if any fragments or echoes of a memory, any small trail of insight might remain.

The following day we went to the embassy, which was full of chattering Nepalese people lined up at the counters, keen to apply for UK visas. I was rendered speechless, so Wendie took over and said to the woman at the counter that we were there because 'our' brother had died; we had sent a letter to alert them to our visit. Instantly, a hush fell over every person crammed into the under-sized space. I was so touched by the compassion and kindliness exuding from their faces.

It turned out that a tourist had died the previous week, and the assembled crowd assumed we were his relatives. Their empathy was so palpable, it served only to bring me further undone as we were ushered into an office to meet with a diplomat.

'Diplomat' is a great descriptor for this solicitous and gentle man. He was so sweet with us, but his kindness caused me to plunge even deeper into the inarticulate spaces of grief. Wendie had to do all the talking because I simply couldn't get one word out of my mouth. I tried and failed several times to say something, but grief had hollowed me out of coherence—the words just wouldn't form.

Wendie asked whether we might see where Brenden had been cremated. The diplomat gently guided us away from this idea, saying that the river next to where cremations were held had dried up and was filled with crows. He kindly offered a driver and car to take us to where foreigners were buried, but that seemed pointless given we knew Brenden had been cremated.

Through this conversation, we learned that Geoff must have made the decision for Brenden to be cremated. Families are always given the option of having a body repatriated. This news came as a shock, because Geoff had told us that Brenden had already been cremated by the time we heard of his death. He'd clearly decided to protect us from seeing Brenden's body, and I knew he had done this out of kindness.

The diplomat finally suggested that we travel to Boudhanath Stupa on the north-eastern outskirts of Kathmandu, as it is considered the holiest place outside of Tibet; a place of pilgrimage. Perhaps, he suggested, we could purchase prayer flags there to take back to family members in Australia.

Opposite the embassy stood a simple hotel. Brenden had been referred there on the day he'd sought help from the embassy and they'd told him to return in the morning. It was there, in that very building, that he had died, but my heart and legs refused to enter its grounds.

***

We followed the diplomat's advice and travelled to the Boudhanath Stupa in the ancient town of Boudha. My first sight of its extraordinary architecture took my breath away. Situated on the trade route used for centuries between Tibet and Kathmandu, Boudha is now the central town for Tibetans in exile from their own homeland. The imposing stupa is its crown jewel.

As Wendie and I walked into one of the temples surrounding the stupa, a large group of Tibetan monks were chanting their scriptures and playing musical instruments such as the rag-dung (a long and impressive trumpet), drums, cymbals and bells. The air was heavy with incense, and the steady drone of the chanting felt like a balm to us both. We stayed a long time, lost in the heady perfume and mesmerised by the combination of sounds. Finally we emerged, refreshed and soothed.

We purchased prayer flags to deliver back to my parents and Ross, and as a gift for ourselves. They hung for many years in our garden before the wind and rain shredded the fabric and delivered the written prayers for peace into the ether.

Back in Kathmandu, we went to the only English newspaper office to see if there were any records dating back to 1982. We ascended five floors of creaky wooden stairs and entered a small timber-panelled office where the four staff were very welcoming.

When I told them I was looking for news of my dead brother, their postures softened into the subtle language of compassion. They respectfully located editions from April 1982, and we scanned the pages of the days surrounding Brenden's death. We found all sorts of titbits and news about tourists, but no news detailing the demise of a foreigner in such circumstances. We thanked the staff warmly and, with much smiling and bowing, we took our leave.

As we descended the creaking steps and emerged into the brightness of the day, I felt we had done what we could to find echoes of Brenden's life and death, and this was enough to put it to rest. A weight had lifted from my heart.

***

Later that same year we travelled to Montreal for a conference on death and dying with the Dalai Lama and many other wonderful speakers, including Sogyal Rinpoche.

At this conference we met a researcher, Caryle Hirshberg, who had been looking for commonalities among people who had achieved a 'spontaneous remission' from their disease. Through funding from the Institute of Noetic Sciences in Sausalito, Caryle and Brendan O'Regan studied two and a half thousand cases of people who'd been given three or fewer months to live and who were now—five, ten or twenty years later—alive and free of their disease. Brendan and Carlye were looking to see whether these people *did* something or *had* something in common, and they wanted to know if their findings could be replicated for others with a poor prognosis.

It so happened that a documentary about my life and work, *A Year in the Life of Petrea King*, was shown at this conference to wide acclaim. In 1992, the ABC and Channel 4 in the UK had jointly funded this documentary through their Visionaries series; two filmmakers had spent a year with me, from one birthday to the next, and also followed several of my clients during that time.

When Caryle saw the documentary, she sought me out. We realised that she had discovered from studying case histories what I had discovered in my clinical practice. Our findings supported the notion that there are similar characteristics in people who achieve unexpected remissions or far outlive their prognoses. I call them the four Cs—control, commitment, challenge, connection— and have written and spoken extensively about them online, on the radio, in articles and in books. These characteristics and their culti- vation have continued to underpin my life and work to this day.

CHAPTER 35

A dream come true

Wendie and I had only been living in Bundanoon for a couple of years when Killarney House came onto the market. It's a beautiful property, right in the heart of the town, and it served then as a forty-bed guesthouse and motel, caravan park and theatre restaurant set in nine acres of lawns and gardens.

I was quite excited by the idea of finally offering a large, safe place of nurturing, support and education to people facing life's greatest challenges. However, Wendie was less excited—or, perhaps, just more realistic. She agreed that Killarney would be ideal as a place to expand the work of the Quest for Life Foundation, but she reminded me of its price tag of $1.5 million. Quest had, at that time, $15,000 in its bank account—so we had the 1 and the 5, but we clearly needed a lot more zeroes.

Undaunted and still full of enthusiasm, I phoned the chair of the Foundation's board, Chris Levy. Wendie and I have always considered Chris to be a trusted adviser, and he has mentored me through some challenging times in managing business affairs. He's also become a dear friend, along with his wife, Anita. When I called him that day, he listened patiently and, towards the end of our conversation, reminded me of our limited financial resources. I said, 'Yes, I know, Chris, but I'm sure this place is meant for Quest.'

Wendie thought I was 'out of my tree' in setting my sights on the acquisition of the property, given our poor record of fundraising. It wasn't something I had any expertise or interest in. Anyway, we always seemed to have sufficient funds to do what we needed, and the accumulation of money for its own sake was never a priority for me.

I often drove to Killarney House on my way home from my practice to savour the possibilities in my mind. I told the owners that we didn't have the necessary funds, just the certainty that this property was destined to be a safe harbour for many people, as the Eremo had been for me all those years ago.

***

Weeks passed and Killarney House was soon to go to auction.

About this time, I attended a function at Prince of Wales Hospital because a patient of mine, a breast-cancer survivor, was being celebrated for her service to the hospital as a researcher. The Barbara Gross Research Unit was established that day in recognition of her many years of dedication to the health and wellbeing of women and their infants. When I went to congratulate her, Barbara pressed into my hand a small slip of torn-off paper with a name and phone number upon it, saying to me, 'If you're serious about purchasing Killarney House for the purpose you say, then ring this person.' On a day dedicated to celebrating her achievements, Barbara was thinking of those who'd suffered like her and she wanted to help them.

I came home from the function and shared with Wendie what had happened. We talked about the reality of Quest owning Killarney, and whether or not we felt we were up to the challenge of creating the dream that lay more in my heart than in hers. I then waited for a week to make the phone call, as we needed to be sure that we were unanimously certain about this. We knew if the purchase happened, this dream would absorb every ounce of our time, money and energy for the foreseeable future.

The day came when it felt right for me to phone the person whose scrawled name graced the torn-off slip of paper.

Clare patiently listened to my story. I told her of the work I had done with thousands of people and the dream I held of creating a safe harbour for many more. I told her about my desire to encourage, inspire and educate people to more consciously embrace their challenge so they can find peace and healing. At the end of my story, Clare asked me to put what I had said into a one-page document and fax it through to her. She would see if she and her husband were interested or able to help us.

Days passed before Clare called back to say that her husband, Geoff, would visit so we could show him Killarney House.

***

Geoff arrived an hour later than expected. Wendie, two other board members and I greeted him warmly, but he seemed hesitant as we sat in my rooms in town and dealt with introductions. After a brief conversation, we drove to Killarney—which, given our lateness, was deserted and lay in complete darkness; the manager and her son lived on the property, but she had given up waiting for us and had gone out for the evening. Her son said he knew how to break into the building, so he climbed through a window to allow us entry. Geoff was silent as we began our tour of the dishevelled premises.

Killarney's decor needed a complete upgrade. Its furnishings were tired and of a bygone era. Its walls were painted in apricots, pinks, limes and mauves, which did nothing to complement the brown sticky carpet or the orange chenille bedspreads that were all in disarray.

Geoff still said nothing while I chattered on about the potential I could see in the place. I flashed the torchlight into the dark distance to give him some idea of the shape and size of the property, but this did nothing to enliven the gloomy landscape.

Finally, our tour was complete and my patter exhausted. We invited the still-silent Geoff home for a meal before he returned to Sydney.

Our friends Sue and Bill were staying with us at home. Sue was living with breast cancer, and they frequently visited from Melbourne for counselling and advice about managing her health. That night, she prepared a fish pasta and a fresh salad from the garden. While we chatted over dinner, Geoff still said nothing about Killarney.

After we'd eaten, we moved to the lounge room. Geoff requested pen and paper. He asked the dollar amount that the vendors hoped to secure and jotted down some perfunctory calculations. He believed that the property could be purchased for less than was expected, with the addition of a few hundred thousand dollars for refurbishment. Then he wrote '$1.5m', sat back and said, without fanfare, 'Yes, we can do that.'

Wendie and I were gobsmacked but grateful. In that moment, our lives changed.

We couldn't have imagined how significant a challenge it would prove to be.

***

It turned out that two of Geoff and Clare Loudon's closest friends had been patients of mine. The couple simply wanted more people to benefit from what Quest and I had to offer. I remain deeply grateful to them for their generosity of spirit and for the faith they showed in Wendie and me.

These extraordinary people, who chose to remain anonymous until now, made available the money—which grew to $1.67 million—in a non-recourse loan, without a business plan and knowing we had no experience in undertaking an endeavour like the Quest for Life Centre. The terms of the loan were very generous—and, several years later, Clare and Geoff forgave the loan. Since then, the property has been owned outright with no debt by the Quest for Life Foundation.

When I rang Chris Levy to let him know what had happened, he was as surprised and delighted as we were. Chris thinks I have fairy dust in my pockets.

With two friends who lived nearby and were also board members, Wendie and I sat at a computer and plucked figures out of thin air for a budget to refurbish the property. Lights? $25,000. Carpet? $60,000. Paint? $45,000. Raising floors? $30,000. And, though none of us were builders, we pulled together a budget based on our best guesstimations: $865,000. We ended up being $5000 out in our calculations.

Some things were donated, such as the paint from Dulux, which allowed us to allocate more funds where needed. For instance, the initial building inspection said the roof didn't need replacing, which turned out not to be the case.

The property was abuzz with activity from many people who gave generously of their time and expertise. Patients, friends, members of the local community and others volunteered to empty the building of rubbish, and to clean and prepare it for painting and refurbishing. Clare and Geoff often worked alongside these volunteers, though none of them knew they were the benefactors who had made it all possible. Geoff lugged mattresses and other paraphernalia here and there, and Clare was down on her knees scraping out the ancient dirt and nails from the floorboards.

Wendie and I worked with a fabulous local project manager, Roy Burton, to completely refurbish the main building and accommodation lodges so that it was wheelchair accessible and safe for unwell people. Roy told us we were some of the easiest people he'd worked with because we were decisive. With his advice, we sealed up doorways and established new ones, changing the traffic flow within the building, and replaced glass bricks—along with a thousand other changes. Today, after more than twenty years of running the Quest for Life Centre, we would make the same choices.

There were times when we didn't have the funds to accommodate unexpected contingencies associated with the refurbishment. Rae and Geoff donated all the front windows and the main doors at the entrances. Like my parents, Dame Elisabeth Murdoch, a dear friend and supporter of Quest, contributed significant funds to complete the extensive tiling of the walkways and front companionway.

Wendie and I found the whole process to be energising and uplifting. We were excited to create a beautiful place where people could find peace and healing. None of it would have been accomplished without Wendie's love, commitment and support. We always discussed things and never had difficulty in arriving at a united front, as we mostly held the same tastes and sensibilities. Wendie has a great eye for design, and I'm often happy to be guided by her.

CHAPTER 36

Never smooth sailing

Amid all the buzz of activity and the preparations for the opening of the Quest for Life Centre, I discovered a group of lumps high in the tail of my breast near my armpit, along with a lump in my neck. I was loath to tell Wendie—I couldn't bear the thought of her losing another partner.

I wasn't particularly stressed by the possibility, as I was no longer a worrier. After I'd faced my mortality in my thirties and journeyed with hundreds of people who likewise had faced theirs, death no longer held any sting for me. It would be profoundly inconvenient for me to be ill when the Centre was about to open, but I had no fear and would just be disappointed for Wendie and our project.

Finally, I broached the subject with Wendie, and we consulted with one of the best breast surgeons in Sydney. He was a man I'd heard only the loveliest of comments about from his patients, and he knew of my work; I had written a book for women with breast cancer, and many of his patients had come to see me over the years. He was gracious and kind when he told me he was certain these breast lumps would prove to be cancer and was also concerned about the neck lump. He held a mirror for me to see the dimpling around the lumps, which he said was a sign they were cancerous. He referred me to the breast clinic in the city, and Wendie and I dutifully went off to have a mammogram and needle biopsy. I tried to jolly her along while feeling miserable that I was the cause of her having to sit in a breast cancer clinic again. None of it was funny.

My intuition shrieked at me not to have the needle biopsy. I was lying down while the specialist, needle in hand, was standing over me. I said to her, 'Why do I need to have the needle biopsy given the surgeon wants to remove the lumps anyway?'

'He wants it,' she replied.

'But I don't want to have the biopsy given he's scheduled me for surgery,' I feebly replied. It's so hard to stay true to your intuition when you're lying down, half naked, and a specialist is standing over you with needle poised in hand.

'He wants it,' she repeated. The echo of 'he wants it' stirred a thousand memories of being unable to speak up when a man had needs that obliterated my own.

Reluctantly, I again surrendered to what was done to me.

During the biopsy, the specialist punctured a blood vessel, contaminating the specimen and making it useless for diagnosis.

I was disappointed with myself for sacrificing my own sense of things and giving my power to someone who appeared to know better. When would I learn to trust my intuition and not be swayed by others who expressed their view more forcefully? It seems to be a lifelong learning for me to stay true to what I know.

Some people believe I must have had a blinding flash of insight in the Grotto of St Francis and that my life was instantly and permanently transformed; that no trial or tribulation would ever ruffle my peace.

Worse still, over the years, some people have put me on a pedestal, only to be terribly disappointed or angry when I don't measure up to their expectations—perhaps, for some, making me or anyone 'special' becomes an excuse to avoid putting in the necessary effort to challenge their own beliefs or judgements. I've been luckier than most in having circumstances challenge my own cherished but often limiting beliefs and judgements. Each moment is a choice: do I go with my cherished but limiting beliefs that are second nature to me, or let go and cultivate a larger experience of life? I thought it interesting that we refer to these beliefs, judgements, reactions and feelings as 'second nature' to us without any questioning of what our 'first nature' might be. Yoga philosophy supports the notion that, to find peace, we need to relinquish whatever has become second nature to us, in order to experience our essential nature, our first nature. The qualities of our first nature include wisdom, humour, insight, intuition, spontaneity, authenticity and creativity.

I refuse to go to my grave trading off the limitations, anxieties and beliefs I accumulated as a child. I want to grow into the fullness of this life. And so I continue to choose life every day.

While there were flashes of insight and experiences of the peace that passes all understanding in my time in the cave, like everyone else who wants to find that peace as a permanent state, it continues to be a journey of choice. These patterns of the past are deeply ingrained in all of us. They had shaped and moulded me into who I had become. But I know that I am more than my story.

I wouldn't change one bit of my story. Those tragedies, difficulties, traumas, joys and challenges have brought me to now. I had discharged a multitude of powerful emotions during my time of isolation in the cave. That cathartic journey had hollowed me out and taken me to the heights and depths of human emotional experience.

It is great to have a story. My story had broken me open and laid me bare. Long years of practising meditation had given me the skill to witness the expression of long-held grief and sadness as it ravaged my body. I watched as my body shook and shuddered through an emotional roller-coaster of emotions. Expressing them had been a blessing as it was the means by which I understood myself so deeply. My story had broken me open.

The more I aligned with being the witness of this experience, the more peace I felt. Finally, the witness became my more stable, authentic and peaceful expression of my essential nature. I could have a story without having to *be* my story.

My intention is simple; no moment will pass when I am not aware of any temptation to react from past conditioning. This is the path of yoga that I embraced wholeheartedly. It provides the only certain journey into peace.

***

A few days later, I entered hospital for the lumpectomy and the removal of the node in my neck. Because of the burst blood vessel, the lumpectomy was larger than anticipated so that clear margins could be obtained.

In the hospital bed opposite mine lay a woman who was in for a second lot of surgery after a positive diagnosis of breast cancer. She noticed my name on the card at the head of my bed and inquired, 'You're not the Petrea King who wrote *Spirited Women*, are you?' When I said yes, she came over to my bed with her copy of my book for me to sign, telling me it had become her bible as she went through the experience of breast cancer. She asked why I was in hospital, and I told her, 'First write the book, then have the experience!' and we both laughed at the not-so-funny situation.

The following morning, I was on the gurney ready for the anaesthetist to make his observations outside the operating theatre.

He took my pulse and blood pressure, then asked if I knew why I was having surgery. I told him that my surgeon believed I had breast cancer with the possibility of a secondary node in my neck. The anaesthetist said, 'Your body is completely relaxed and your blood pressure is normal.' I told him I meditated and had done so for decades. Looking surprised, he emphasised that my pulse rate was slow: was I sure I understood what was about to happen to me? He seemed quite bemused, perhaps not quite believing me when I told him that meditation helps me to remain calm in difficult or stressful circumstances.

When I awoke from the anaesthetic, my surgeon was standing by my bed. He was more than a little agitated as he profusely apologised for frightening me. He had sent off a frozen section for biopsy during the surgery, and it appeared that while the cells were unusual, they were not cancerous. He said he still wasn't convinced, as he'd been so certain of his initial diagnosis, and he promised to phone me in a few days with the definitive result.

Much to everyone's relief, the thorough biopsy revealed no cancer. Rae believes her prayers are very powerful.

Wendie and I had recently attended the birth of our first grandchild, Matteo. His delightful presence in our lives was a great antidote to everyone's upset over my surgery. During my recovery I cuddled him as he fell asleep in my arms. Holding him was a blissful balm in my heart.

Once fully recovered from the surgery, we attended to the last preparations before the opening of the Quest for Life Centre.

CHAPTER 37

Without a dream, nothing happens

Beyond all expectations, we opened the doors of the Quest for Life Centre eight months after the purchase of Killarney House. Wendie and I had never undertaken such a mammoth project before, and we were grateful when the day of the opening dawned sunny and clear.

Dr Jerry Jampolsky and his wife, Diane Cirincione, from the Center for Attitudinal Healing in Sausalito were visiting Australia at the time, and they did the honours of officiating at the opening ceremony. This was most fitting, as the Twelve Principles of Attitudinal Healing that Jerry distilled in his bestselling book *Love Is Letting Go of Fear* have been a foundation in my own life and lie at the heart of our educational programs at Quest. So much of my life and my work with other people has been about changing attitudes to whatever the crisis or upset might be.

Many of my patients, colleagues, board members, volunteers, friends, local community members and supporters from farther afield gathered for the auspicious occasion. We planted a hawthorn tree in the grounds, as the hawthorn has several positive associations, including being the tree of love and protection in Celtic lore.

***

There was little time for us to celebrate our accomplishment before the real work began. We opened the Centre with a mere $50,000 in the bank and no active fundraising on the horizon. Anyone who knows anything about business would understand that those are slim pickings for starting up such a venture from scratch.

Along with our board members, I was loath for Quest to have an overdraft, as the business model would always be reliant on donations, bequests and program fees. The Foundation would subsidise people's attendance at the five-day residential programs so we only ever charged half the actual cost to house, feed and educate people. Given the stories of tragedy, trauma, life-threatening illness, grief, loss, despair, anxiety and depression that people brought to Quest, our ratio of program team members to participants has always been high out of necessity.

Wendie and I worked virtually seven days a week for the first few years, as it took every ounce of our energy and time to attend to every detail. She became the first general manager, and I focused on the development of the educational programs that we would conduct. We answered phones, made beds, cleaned toilets, ran programs and generally did whatever was necessary to make the dream become a reality. There were dozens of policies and procedures to be written; there were behind-the-scenes accounting structures and administration processes to be developed. We enjoyed the challenge of helping to bring it all to fruition. Without a dream, nothing happens!

Of course, the realisation of this type of dream takes a great deal of effort from more than two people, and so it was with the Quest for Life Centre. Friends, colleagues and past patients all stepped forward to assist with accounting and other procedures, and together we created the safe harbour that I had long wished for.

In the first two years, Wendie and I lived on our paltry savings as there were insufficient funds to pay us salaries when Quest had so many pressing financial commitments. My private practice was put on hold—there weren't enough hours in the day—while sales of my books and recordings kept us going financially; we packed orders at night after returning home from our day's labours.

***

After we'd put in so much time, money and effort, we were delighted when so many people wanted to visit our safe haven. They travelled from all over Australia and sometimes beyond to attend Quest's programs at the Centre. These programs have evolved over the past nineteen years to meet the growing and changing needs of our communities, and the evolution hasn't always been easy.

We hadn't been open for very long when we were inundated with people desperate to attend our programs but unable to pay anything towards the costs. I found it painful to turn anyone away on financial grounds, but we were so busy that it was impossible to arrange any substantial fundraising in addition to the day-to-day running of the Centre. We could hardly expect the people who sought our assistance to be concerned with how we were funding our services. They were already preoccupied with major health or other concerns, so Quest's precarious financial position was not on their radar.

Over the years, more than one board of the Foundation thought that the best option for solving Quest's financial difficulties was to sell the property; from the funds left over after repaying Geoff and Clare Loudon's loan (this was before they had gifted the property to Quest), we could tailor our services to our financial realities. Undoubtedly, this would have been the fiscally responsible thing to do, but I couldn't bring myself to sell the property for two reasons:

first, I knew how important it was to provide a safe harbour; second, I wanted to honour the enormous gesture of trust and generosity that the Loudons had made by supporting me and Quest to provide this special place.

At one stage, a whole board resigned because I refused to sell the property. Understandably, they felt that they had provided their best advice and my refusal left them little option. With my history of avoiding angry encounters at all costs, I found some of these meetings quite intimidating and stressful—but they also helped me grow as a woman and leader. I learned to stand firm and stay true to what I most valued and believed in. I am sure some board members found me infuriating at times, though I doubt any would question my dedication to the vision and ideals of Quest.

The decision to keep going, even though we couldn't see a financially sustainable model on the horizon, meant we continued to provide our services at the Centre week by week. Often a donation would come in at a critical time to pay some outstanding invoice, and while this unpredictable income could be a little hair-raising for staff and board members, I became used to trusting that life or love would always find a way.

On one occasion, a wonderful group of women who had attended programs for cancer sufferers came to the rescue. They formed another board as well as a fundraising committee, and together we continued to provide Quest's life-changing services.

***

In the first few years, Wendie and I conducted almost all of the Quest programs. The other facilitators included Pat Moss and Peg MacLeod, a clinical psychologist who was steeped in the principles of attitudinal healing.

Wendie and I soon realised that if the Centre was to flourish long into the future, we would need to train more people to do the work that had so long preoccupied us. We focused on training others who could facilitate, counsel, massage and generally support the participants of our programs without our direct involvement.

Our staff at Quest grew to manage the administrative and practical aspects of running a large and busy centre. In time, we replaced Wendie with a centre manager so she could more fully devote herself to co-facilitating programs with me.

We loved the work and spent most of our time ensuring the success of the programs and the smooth running of the Centre. Mostly we navigated times of high financial stress together, although once or twice we agreed not to discuss Quest outside business hours as we both saw the situation so differently—especially when Wendie was ready to give up the struggle to keep the Centre open. It was painful when we had such differing perspectives, as we were always so much in accord in every other way.

Over weekly dinners, some dear friends provided us with a sounding board to our ideas and offered advice about dealing with the daily challenges of managing such an ambitious enterprise. They listened to us endlessly and supported us as we grew into the roles needed for the successful running of the Centre and its programs.

CHAPTER 38

Out and about

Wendie and I have conducted workshops in every city and in dozens of towns, both large and small, throughout our wonderful country. I've found good people everywhere, and it has been such a privilege to share in their struggles, their challenges and their hopes. Wendie and I, and now other facilitators, have taken Quest's work into communities dealing with illness, depression, natural disasters and other life-sapping challenges. We've delivered workshops in all kinds of places, including RSL clubs, church halls, CWA rooms, community health centres, agricultural stations, churches, pubs and clubs—and in a room while jackhammers were operating outside!

The two of us were once invited to a small, remote town interstate that had been experiencing many deaths through a variety of causes. Grief was putting a strain on the whole community. Domestic violence was escalating, along with drug and alcohol abuse, depression, hopelessness, isolation and anxiety.

Out in the bush, it's not uncommon for people to wait a long time before getting a cancer diagnosis; several people in this community had been dealing with advanced illness and had recently died in a relatively short space of time. In addition, a young farming father had crashed his small plane and died. A child had fallen off the back of a truck and been killed; a young man had tried to beat the train to the crossing without success; and there had been several suicides among farming men who had found the drought, falling stock prices, flood, then another flood, too much to bear.

I sat on a pile of hay bales in a shed while two hundred locals gathered for a two-day workshop. After we'd established the guidelines for our time together—confidentiality, listening 100 per cent, not judging, staying with our experience rather than our theories—the first man stood up and, from under his akubra hat, described how he had been planning the murder of the local police officer for two years.

A deep hush fell on the crowd as they all knew one another quite well, including the police officer in question, who was also present.

The farmer described how his young daughter had died in a dreadful accident on their farm. The police officer had taken two hours to arrive and then asked some routine questions to ensure this horrifying tragedy was indeed an accident and that neither parent was involved in any way. The distraught farmer railed at the copper for taking so long to get there. The officer responded that there hadn't been a rush—the farmer's daughter was already dead, and the officer had to pick his own daughter up from school before coming over. The farmer was further enraged because the officer had questioned the cause of death and was outraged he should infer that either parent could conceivably have been involved.

Clearly, the farmer had shifted his grief into rage against the police officer for what he perceived to be a callous response, though the poor officer had undoubtedly been lost for words.

At our workshop, the farmer described in detail how he intended to kill the officer. But by the end of his outpouring of emotion, they were both weeping openly in each other's arms.

To witness such events is an extraordinary privilege and always leaves me humbled by the capacities of the human spirit to reconcile, forgive and heal.

***

Another time, Wendie and I were asked by the Loddon Mallee Integrated Cancer Service to facilitate a series of workshops across Victoria. Illness, depression and the drought had left many families at the end of their collective tethers. We were gone from home for a month and, in that time, conducted thirty-two workshops or talks starting in Lorne, then Kyneton, Bendigo, Echuca, Kerang, Swan Hill, Mildura, Wangaratta and finally Albury. Sometimes we had two or more commitments in one day, with evening and breakfast lectures as well as all-day workshops. Plus, of course, we travelled in between.

Our motel accommodation ranged from rustic to plush, and occasionally we were housed in a beautiful B&B. The owners of one were quite nonplussed by us as a couple—they couldn't reconcile their Christian prejudices about gay people with the fact we were so friendly and interested in them and their lifestyle, along with helping their local community. Hopefully we melted some of the judgements that cause so much unnecessary pain to people.

We had no fewer than two hundred people at every event, as resilience was low and tempers were fraying. Some events were attended by over four hundred people, many of them men, angry and frustrated with the government over water allocations. In situations where tempers were short and the atmosphere tense, I always started by naming what I thought people might be thinking: 'Now, I know you're probably thinking, what does a woman like me think she's got to say to men like you? But let me share a little of my background before you make up your mind that I'm not worth listening to.'

At these times, the complexities of my life experience were of such value. I had lived on and loved the land. I knew about sheep, the value of water, cattle, fencing, droving, mustering, drought, and the despair of losing crops and stock. I understood rural communities, both their strengths and frailties.

***

I have Wendie to thank for many of the skills I've gained to be effective in volatile environments. My habitual inclination is to run when conflict is on the horizon, while Wendie stands firm, and I am so grateful for what I've learned from her. Her direct approach has helped me understand how to remain available and useful in difficult circumstances, without reacting from the habitual.

We are so different from and complementary to each other, and there is a lovely story that demonstrates this contrast.

We were on one of our long driving trips, out into the desert areas of Australia, when I asked Wendie the question, 'If the children born today were the last to be born, what do you think would happen on the planet?'

In my reflection on this question, I had played out in my mind that people would cherish each other more; they would be loving, supportive and kind to one another, considering the certainty of humanity's limited future; they would all do what they could to rise to the occasion and face the challenge presented by the end of humanity. These could, just possibly, be the most peaceful and enlightening years on Earth.

Wendie's response had us laughing so hard we had tears in our eyes. Her take on the idea was simply, 'There'd be complete and utter chaos as everyone grabs whatever they can for themselves—there'd be anarchy, mayhem and murder in the streets!'

The fact that we often see things from such different perspectives has provided us with much amusement and plenty of discussion.

But our values are entirely aligned, something that provides a solid foundation for any meaningful relationship.

Wendie is comfortable in the world: when she wants something out on the table, there's no sense in trying to postpone the meal. I may as well surrender and pull up a chair. We resolve whatever it is, so we are always emotionally up to date with each other. There's nothing left unsaid or undone between us. This leaves us free to embrace each day completely at one with each other.

Though, to continue the analogy, Simon once said of Wendie, 'The problem with Wen is that she wants to plate up before the food's fully cooked!' as she swiftly focuses on all the problems that could arise with any decision or plan and usually voices these, even before she's grasped the whole concept.

We seem to be completely co-dependent, as I am at a loss without her when I need to travel alone. I misplace and forget things, feeling discombobulated and sure that the most functional part of me is missing. She, on the other hand, doesn't sleep unless our rescue cattle-dogs, Meg and Maxi, are beside her; she hears strange noises that only seem to occur when I am away; she finds excuses not to go to bed, and then we play online Scrabble until the wee hours. We simply don't like being apart. Living and working together places a great strain on many couples, but we love doing everything together. We accomplish far more than most because of our shared commitment to each other and to our work, which we both find deeply meaningful.

***

Our lecture and workshop tours were opportunities for us to meet some wonderful characters who truly love their land and their communities. We so appreciated the trust they placed in us when we, two strangers, arrived in their towns and laid down the four guidelines, then listened as they shared their vulnerabilities and grief, their rage and frustration, and finally worked with them to explore healthier pathways to peace.

On our tour through rural Victoria, we sold all my books and CDs at cost so we could get these practical resources out as widely as possible into struggling communities. Staff at Quest had to bring down two more full carloads of resources as we sold $45,000 worth of stock. People were hungry for anything to help them in practical and tangible ways to get to sleep, to communicate more skilfully around difficult subjects, and to manage their anxiety, anger, grief, fear and despair.

One of the dozen principles of Attitudinal Healing that Dr Jerry Jampolsky has written extensively about is: 'I can always perceive anger in myself or in others as a call for help, rather than as an attack.' That is a fabulous reminder to look past frayed tempers and harsh words. We can always consider an appropriate response to such outbursts, recognising we may have come close to someone's vulnerability, rather than hurling back a defence that serves only to escalate the upset.

Given the fluctuations of a changing climate, the resilience and tenacity of people in the bush is extraordinary. We returned to some of these areas a few years later when they were dealing with the consequences of floods. Our workshops also took us to the flood-affected communities of Theodore and St George in Queensland.

***

While I was conducting a workshop in the Gunnedah tourist centre, a truckie stopped off to use their facilities. He stood behind an educational display, listening in to what I was saying. He then came forward and asked if he could join us for the day—all the participants happened to be women. We welcomed him.

After the workshop, the truckie admitted to me that he'd been thinking about driving headlong into a tree or over an embankment to end his life. He had been playing out in his mind a good place for this 'accident' that would ensure he didn't survive. He felt the awful pressure of the clock to deliver his loads and believed that the company he worked for regarded him merely as a commodity.

A few months later, we were relieved when he attended a program at the Centre; he has gone on to find more meaningful work in a managerial role.

***

Wendie and I have been invited into many diverse communities, all of which were looking for healing and peace. We have worked with beautiful Aboriginal women from the Stolen Generations or who have been victims of domestic or institutional violence. These women often have devastating stories of trauma, abuse, grief, loss and violence—but, paradoxically, they usually laugh more than any other group. They have the most amazing sense of humour, and I'm sure it is why they have survived such appalling and inhumane treatment over the many decades since European settlement.

We've often had Aboriginal women attend residential programs at the Quest for Life Centre, and we always learn more from them than they could ever learn from us. Our workshops provide an opportunity for them to interact in a supportive space, where together they can reflect upon what is happening in their communities and families, and develop practical strategies that might make a positive difference back home. They're hungry to understand neuroplasticity, which is the ability to change our brain by consciously choosing new and healthier responses, along with epigenetics and how epigenetic consequences are passed on through the generations; this generational grief and trauma is a major stumbling block in the long journey towards healing and reconciliation.

Indigenous people understand the concept of connectedness better than any of us blow-ins. When Wendie and I were working with a group of Aboriginal women on the north coast of New South Wales, they described some of the ways in which they traditionally gathered their food. What to us might seem a delicacy was, for them, their daily fare—most of them had grown up eating oysters and laughed heartily when Wendie told them she'd paid $5 per oyster in a restaurant.

The women said that when the pipis were up the northern end of the beach, they would cross two rivers to the south, and they were bound to find fruit ripe and ready for eating. But, when the pipis were at the opposite end, they knew they needed to cross the mountain to the north to find nuts ready for picking, storing or eating.

This constant 'reading' and interpretation of the environment demonstrates a level of connectedness that most of us have long lost, though all Indigenous ancestors well understood the interconnectedness of life.

CHAPTER 39

Meetings in the ether

While travelling around the country facilitating workshops or giving lectures, I've been interviewed dozens of times on radio stations in every state and territory. Sometimes these interviews were conducted before Wendie and I were to run workshops in local country areas. At other times, a community had been through a particularly difficult period and the topic of resilience, or euthanasia, or dealing with death and dying or looking after carers or being aware of your mates when depression is rife would be our focus.

I have also done many interviews for ABC Radio with most of their regular broadcasters, starting in the 1980s with Caroline Jones on *The Search for Meaning*, then with Margaret Throsby on *Midday*, Dr Rachael Kohn on *The Spirit of Things* and Richard Fidler on *Conversations*.

Caroline Jones is a wonderful interviewer, as her calm and quiet manner underpin her skilful questioning. When I was interviewed by her for *The Search for Meaning*, she introduced me as having suffered through the suicide of my brother, Brenden, among other things. After the interview went to air, I rang my parents to see how they felt it had gone—it being my first major radio interview about my life.

Geoff sounded breathless, his blood pressure surely sky-rocketing, and all he could say was, 'Why did you have to say *that*?'

'What did I say?' I replied, somewhat alarmed.

All he could do was repeat the question a couple of times, then he handed the phone to Rae, too upset and angry to talk to me.

'What did I say to upset him so badly?' I asked her.

Unbeknown to me in the five years since Brenden's death, Geoff had never told his friends and colleagues that my brother had taken his own life. Geoff had told them, 'Brenden died in a mountain-climbing accident.' The stigma of suicide runs deep for many people, and Geoff had seen it as a potentially negative reflection on his family.

He rang me uncharacteristically early the following morning and said he'd had a sleepless night. He was relieved that the truth was now 'out' rather than kept as an agonising secret through some sense of dreadful shame.

Families have complex structures, and it has been a long and difficult journey for our family to speak openly about painful subjects. We always assumed that we loved one another and gave kisses on the cheek that missed. Since making our journey to emotional vulnerability, we've had no difficulty in expressing our deep love and care for one another, and the ructions so common in many families have long been put to rest. It took the tumult of Brenden's long mental illness and suicide, my near death and many other challenges to bring us to this place.

Every time I spoke about suicide publicly, it was difficult for Geoff. Sometimes he wouldn't speak to me for days if there was an article in the print media or a radio interview in which Brenden's suicide was mentioned.

After my interview with Margaret Throsby went to air, two women called Quest to say that they had planned to end their lives that day, but on hearing about the terrible distress that suicide causes families, they changed their minds and reached out for help.

One of the women, a young mother, described how she'd prepared her children's school lunches that morning. She had put notes in their lunchboxes telling them how much she loved them and always would, her intention being to take her life before their return home. Both these women attended programs with us at the Centre, where they were given more personal resources and connection to services.

When Geoff learned of their stories, he understood how important it is to speak about the consequences of suicide, and from then on he fully supported me in this.

***

There were many television interviews too, starting with Ray Martin and *The Midday Show*, where I was a regular guest; I spoke about living with illness and grief and many other issues that cause us to suffer. Then, when I lived in Crows Nest, I was often interviewed on the news broadcasts of nearby Channel 9 about topical issues such as the importance of a nourishing diet when you're living with illness. I was also interviewed on *Compass*, *A Current Affair* and *Stateline*, and twice on *Australian Story*.

Sadly, *A Year in the Life of Petrea King* never aired in Australia. Many years after its production, the ABC decided to broadcast it after all, but fortunately reconsidered when I asked them not to. I had no way of contacting many of the families involved in the making of the film, and it would have come as a shock for them to see their loved ones onscreen without warning. When the documentary aired in the United Kingdom, it was enthusiastically received, and I was sent many letters of support and encouragement afterwards from people touched by the story.

Everyone loves to share their stories with people who 'get' them. I've received thousands of such letters over the past thirty-plus years, and I have answered all of them. I think it is essential that we communicate around things we find difficult or painful. And, whether we speak or write them, our stories can become avenues for deeper reflection and understanding. I am often called upon in complex family situations where there is conflict and the potential for escalating angst among members with opposing views.

***

Naturally, *This Is Your Life* came as a surprise.

I thought I was meeting a marketing executive with one of our board members, Bob, and we were standing in the foyer of a Sydney hotel when I saw Mike Munro walking up the stairs, film crew in tow. I said to Bob, 'Some poor bugger is about to get sprung!' as Mike continued to walk towards me. I thought he was going to ask me directions to someone else and was shocked when I was the subject of his attention. If there was even a hint that the program's subject knew about the surprise, the show was cancelled no matter how many months had gone into the research and preparations.

Mike left me with a 'minder' while he returned to the studio to prepare for my arrival. I wasn't allowed to make any phone calls, and even when I went to the bathroom, the minder accompanied me to ensure I didn't 'do a runner'.

While I waited, I considered several things. The first was that Mike would undoubtedly talk about Brenden's suicide on national television, and that would be very difficult for my parents who I imagined weren't in Brisbane as they had led me to believe—

I thought it likely that they were aware of the surprise and might be part of the program.

The second thought I had was, *What if they don't mention that Wendie is my partner?* as that would be appalling. I was reassured on that account when I arrived at the studios and saw my suit bag hanging up in the room where I was to shower and change; this meant Wendie had to know about the program.

Beyond that, it was all a complete and utter surprise, as well as a wonderful delight to be reminded of so many special people in my life.

They had even found Padre Ilarino. In addition to his contribution to the program, he sent another half-hour talk to me on video. My Italian son-in-law translated it for me—and, in part, Padre Ilarino asked me to return to Italy and visit him.

A viewer of the program wrote to me after it aired; she owned a small fourteenth-century farmhouse outside of Assisi, and she told us that we were welcome to use it if we ever decided to visit. We were touched by her kind gesture and gratefully took her up on her generous offer, making this beautiful stone house—which overlooked soft hills and gentle green pastures—our base for a wonderful holiday when we returned to see Padre Ilarino. He now lived in a monastery for elderly or retired priests outside the beautiful town of Amelia, a couple of hours' drive from Assisi.

The only thing I could ever do for Padre Ilarino was to send him possum socks—a warm blend of wool and possum fur—every year, as the Assisi winters are harsh and his vow of poverty meant he bought nothing for himself. I had brought possum socks with me on this final visit.

While Padre Ilarino looked content, he was obviously very unwell and quite jaundiced. His carer, Pepino, had helped him out of bed and to dress just to see me.

In the delight of reunion, we again talked with and over each other. I thanked him for caring for me, a stranger, all those years ago, and for seeing something of value in me when I'd held so little regard for myself.

As I lifted his brown habit, his swollen ankles and cold purple feet were revealed. With tears of gratitude and much love, I gently put the possum socks on his feet. Later, after we had lunch with the priests downstairs, I returned to his bedroom for his last blessing.

Pepino told me that Padre Ilarino refused to have anyone remove his possum socks from his feet, and he was buried in them two weeks later.

***

Dozens of articles have been written about my work in almost every Australian newspaper and magazine. Most of them have been done very respectfully.

I was disappointed, to say the least, when the *Daily Telegraph* published a picture of me, on page three, sitting at my desk with the grim reaper superimposed above me and the headline: 'Woman helps AIDS innocents to die'.

The story was about my work with AIDS sufferers who had been infected through blood or its products, and it described children or the people who were haemophiliacs or recipients of blood transfusions as 'the innocent ones'. This was so *not* how I thought or will ever think. I am yet to meet the person deserving of their suffering.

On page four was a picture of me with my head thrown back laughing, accompanied by the caption: 'Eight of her patients died in one week.'

***

In 2000, Richard Glover invited me and Michael Rennie from McKinsey's onto his ABC 702 program for a segment called *Midweek Conference*.

Like me, Michael had survived cancer, and we had both used the valuable practice of meditation to make peace and find respite during the turbulence of illness. We discussed the benefits of meditation and how helpful the ability to quieten the mind becomes during times of high stress. Listeners would call in with various issues and stories that related to their own lives, and these interviews proved very popular.

After a few weeks, Michael left the program when he relocated to New York. Richard and I have continued with it about once every six weeks to this day.

Over the past seventeen years, we have discussed many challenging topics. These include how to deal with angry people, what is helpful to say when a loved one is diagnosed with a serious illness, how to manage Christmas when there is conflict or a family member has died in the previous year, sibling rivalry, living with someone who has a mental illness, how to cope when someone you love ends their life, what to say when you no longer want to continue a friendship or see a person, living with chronic pain, dealing with a diagnosis, loving someone with post-traumatic stress disorder, the impact of family secrets, the effect that childhood trauma has on how we live as adults, why some people crumble under stress and others thrive, and how to move on after major disappointments— to name just a few!

I'm usually in Bundanoon when Richard rings around midday to choose a subject for *Midweek Conference* that afternoon. While driving to Sydney, I reflect on the topic so that I'm prepared for the interview at 5.30 pm. Richard is a wonderful interviewer and a good-hearted man, so working with him is always a pleasure.

Recently we were discussing how childhood trauma impacts on people as adults, when a caller rang in to describe the awful abuse she suffered as a child and the terrible impact it had on her self-esteem and relationships. She sounded despairing, and we chatted for a while about her options to heal some of her past trauma. I encouraged her to call the Quest for Life Centre to talk about attending a program with us. Our caller said that while she would love to attend, there was no way she could afford to come. I suggested she call anyway and we would see what we could do to help her. I also suggested that she get my book *Your Life Matters* from her local library, as many people find that it provides light and direction in challenging circumstances, along with a perspective that fosters us to grow through adversity.

Much to the surprise of Richard, the producers and me, listeners started ringing in to make donations so our caller could attend a program at Quest. The caller was so touched by strangers caring about her that she immediately began to take better care of herself. Since then, she has attended a couple of programs at Quest for people with symptoms of post-traumatic stress, and she has completely turned her life around.

It is so gratifying to have these deeper conversations with people about the issues that cause us so much pain and suffering. In each program at Quest, we have a session that gives attendees the opportunity to tell a little of their story and what they hope to achieve by participating in the program.

Many years ago, at a *Healing Your Life* program that I was facilitating, the first person to speak was a man in his forties. He started off by saying that he'd been sitting in his car with a pistol. He had fired the test shot. He didn't know what had possessed him to turn on the radio, but he had, and I was talking. And, 'It just made sense, so that's why I'm here.'

A woman in her fifties and to his left spoke next. She declared that she was terribly depressed. She and her daughter looked like mirror images of each other, and her daughter had also been depressed. Her daughter had been found dead, and the family would never know whether she had fallen accidentally or jumped. The woman told the group that at times she couldn't bring herself to see her family because she reminded her husband of his daughter and her other children of their sister, and she didn't want to bring them all down. She had been sitting in her car and eating takeaway food when she turned on the radio, and I was talking. 'It just made sense,' she said, and that was why she had come to the program.

The next man had been driving to the hospital to make the heart-breaking decision to turn off his son's life support machine, having already lost a daughter and another son to an overdose, and his wife to cancer. He couldn't bring himself to go into another intensive care unit; he could not, would not make the decision to turn off life support for the third and last time. He had been sobbing in his car in the hospital carpark. He too didn't know why he'd turned on the radio, but I was talking and, 'It just made sense,' hence his arrival at the program.

There were ten such stories, one after the other, of people sitting in their cars in various states of despair, anguish and hopelessness, and they had turned on the radio.

Although I drive an hour and a half to Sydney, do about fifteen minutes on radio with Richard, then drive an hour and a half back to Bundanoon, it seems a worthwhile journey to make.

***

At the same time in 2000, I became a regular guest on Tony Delroy's *Nightlife* program. Tony and I also discussed the challenges of living a meaningful life in difficult circumstances. However, because his interviews with me ran for a full fifty minutes, we could unpack the topics in much greater depth before we took listeners' phone calls.

I was always very mindful that Tony's program was beamed across the country at 10 pm. Our discussion was heard in remote homesteads by solitary individuals as well as in cities and houses in rural and regional areas. And I love the radio for that reason—it is such an intimate conversation. Often people who lie awake listening to the radio may find sleep elusive due to pain, loneliness, depression, grief or despair, and a warm and friendly voice in the ether can be a lifeline for them. I have had many letters from people all over the world who have listened to these interviews via the podcasts.

When Tony retired in 2016, his listeners were devastated. He had been such an important part of so many people's lives for such a long time. They were often in bed or alone when he went on air. Tony was their friend, a constant in their life, a warm and familiar voice in the night. His show is missed by many, many people, including me, although I am happy to continue my *Nightlife* conversations with Sarah Macdonald on Sunday evenings.

Perhaps the strangest call that Tony and I ever had came from a man who was very angry because people judged him harshly for not working—because he was a drug addict. 'People say I don't work,' he said. 'I have to work bloody hard to knock off enough houses to get stuff that I then have to flog off at the pub. I have a $200-a-day habit!' Tony and I looked at each other, trying to decide who should talk to our caller. Finally, I said something along the lines of, 'When you're ready to get help for your drug habit, your life can change for the better,' and we both had a good laugh about it later.

Some of our listeners had imbibed a tipple or two by the time we were on air, and that added a whole other layer to understanding the complexities of their stories. We had so many wonderful conversations both sober and sobering with callers from across this vast land.

CHAPTER 40

The quest for peace

Given I have had no training in managing the various aspects of developing educational programs, establishing a happy, thriving workplace, creating and managing budgets and cash flows, liaising with architects and project managers, and a thousand other tasks that I've needed to address in the successful running of Quest, I have been grateful for the mentoring, support and guidance of many people, Wendie foremost among them.

As the founder and CEO, my role is focused on the mentoring and supervision of the facilitators, counsellors, support teams and therapists who deliver our programs and workshops, the development of the educational and support programs that the Foundation delivers and, in conjunction with our board, the overall direction and development of Quest.

My training in the School of Philosophy gave me an insight into the value of attention to detail, whether reflected in our printed materials, the way a stamp is placed on an envelope, the cleanliness of the building, the care of the grounds, the way a tablecloth hangs or the presentation of the food. The divine is in the detail.

Years ago, Quest was going through a quality review process, and

I met with our housekeeping staff to see how they brought 'quality' to their work. There was silence for a while, and then one of our cleaners said, 'Is that when I've finished cleaning a bedroom and I stand in the doorway and radiate love into the room?' And another hesitantly offered, 'Is that when I make a little pocket in the sheets for someone's toes?' What a pleasure it is to work with people who love what they do and who transmit that care and attention into their work.

What makes the professional staff of Quest unique is that regardless of our training in psychology, social work, psychotherapy, yoga and meditation teaching, counselling, medicine, massage or naturopathy, we have all had our own suffering. We are all a 'work in progress', and we do our best not to create a sense of professional separation from the people who seek our services. We are all students and teachers to one another. As health professionals, we don't remain detached from participants—we recognise that we can all grow and change for the better through adversity. Everyone flourishes in an atmosphere of love and compassion, and participants feel nurtured by the deep level of care they experience during their time with us.

In our programs, we don't presume to know what's best for people. We trust that people will find their own best answer. Our work is to share a perspective on life that empowers a person to heal the past, build resilience for the future and live more in the present. Participants pick the information, techniques, skills and strategies that feel right for them, and we encourage them to put these into practice in their lives to see if they're useful. We stay current with the latest research in epigenetics and neuroplasticity.

Up until now, participants may have reacted to the circumstances that have beset them—but, with understanding and education, they can choose new and healthier options so they move into the driver's seat of their own life. There are many things in life that cannot be fixed, cannot be changed, cannot be made better, *and* there are a host of things we can do to shift from feeling like a victim, to feeling empowered.

Over the years, talented and experienced professionals have been drawn to our work at Quest, sometimes because they had clients who reported their positive experience from attending our programs or reading my books. Some of our facilitators and staff have been working with Quest for a decade or more, while facilitators, counsellors and therapists continue to be added to our professional teams. This forms a large part of Wendie's and my time at Quest, as we work to ensure that the future is secured through competent and experienced hands, minds and hearts. Wendie assesses facilitators and therapists so that we maintain our high standards, and she ensures that the educational aspects of the programs are consistently delivered and updated.

I know of no other facility in Australia that does similar work, and the need for these intensive residential lifestyle, support and educational programs is enormous. People are hungry for information about resilience, rebuilding their health and establishing peace of mind. It's extraordinary to see participants arrive at the Centre feeling anxious, perhaps unable to make eye contact, nervous about being with other people who, like them, are suffering in some way—and then to see them leave five days later with a spring in their step, hope in their eyes and a smile on their face.

The financial future of Quest is also a large focus of my energy. When the time comes for me to retire, I would like to see the Foundation financially secure so the full vision of Quest can be accomplished: there is still so much that can be done to educate, empower and encourage people to improve their health and well-being. The nurturing of our staff and the program teams also lies close to my heart.

With public speaking, radio interviews, writing and my responsibilities at the Quest for Life Centre, my career continues to be full and rich.

✶✶✶

Participants enjoy the beautiful grounds of the Centre and the opportunity to reconnect with nature. All around the grounds are places to reflect, to write, to weep or to dream, and a magnificent labyrinth for those who find that a walking meditation suits them better than sitting still.

One of our participants' favourite places to sit and contemplate is a lovely garden with a pond installed by Ruth Cracknell's family in her memory. Ruth was a dear friend as well as the first Patron of the Quest for Life Foundation.

Ruth first contacted me when her beloved husband, Eric, fell ill in Venice and was subsequently diagnosed with a life-threatening illness. I visited Eric and his family during this difficult time. Some years later, Ruth herself fell ill.

Wendie, Ruth and I were on our way to give a talk in Newcastle at a palliative care conference when it was obvious that Ruth, sitting beside me while I drove, was very unwell, even though she seemed oblivious to her own breathlessness. I knew that everyone would want a photo with her or to have her sign a book after she had given her talk, and it would be difficult for her to say 'no'. We whisked her away immediately after her presentation, and Wendie drove her home again, much to her relief.

I visited Ruth several times at her house and encouraged her to seek assistance for her health. She felt despondent about the world and its sad madness and missed Eric terribly after he died.

A few weeks after the conference, I received a distressed phone call from her daughter Anna: Ruth had been hospitalised. The family were at a loss to know what was happening, as Ruth found it hard to discuss her health and her doctor wasn't obliged to enlighten them. I agreed to visit Ruth in hospital on our way to the airport—Wendie and I were leaving that afternoon for a holiday in the United States.

I was shocked when I entered the room and saw Ruth on oxygen. She was finding it difficult to breathe, let alone talk. I sat with her for a bit, then spoke about the effect of not knowing what was happening to her was having on her very worried children. I outlined some ways in which she—or I, if she was willing—could include them in this unexpected and frightening deterioration in her health. Fortunately, she allowed me to talk to her family and inform them of the seriousness of her situation.

I loved Ruth and was a great admirer of her, both professionally as a much-loved actor and personally as a dear friend. It was an agony for me to tell her that I was leaving for the States and wouldn't return for six weeks. Until then, I had done all the talking, with only meaningful looks, nods, headshakes and hand-squeezing from Ruth as I made my various suggestions. When I told her of my flight to the other side of the Pacific that afternoon, she gave me a direct and stern look, took off her oxygen mask and said, in a tone straight out of *Mother and Son*, 'How could you?'

I felt mortified to be abandoning her at such a critical time. It was clearly impossible for us to talk on the phone, but I wrote to her regularly.

On my return, Wendie and I went straight to the hospital from the airport. The moment I walked into Ruth's room, she took off her oxygen mask and said, in a slightly weaker voice this time, 'I waited.'

It was a privilege to journey with her through those last weeks of her life. Most of our communications were simply through touch; I had to trust that my words to her about the letting go of a life lovingly lived were received gently and kindly, as they were surely offered with great love and compassion. Perhaps the warmth in her eyes and the tenderness of her embrace conveyed more than words could anyway. Ruth, who could deliver a line like no other, had also perfected the unutterable arts of love.

***

Family life always presents its complexities, challenges, griefs and joys. As the years unfolded, it was a joy to welcome more family members into the fold of our love as children gained partners and then had children of their own. Family gatherings are always precious occasions because we are far-flung and rarely all present at once.

There have been sad times too. Leo, then Geoff, died.

Leo lived another twenty years after the removal of his lump. It never returned, though he suffered with circulatory problems due to the frequent peripheral shutdowns he had endured. In his later years, Leo became mentally unwell and paranoid about many things—but regardless of how difficult he became, Simon and Kate spoke with him regularly, visited him when he would allow it, and were both by his side when he died aged seventy-six.

Wendie and I were on a ship many miles from shore when the text arrived from Kate telling us of Leo's death. We knew he was likely to die while we were on this lecture cruise. Simon, Kate and I had spoken about the likelihood of my being away at that time, and they were fine about this. It was perfect just as it was.

Silently, I wished Leo well on his journey and asked him to send me a sign that he was alright.

Leo had always loved the colour orange. And he used to say that if you admired a butterfly, it would always return close to you for a second viewing; I had practised this throughout my life and found it to be largely true.

As we stepped out of the lift on the top floor of the ship, two sets of automatic doors opened to the outside deck: one pair sliding open, the others opening outwards, though no person appeared to activate them—and in flew an orange and black butterfly. This beautiful creature alighted on the wall in front of us and spread its wings wide. We admired it and reflected on Leo's presence in our lives.

Finally, the butterfly put its wings together so I could gently pick it up and deliver it outside. It didn't struggle and seemed quite content to be held gently.

Then we went inside to the bar where we made a toast to Leo and wished him well on his journey. As we lifted our glasses, a pesky fly started buzzing around me and Wendie. It wouldn't leave us alone no matter how much we waved it away. It didn't go near our friends, just us. Zzzzzzzz it went, right in front of our faces, finally landing on my nose. We laughed heartily as both the butterfly and the fly signified different aspects of Leo so perfectly.

Only after Leo's death was I reunited with some of Granny's china, furniture and trinkets. None of them were valuable to anyone but me, but they were imbued with sentimentality and a host of happy memories and stories. Peter, Granny's companion, had made a blanket chest out of a beautiful silky oak tree, and this finally came home to me after Leo died in 2013.

Geoff also died while we were away, this time on a fundraising trip for Quest in Bhutan. Ross, who has always been an incredible support to my parents, was present with Geoff when he died. Geoff and Ross had long ago put their differences to rest—and, indeed, we were all emotionally up to date with him before he took his leave.

My last phone call to him just before he died was painful, given all I wanted to do was gather him up in my arms once more and assure him of my love. Geoff wasn't easy in my young life, but as adults we had become very close. I couldn't have wished for a more loving, supportive and generous father, and we miss him. Kate and Simon adored Geoff, as he was loving, supportive and generous as a grandparent too, taking interest in their goals and aspirations. His final year was shared with the first year of his great-granddaughter, Olivia, and she brought him enormous joy and contentment.

We are blessed with increasing numbers of grandchildren—seven so far, ranging from eighteen down to a little one about to arrive. Kate and Simon have returned to the state of our family's origins, Queensland, and they and their partners have grown into wonderful people and parents.

Rae once more lives in Bundanoon, after several intervening years living with Geoff in Bowral. At ninety-five she is as bright, loving and wise as ever, and we are so grateful to still have her with us.

Ross continues to provide loving support and practical assistance to Rae and is the best brother I could wish for. We may have been strangers to each other during our formative years because of circumstances beyond our control, but now we are close and grateful to have each other's love and support.

The mystery of love continues to weave its magic throughout our extended family. We are not all related through blood, but our shared stories and history create a loving foundation upon which we are all enabled to flourish, grow and weather the challenges of life together.

***

Every chapter of my life has leant value to my work. There are still challenges, of course, both personally and in running an organisation. It is nearly always through challenges that we learn about ourselves, other people and what really matters. I am blessed to have a wonderful relationship with Wendie, a loving family, good friends and work that brings me great fulfilment. All those things leave me feeling grateful and humble to play a small part in the journey of others, whether personally or professionally.

I have been ministered to as well as ministering to others. In 2013 I chose to have both my knees replaced, one at a time. I had postponed this surgery for many years as it was the only option I was offered and I wanted the techniques to be as advanced as possible. Also, I was quite young to contemplate knee replacements because they generally last fifteen to twenty years before needing further replacement.

While I could walk quite well, the subtle, tiny movements in the joints became too painful—rolling over in bed, going around a corner in the car, even the slightest shift while I was sitting could cause a 'sproing-ing' in my knee, a bit like having your funny bone whacked a few hundred times a day. I could still walk, but not far; I could still stand, but not for long. Stairs were becoming increasingly difficult to negotiate.

Again my orthopaedic surgeon had retired, so I sourced another one who had an excellent reputation for his work with knee replacements. When Wendie and I walked into his office, he looked surprised. He asked which of the two of us belonged to the X-rays on the light box. When I claimed them, he said, 'I expected an elderly person in a wheelchair to belong to these X-rays. I've never seen worse arthritis. Either keep doing whatever you're doing or have knee replacements—there's nothing in between.'

The surgeries went well, but afterwards the pain was excruciating: not in my knees but each time in my hip socket. The hammering to fix the prosthesis in place had traumatised the ligaments in my hip joints, which no doubt had been under stress for years. Gradually my hip pain settled into a chronic bursitis.

When I told the surgeon about my hip pain, he said, 'No, that doesn't happen.' If I hadn't been in so much pain, I would have felt even more deflated by his negation of my experience. When it happened the second time, three months later, after the second knee was replaced, his only reply was to say with a quizzical look, 'Oh yes, that happened last time, didn't it?'

After I had this second knee replacement, an off-duty nurse found me whimpering with pain. She immediately knelt by my bed to ask why I was crying, taking my hands in hers. I was touched by her compassion, and when I cited pain as the cause of my tears, she said, 'I'm so sorry you're in so much pain. Can you give some of it to me?' Through my tears, I told her how healing and helpful her words were—indeed, far more so than the pain medication, which did little to relieve the agony.

Fortunately, one cannot relive the intensity of pain. Over the following weeks and months, while the pain subsided, it settled into a central nervous system sensitisation that extends from my lower spine to my toes; it's a little like very intense pins and needles. Perhaps my legs have endured so much trauma over such a long time and have been subjected to so much manipulation and change that the nerve endings have become super-sensitised.

I can walk well now and without limping. However, chronic pain is a constant.

During my recovery from the second knee replacement I was plagued with severe stomach cramps, which reduced me to a sweating heap on the floor. Twice we went to the hospital, where they gave me an anaesthetic draught to drink. This helped but, within days, I was assailed by more painful cramps. I could barely think straight for pain. It was difficult to sort out the cause but I put it down to the powerful analgesia I was taking for the appalling pain in my hip. Finally, my doctor ordered an ultrasound, which revealed gallstones. I was relieved to have them removed and Wendie, as always, cared for me during my recovery.

✳✳✳

So much of my childhood was based around the limiting belief I had to do everything myself; I had to earn my right to exist, that my value lay in what I did, not who I am. Yet, so much more can be achieved through collaboration.

When I started out as a naturopath, yoga and meditation teacher over thirty years ago, my work was initially with cancer and HIV/AIDS sufferers. Having just confronted my own mortality and having prepared to die, I found I had much in common with people living at the edge, and I could use my skills, knowledge and training to ease their suffering. In time, every experience in my life became relevant, as people told me their stories of chronic pain, rape, hospitalisations, alcohol and drug abuse, grief, lack of self-esteem, failed marriages, domestic violence, broken hearts, shattered dreams and betrayals.

More than 110,000 people have shared their stories of suffering with me. Most of these extraordinary people have been ordinary people like me. They have been through extraordinary challenges, and together we have achieved great things that would have been beyond each of us on our own. Human creativity is extraordinary—when it is collectively harnessed, solutions to our challenges become achievable. Together, we can more easily awaken to the full capacities of the human spirit to embrace unimaginable challenges. These experiences may shape us but they do not have to define us.

I didn't arrive at a place called 'peace' and unpack. Peace is a moment by moment choice. Every challenge becomes an opportunity to choose peace rather than conflict, peace rather than being right, peace rather than a cure, peace rather than hanging on to what has become second nature to me. The peace that passes all understanding is attainable for each of us, yet it always requires effort and often the love and support of people who 'get' us. I have been abundantly blessed by many different people who 'got' me at different times in my life. Their belief, trust and support has both challenged and enabled me to achieve the vision of providing compassionate care, and a pathway to peace, for many thousands of courageous people.

I hope to arrive on my deathbed with a soft smile in my heart, just like my friend with AIDS who ached to discover how to love before he died—and did.

'Be where you can love the best,' said Padre Luigi. Love turns out to be a moment by moment choice. Love for ourselves, love for one another, love of our precious home—this blue jewel of a planet—love is always the answer. And with love, all things are possible.

Epilogue

There are many things we can do in our lives to make us less vulnerable to disease and illness. None of those things come out of a prescription pill. We can learn to know and understand ourselves better. We can find what gives us joy and fulfilment, and pursue those large and small things that give our lives purpose and meaning.

Finding our own personal truth and living from the authenticity of that, regardless of other people's opinions, is the path to fulfilment and peace. I have always liked the saying, 'Other people's opinion of us is none of our business,' but recognise there have been many times in my life when I lived as though the opposite was true.

When I reflect on the pain and anguish I see in both the micro world of our relationships or the larger world of nations, it seems to me that we have lost our spiritual compass. We look for personal, political, military or economic solutions to what are really spiritual matters. It is no longer appropriate to do what we have always done because it simply doesn't work.

Until we recognise the power of love and the interconnectedness of all life, we will flounder in the world of 'us' and 'them'. As the great Indian sage Mahatma Gandhi said, 'An eye for an eye makes the whole world blind.' Until we can see the other as ourselves, we are destined to judge one another according to colour, creed and difference.

We do not need to be well or free of pain to find 'the peace that passes all understanding'. No matter whether we live with pain, sickness or disability, or are in great health, we can all learn to live passionately, to live a life of purpose.

Good health is wonderful, but I have known many people in exceedingly good physical health who are miserable. Sometimes people grasp at life or believe they will only be happy if they have life unfold in the way they believe it 'should'.

345

I have entered many a mansion where heartache lies behind the magnificent door and many a hut without a door in the Indian desert. I have been blessed to be at bedsides, welcomed into homes and country towns where grief or potential loss are similarly experienced. Beyond the trappings, assets and accumulations of our lives, we all face our inevitable suffering, whether with our health, wealth or lack of it, with our loved ones and their challenges or life's proclivities when the unexpected or unimagined darkens our doorway.

Happiness is found when our sense of self is anchored not in our physical bodies, with all their idiosyncrasies and challenges, not in the fluctuations of our busy brains with their thoughts and feelings, and not in the prescriptions and judgements we project onto life, ourselves or each other.

Real joy and wisdom are found in moments of gratitude or kindness, in moments of connection, in moments of wonder and awe. When we take the risk to let go of what we have outgrown instead of clinging to it, we find the freedom to embrace the dream of who we are yet to become. Deepening wisdom and personal growth are possible for everyone, even though a cure for what ails the body may not be.

What small suffering I have had has made me a better companion to other people who likewise suffer; not because I know what it is like for them but because I am willing to hear their suffering without trying to fix it, change it or make it better. Providing a safe environment in which people can utter the unutterable enables the emergence of their courage. Once we can name it, we are already more than it.

If ever we can be of service to you or those you love, please be in touch.

Quest for Life Centre

Well over 110,000 people have benefited from workshops, counselling, groups and programs that Petrea and the Quest for Life Foundation have provided. For the past few years, Quest has used a well-recognised evaluation tool called the Kessler 10 (K10), which comprises ten questions that participants answer before attending a Quest program; and four weeks after the program, they answer the same ten questions. In our program for people suffering with symptoms of post-traumatic stress (PTSD), our evaluations include an additional and more targeted evaluation tool, and the evaluation process continues beyond the month to three, six and twelve months later.

Across our residential programs, participants experience an average of a 27 per cent increase in quantified mental wellbeing four weeks after attending a program. That figure continues to increase substantially at the three, six and twelve month evaluation interviews. These results demonstrate that the framework we use, based on the latest research into neuroplasticity and epigenetics, plus the skills, practical strategies and tools that participants learn about on Quest programs are not only highly beneficial, but benefits increase as participants continue to utilise what they've learned on the program.

Quest's current intensive, educational and support residential programs include:

Healing Your Life—for people living with depression, anxiety, loss, the consequences of abuse, relationship breakdown, grief and other unexpected difficulties.

Quest for Life—for people living with cancer, life-threatening illness, chronic pain/illness.

Moving Beyond Trauma—for people suffering the consequences of post-trauma symptoms or PTSD (DVA and Worker's Comp cover costs for eligible people).

The Quest for Life Foundation is a National Disability Insurance Scheme (NDIS) Provider.

If Quest can be of service to you or your loved ones, please be in touch.

URL: www.questforlife.com.au
Facebook: facebook.com/QuestforLifeAus
Ph: 1300-941-488
Ph: 61-2-4883-6599

Quest for Life Foundation

The Quest for Life Foundation is a DG1 registered charity which relies on donations, bequests and fundraising to continue and further its vision. All donations over $2 are tax deductible.

Our programs and community workshops enable people to feel empowered and capable of embracing their challenges. All programs are tailored to the specific needs of people living with grief, loss, trauma, tragedy or physical and mental illnesses. People leave our programs with a lighter heart and an abundance of practical tools and strategies for healing, resilience, forgiveness and creating peace of mind.

Donations and bequests

Your donation or bequest ensures:
- Quest services are made available to as many people as possible
- helps train more people in Quest's skills, tools and strategies; and
- enables the vision of Quest to grow and expand.

Rainbow Club

Your regular financial contribution—whether large or small—through our Rainbow Club, ensures that we can accommodate everyone in need of our services. Please consider donating to the Quest for Life Foundation.

Acknowledgements

So many people have been a part of both my personal journey and the formation of the Quest for Life Centre and Foundation that it would take another book to list them. The collective efforts of our staff, volunteers, board members, supporters, donors and past participants have together enabled a vision to be enlivened and brought into being.

One such volunteer is Robyn Fagan, who attended a program for people with cancer in 1996. She returned for a second program, when Quest had just purchased Killarney House, and was so inspired by the dream of what we were creating that she moved to Bundanoon to volunteer her time. Since the opening of Quest, Robyn has—on a voluntary basis—picked and arranged flowers throughout the buildings for every program. Such gestures of kindness and generosity are treasures beyond measure and demonstrate the good-heartedness of people. When the heart is touched, it is natural for us to want to pay it forward in some way.

There are many such stories of people like Robyn who, having suffered some illness or calamity, have made meaning of their experience by doing something to benefit others who likewise are hurting.

Angela Belgiorno-Zegna, Liz Lynch, Annie Robinson and Mili Legge were four extraordinary women who wanted to see Quest succeed with its vision. They served as board members and were active fundraisers for several events that enabled Quest to continue. To this day, Mili continues her support of the Foundation; in 2015, she organised and led a wonderful fundraising tour to Italy where we revisited the monastery and cave in Assisi, and then travelled on to the country of her birth, Slovenia and Croatia.

Our staff and volunteers create the ideal environment for our participants to learn valuable life-skills, tools and strategies for living well in challenging circumstances. Everyone plays a valuable role, whether it's in the way they clean a room or make a bed, prepare a meal, greet our participants on arrival, help with administrative tasks, speak on the phone, do our accounts, tend the grounds or something else that enables people to feel loved and cared for when they visit us. People are so relieved when they feel the warmth and care on their arrival. They find it easy to relax into being nurtured, encouraged and inspired. Without our wonderful staff and volunteers, we simply couldn't accomplish as much as we do at Quest. My thanks to everyone who has made Quest into the amazing healing place it has become. I count it as a privilege to work with such special people who all give so generously of their time and hearts.

***

Marcus Blackmore has continued to be a friend and supporter of me personally and the work we do at the Quest for Life Centre.

Some years ago, I sought Marcus's advice when we were reviewing Quest's business model and the issues around our financial sustainability. Remembering back to when the Loudons had made it possible for us to purchase and refurbish the Centre, we knew then that this work would completely absorb our time, finances and energy—and indeed it had. Perhaps after thirty years, we had done what we could to make a difference and it was time to let the Centre go. It is not (financially) easy to keep such an enterprise going given that many of the people most in need of our services are those who are least able to afford the cost of a program.

Marcus heard me out. At first, he suggested that Blackmores do with Quest what they had done with the Macular Degeneration Foundation (MDF), which receives 5 per cent of net retail sales from their product Macuvision. Marcus suggested that if I, as a naturopath, developed some formulas for the benefit of people attending our programs, then Blackmores would donate 5 per cent of net retail sales from this range to Quest. This would enable a passive income stream into Quest, and for that I was very grateful.

I met with the Blackmores formulations team and the marketing people, and we progressed the conversation over several months. Then Marcus unexpectedly declared, 'Petrea, I don't want to go down this pathway with you at all. We (Blackmores Ltd) should be supporting Quest just because it does great work in the community. I don't want you associated with a product.'

I hugged him. This is testament to the great man he is. Many, many years ago, Marcus had said to me, 'The reason you're so trusted by people in Australia is because you're not associated with a product. *Never* become associated with a product, not even with Blackmores.' I was touched that Marcus was so keen to support Quest without wanting anything in return, other than to know their support makes a profound and positive difference in thousands of people's lives. Blackmores Ltd have been Quest's major corporate sponsor since 2012.

In addition to Blackmores' wonderful support, given so freely, Marcus and his wife Caroline recently donated sufficient funds to completely refurbish the Quest for Life Centre. So, with new beds and furniture, paint, carpet and artwork, as well as upgrading our infrastructure, including computers, phone system, a therapy building and caretaker's cottage, the Centre has never looked so beautiful.

The leadership team from Blackmores completely renovated the main program room with new paint and carpet, furniture and artwork. Each of them knew someone suffering with cancer, grief, depression or loss within their own family or community. Preparing a beautiful and comfortable place for such people made their work a joy.

I am deeply grateful for the tremendous support that Marcus and Caroline have provided for Quest, along with their staff. Marcus is passionate about Quest's work, particularly our work with post-traumatic stress sufferers as many of his mates from his Vietnam days have struggled with its effects over the years. I hold Marcus in the highest respect and with an unshakeable fondness.

***

The writing of this memoir required revisiting many events and difficulties, and I am grateful to my mother, Rae, for providing dates and details that helped clarify my memory. It's wonderful that at ninety-five, she remembers things I don't! Thank you, Rae, for your willingness to revisit challenges from our shared past and for your unending love and support. As you know, you have fished me out of even more pickles than are detailed in this memoir and have always stood beside me, lifted me up, settled me down and held the vision of a future when I couldn't see one myself. I will forever be grateful that you are my mother and friend.

I'm grateful too for Ross's willingness to bring some of our past to the page. Exposing my past automatically exposes his, so thank you for your consent to have our story shared, Ross—and for being the best brother a sister could have. Thanks too to my sister-in-law Dianne King, an avid reader, whose encouragement of my writing at an early stage meant so much to me.

My heartfelt thanks to Kate and Simon, whose father, Leo, was a complex and difficult man who nonetheless loved his children dearly. Their commitment to loving *him* is testament to their good hearts. Thank you for letting me share some of our life together with a wider audience. I couldn't be prouder of you both and the beautiful families you have each created.

My thanks too to the thousands of people who have shared their stories with me and those who have been included in my memoir. Through your permission to share them with a larger audience,

Acknowledgements

I know you will have touched the hearts of many more people than you can imagine. Thank you for your courage. I know we are all ordinary people living through extraordinary circumstances. Together, and by shedding light on one another's paths, we can all find our way home.

Keri Ahmet, my assistant at Quest, was a great support too in giving input and feedback as she patiently read and re-read the manuscript. Thank you, Keri, for your patience, suggestions and good humour.

Kate Goldsworthy brought amazing skills to forming my brain dump into coherency and structure. Thank you, Kate, for your support, encouragement and suggestions, which brought my memoir to life. You teased out the details of my story and then skilfully pruned and shaped its form. And you did it all with such care and good grace!

The staff at Allen & Unwin have been a pleasure to work with. Thank you especially to Louise Thurtell for your encouragement from the beginning and for overseeing the memoir into existence. And my thanks too to Sarah Baker, who shepherded my book through each stage.

And last but never least, my thanks to Wendie who fed, watered and encouraged me while I wrote this memoir in three solid weeks of work plus evenings, weekends and any other moments I created among the busyness of our lives. I can only be the best version of me because you are by my side. My eternal thanks for your love, wit and precious companionship—all of which are major blessings in my life. Twenty-four years ago, we thought we would be mad not to give our love a chance to grow and blossom. I'm so grateful that we jumped right in as together—and with love—all things have proved possible.